# Tradition & Change
## on the
## Northwest Coast

# Tradition & Change on the Northwest Coast

## The Makah, Nuu-chah-nulth, Southern Kwakiutl and Nuxalk

# RUTH KIRK

University of Washington Press
Seattle

*in association with*
The Royal British Columbia Museum

*To Ada and Margaret and Felicity—and all the
elders—for their forebearance and faith*

University of Washington Press
Seattle

**Library of Congress Cataloging-in-Publication Data**

Kirk, Ruth.
  Tradition and change on the Northwest Coast.

  Bibliography: p.
  Includes index.

  1. Indians of North America–Northwest Coast of
North America–Social life and customs. I. Title.
E78.N78K57 1986      979.5′00497      86-9284
ISBN 0-295-96628-9

Design by Fiona MacGregor
Typeset by Typeworks
Printed and bound in Hong Kong

# Contents

| | | |
|---|---|---|
| *Foreword* | | 7 |
| *Preface* | | 8 |
| *Acknowledgements* | | 10 |

**PART I   PEOPLE OF THE TRANSITION**

| | | |
|---|---|---|
| *Chapter 1* | Today's Elders | 12 |

**PART II   THE WORLD THAT WAS**

| | | |
|---|---|---|
| *Chapter 2* | Kinship, Rank and Privilege | 36 |
| *Chapter 3* | Ceremonials and Religion | 57 |
| | *A Sense of Place and Past* | 89 |
| *Chapter 4* | Daily Life | 105 |
| *Chapter 5* | Dealing with Others: Trade, Conflict and Marriage | 139 |

**PART III   TIME'S FLOW**

| | | |
|---|---|---|
| *Chapter 6* | Seeing the Past from the Present | 158 |
| | *To Carry on the Legacy* | 185 |
| *Chapter 7* | The Dawn of a New Era | 201 |
| *Chapter 8* | A Changing World | 214 |
| *Chapter 9* | Today and Tomorrow | 244 |

| | | |
|---|---|---|
| *Selected Bibliography* | | 250 |
| *Index* | | 252 |

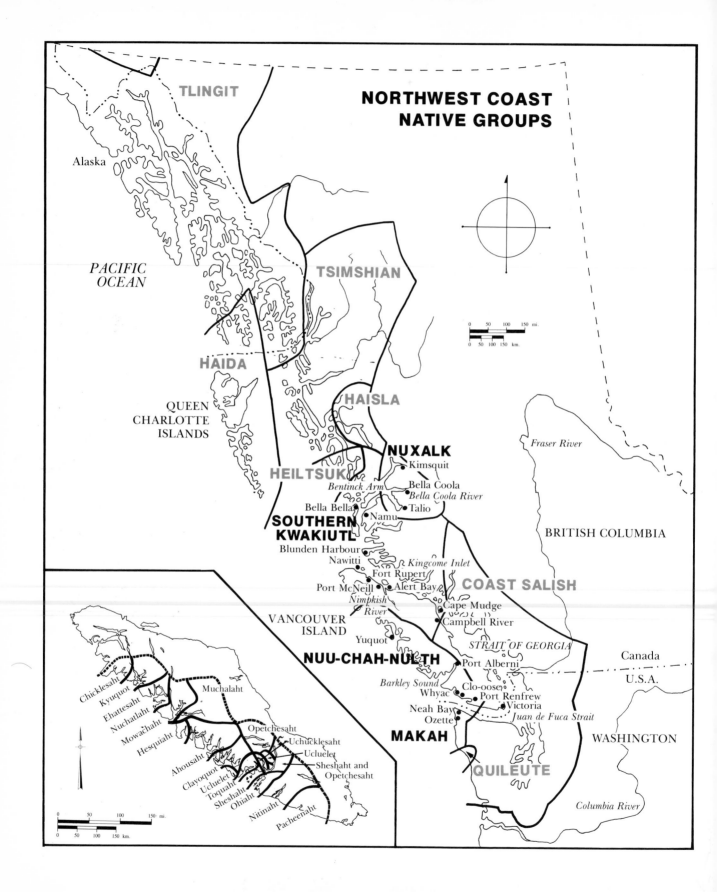

NORTHWEST COAST
NATIVE GROUPS

TLINGIT

Alaska

PACIFIC
OCEAN

TSIMSHIAN

HAIDA

QUEEN
CHARLOTTE
ISLANDS

HAISLA

NUXALK

HEILTSUK • Kimsquit

Bentinck Arm • Bella Coola
• Bella Coola River
Bella Bella • • Talio
• Namu

SOUTHERN
KWAKIUTL

Blunden Harbour •
Nawitti •

Fort Rupert
Port McNeill • • Alert Bay
Nimpkish
River

VANCOUVER
ISLAND

Yuquot

NUU-CHAH-NULTH

Kingcome Inlet

Cape Mudge
• Campbell River

COAST SALISH

STRAIT OF GEORGIA

Port Alberni

Barkley Sound    • Clo-oose
Whyac • • Port Renfrew
• Victoria
Neah Bay •
Ozette •

MAKAH

QUILEUTE

BRITISH COLUMBIA

Fraser River

Canada
U.S.A.

Juan de Fuca Strait

WASHINGTON

Columbia River

Chicklesaht
Kyuquot
Ehattesaht
Nuchatlaht
Mowachaht
Hesquiaht
Ahousaht
Clayoquot
Ucluelet
Toquaht
Sheshaht
Ohiaht
Nitinaht

Muchalaht

Opetchesaht
Uchucklesaht
Ucluelet
Sheshaht and
Opetchesaht

Pacheenaht

0    50    100    150 mi.

0    50    100    150 km.

0    50    100    150 mi.
0    50    100    150 km.

# Foreword

The native people who lived on the Pacific Coast of British Columbia—as well as in the northwest corner of Washington and in coastal Alaska adjacent to British Columbia—inhabited a region with a remarkable wealth of natural foods. This plenty gave them time and energy not needed for survival and made possible a remarkable cluster of human cultures, each somewhat similar yet distinctive, and each one rich in social ceremony, myth, art and theatre.

The three groups of people who are the focus of this book—the Nuu-chah-nulth, Southern Kwakiutl and Nuxalk—were chosen for several reasons. While they differ in important ways, they share similar coastlines, many common foods and technologies, and some social characteristics through casual contact and marriages.

The need for popular information on native British Columbians was served for several decades by a set of ten small books in the British Columbia Heritage Series, subtitled Our Native Peoples, produced by the Provincial Archives of British Columbia. By the 1970s these texts were dated in social attitude and outdated in factual content, so the Royal British Columbia Museum planned to produce ten new volumes, each written by the most appropriate anthropologist available. This produced just one manuscript, which the museum subsequently published as an excellent work breaking much new ground. *The West Coast People* by Eugene Arima was not attached to an anthropological series, however, for by this time the plan had of necessity evolved into something different.

In this new approach, cultures located in somewhat similar environmental conditions were to be clumped appropriately into a book, possibly to be followed by a series of four or five volumes. Since the books desired were to be that uncommon kind described as good science well written for the public, the solution appeared to be an account written by an experienced and successful writer in the life sciences (a term here intended to include the social sciences) who would be informed by anthropologists throughout the writing process. The first essential of the finished product was that it be a popular account; the great unknown was the extent to which the academic knowledge of anthro-

pologists could be presented in a popular format in a way that was acceptable to them.

The participants in the first book of this experiment were obvious and happy choices: Ruth Kirk, successful author in natural history and anthropology; and four specialized and willing anthropologists on the museum's staff, Richard Inglis, Robert Levine, Peter MacNair and Kevin Neary, who are in the same order an archaeologist, a linguist and two ethnologists.

Ruth Kirk has the rare ability to assemble academic information from many sources, then to blend the whole into good prose for the general reader while still maintaining the factual integrity of the reports. First-hand experience and investigation are always among her sources as well, and from the first she insisted that this book must be partly an Indian account about being Indian. Native people with strong cultural ties to the old ways have supplied the author generously with information on how it once was to be Indian, as well as how it is to be one now in a rapidly changing world. The museum joins the author in thanking these people. Their generosity has given to this book a warmth that comes with comfortable conversations over tea in a living room or while digging out and eating roots in a traditional gathering place.

I think it remarkable that the sciences have no firm tradition for taking their understandings effectively to the public. The Royal British Columbia Museum, however, because of its mandate but also in recognition of its debt to its audiences, has a number of communication programs that strive for effective ways to inform the public, a function that is after all very much a need of the sciences as well. Throughout most scientific institutions, including museums, it is the public that makes most scientific effort possible, because public funds control the extent of most such efforts including whether there will be any efforts at all.

This book, then, is partial payment of a debt to British Columbians for their support of anthropology in this province. If it gives readers accurate information with enjoyment, then this project is a success.

Yorke Edwards, Director (retired)
Royal British Columbia Museum

# Preface

This book deals with continuity. It seeks to highlight the distinctive nature of three of the separate language groups that live along the central British Columbia coast and the adjoining northwestern tip of Washington State. These people—the Nuu-chah-nulth (including the Makah of Washington State), the Southern Kwakiutl and the Nuxalk—partly share language roots and largely share a particular world view and social structure. They are representative of all Northwest Coast cultures, and consequently, curators at the Royal British Columbia Museum felt it reasonable to write about these three groups in a single volume. The book attempts an overview based on at least 10 000 years of these peoples' presence on the coast.

I hope the book rings with the admiration I feel for the cultures and individuals represented and for their refusal to accept assimilation. Not even the social upheaval of losing nine out of every ten people to raging epidemics in the nineteenth century, not even the disorientation of changing to new, cash economy with a more complex technological base, not even the acceptance of a new cosmology and religion—none of these broke native pride in the past or native ties to ancestral lands and waters. This is the remarkable continuity that fills these pages.

The presentation will not please everyone, for one book cannot include all the information available. Additionally, there is enormous audacity in an outsider attempting to summarize anyone's cultural history—and a counterbalancing difficulty when "insiders" attempt the task, for, either way, who is to speak for all? I acknowledge the pitfalls.

Finally, a word concerning spelling. We recognize that any English-based system inevitably does violence to the pronunciation of aboriginal vocabulary. Native languages have many sounds that are lacking in English and therefore require the specialized spelling that linguists use to record native language material. However, since this special spelling is difficult for the rest of us to follow, we have chosen to use a conventional spelling system, even though it fails to accurately convey the pronunciation of native words. For similar reasons of general accessibility, we are not using footnotes or presenting a complete bibliography.

May these decisions, and all the others, work together to increase understanding and to illuminate native tradition and change along the Northwest Coast.

I would like to acknowledge the generosity that underlies these pages, the collective giving of accumulated experience and wisdom that has come from Indian people and also from non-Indian ethnologists, archaeologists, linguists and historians. I know my role is as compiler more than author, and I feel a deep sense of obligation in representing others and have tried to do so faithfully.

It is pleasant to publicly acknowledge the many people who have helped with this book and to thank them. It also is somewhat daunting, for the list is long and the indebtedness greater than mere naming implies.

Sadly, we no longer can hear the voices of many elders except in memory and, in some cases, on tape. Among these elders, for me and for this book, are: in Bella Coola, Margaret Siwallace and Felicity Walkus; along the coast of the Olympic Peninsula, Ada Markishtum, Nora Barker, Mabel Robertson, Harold Ides, Harry McCarty, Ted Hudson and Hal George. There also are many, now gone, who are represented by written manuscripts and published autobiographies and on tapes at the Provincial Archives of British Columbia. They are identified by name within the text.

Scores of native people have allowed me into their homes and taught me, giving insight into their lives, or posed for my camera; and others have graciously authorized the use of material and photographs. Some are long-time friends, others the friends of friends. These many include: among the Southern Kwakiutl, Agnes Alfred, Basil Ambers, Flora Cook, Richard Hunt, Tony Hunt, Robert Joseph, Flora and James Sewid, Daisy Sewid Smith, and J. J. Wallas; among the Nuxalk, Louise Hilland, Ed and Sandy Moody, Joanne Schooner and Cecilia Siwallace; among the Nuu-chah-nulth and Makah, Edward Claplanhoo, Lida and Roger Colfax, Lloyd Colfax, Ben David, Winnifred David, Edith and John Hottowe, John Ides, Isabel Ides, Hubert Markishtum, Alice Paul, Larry Paul, Tim Paul, Charles Peterson,

Helen Peterson, John Thomas, Art Thompson, Marina Tom, Ruth Tom, Bernice Touchie, Margaret and Adam Shewish, Jane Sterritt-Jones, and Jessie and Peter Webster. To all, my deep appreciation.

At the Royal British Columbia Museum, Yorke Edwards, former Director, heads the list of those upon whom this book has depended, and Richard Inglis, archaeologist, has given more patient, continuing input than any other one person. In addition, guidance, information and criticism have come from museum ethnologists Peter Macnair, Alan Hoover and Kevin Neary; linguists Robert Levine and Barbara Efrat, as well as Don Prescott of the Linguistics Division; archaeologists Don Abbott, James Haggarty, Grant Keddie and Thomas Loy; and historian Robert Turner. Harold Hosford gave overall encouragement and specific editing suggestions; Doris Lundy handled innumerable manuscript and illustration details; and Dan Savard, Andrew Niemann, Burton Storey, Grant Holland and Cairn Crockford at the Royal British Columbia Museum and Bob Soderlund of the Nuu-chah-nulth Tribal Council made it possible to assemble and print the large selection of black-and-white photographs.

Outside the museum staff, anthropologists Bill Holm and Carolyn Marr, archaeologists Roy Carlson, Phil Hobler, Gary Wessen and Al Mackey, linguist Peter Wilson and ethnobotanist Nancy Turner all helped with the manuscript, contributing valuable information and suggestions. Hilary Stewart made drawings specifically for this volume.

To all these persons and others who are not named, and to the authors of published and taped material that I have consulted, goes awareness that these pages are something we have created together; also acknowledgement of my responsibility for whatever weaknesses may linger despite the opportunities and help so generously given. Every account passes through the filter of whoever does the recording, compiling, writing: I have tried to be meticulous, but there is no way to succeed totally or to everyone's satisfaction, my own included. A book is only a book. Culture comes from human convictions and experiences; it fits only partially onto paper.

Ruth Kirk

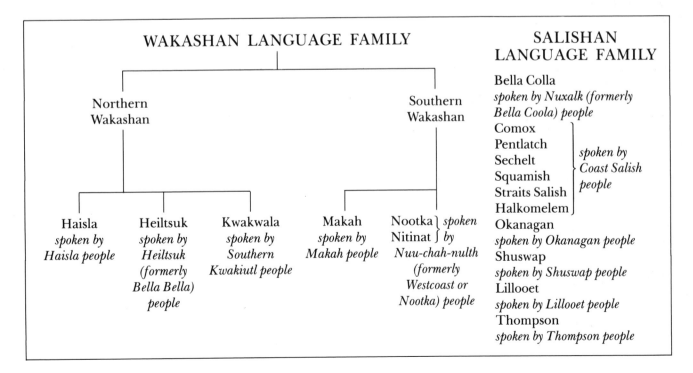

WAKASHAN LANGUAGE FAMILY

Northern Wakashan

Southern Wakashan

Haisla
*spoken by Haisla people*

Heiltsuk
*spoken by Heiltsuk (formerly Bella Bella) people*

Kwakwala
*spoken by Southern Kwakiutl people*

Makah
*spoken by Makah people*

Nootka
Nitinat
*spoken by Nuu-chah-nulth (formerly Westcoast or Nootka) people*

SALISHAN LANGUAGE FAMILY

Bella Colla
*spoken by Nuxalk (formerly Bella Coola) people*

Comox
Pentlatch
Sechelt
Squamish
Straits Salish
Halkomelem
*spoken by Coast Salish people*

Okanagan
*spoken by Okanagan people*

Shuswap
*spoken by Shuswap people*

Lillooet
*spoken by Lillooet people*

Thompson
*spoken by Thompson people*

# Acknowledgements

*A number of publishers, organizations, persons and institutions have generously given permission to reprint material from copyrighted works and sources, as noted below.*

"Ethnology of the Kwakiutl" by Franz Boas, in *Thirty-Fifth Annual Report of the Bureau of American Ethnology to the Secretary of the Smithsonian Institution 1913–14*, by permission of Smithsonian Institution Press. Report on Barkley Sound by George Blenkinsop, Indian Affairs R.G. 10, vol. 3614, file 4105, 1874, by permission Provincial Archives of British Columbia. *Log of the Columbia, 1790–1792* by John Boit, in Proceedings of the Massachusetts Historical Society, October 1919 to June 1920, vol. 53, by permission of the society. *Fighting with Property* by Helen Codere, American Ethnological Society Monograph no. 18, by permission of the society. "Franz Boas and the Bella Coola in Berlin" by Douglas Cole, in *Northwest Anthropological Research Notes*, vol. 16, no. 2, by permission of NARN. Interview with Agnes Cranmer, tape 1015-1, by permission of Provincial Archives of British Columbia. "Contemporary Accounts of Nootka Culture" edited by Barbara S. Efrat and W. J. Langlois, in *Sound Heritage* VII: 2, by permission of Provincial Archives of British Columbia. "Kerf-Bent Boxes: Woodworking Techniques and Carving Tools of the Northwest Coast" by Susan J. Davidson, in *Fine Woodworking*, © 1980 The Taunton Press, by permission of The Taunton Press. "The Fort Victoria Treaties" by Wilson Duff, in *B.C. Studies* no. 3 (autumn 1969), by permission of BCS. *Smoke from Their Fires* by Clellan S. Ford, © 1941, by permission of Yale University Press. "Reminiscences of a Whaler's Wife" edited by Erna Gunther, in *Pacific Northwest Quarterly* 33, by permission of PNQ and University of Washington. *The Outer Shores: Part 1, Ed Ricketts and John Steinbeck Explore the Pacific Coast* edited by Joel W. Hedgpeth, by permission of the editor and Mad River Press Inc. Diary (1882–89) of Kate Hendry, MS, by permission of Provincial Archives of British Columbia. Notes by George Hunt, in Newcombe Family Papers, vol. 40, file 16 and MSS 1077, by permission of Provincial Archives of British Columbia. *Noticias de Nutka: An Account of Nootka Sound in 1792* by José Mariano Mozino, translated by Iris Higbie Wilson, American Ethnological Society Monograph no. 50, by permission of University of Washington Press. "Livelihood of Indians of Nootka" by August Murphy, MS, by permission of Archives Deschâtelets. *Nootka Texts: Tales and Ethnological Narratives with Grammatical Notes and Lexical Material* by Edward Sapir and Morris Swadesh, by permission of the authors' Executors, Philip Sapir and Dr. Evangelina Arana, and Linguistic Society of America. Interview with Bill Scow, tape 1014-1, by permission of Provincial Archives of British Columbia. *Prosecution or Persecution* by Daisy Sewid-Smith (My-yah-nelth), by permission of the author. *Guests Never Leave Hungry: The Autobiography of James Sewid, a Kwakiutl Indian* by James P. Spradley, © 1960, by permission of Yale Univeristy Press. *Bella Coola Stories* edited by Susanne Storie, Report of the B.C. Indian Advisory Committee 1968–69, by permission of First Citizens' Fund Administration. *Bella Coola Ceremony and Art* by Margaret Stott, Canadian Ethnology Service Mercury Paper in Ethnology no. 21, by permission of National Museum of Man, National Museums of Canada. "Frederick Christian Thornberg" by Frederick Christian Thornberg, in *Sound Heritage* 33, by permission Provincial Archives of British Columbia. *An Account of a Voyage to the North West Coast of America in 1795 and 1796* by Alexander Walker, edited by Robin Fisher and J. M. Bumsted, by permission of Douglas & McIntyre. *As Far As I Know: Reminiscences of an Ahousat Elder* by Peter Webster, by permission of the author and Campbell River Museum and Archives. Interview with Peter Webster, tape 2392-6, by permission Provincial Archives of British Columbia.

# Part I
## *People of the Transition*

# CHAPTER ONE
## *Today's Elders*

Ride the ferry between Vancouver and Victoria, or fly aboard the bush planes that serve the British Columbia coast, and you often hear the soft voices of Indian elders speaking their own language. These are people for whom English is a language learned at residential school or through other alien contacts. They are living links with a past that is thousands of years old.

"We were all the time going places by canoe," an elderly native woman told me as she switched off the television news. She started to reminisce about travelling with her grandmother to trade baskets at the Hudson's Bay Company store in Victoria:

Even we children knew how to sit still in a canoe. Maybe those days were better. Everything we needed we had right around us. Fish to dry, herring eggs, seal oil, berries . . . even whale meat. What we didn't have, we could trade for. It was easier than now, with cash.

In the past canoe travel linked one coastal village with another, yet each community was almost a separate social, political and economic unit. Today

*Two women return from digging clams, easily paddling their small canoe and its heavy, wet load.* VANCOUVER PUBLIC LIBRARY, 14101

floatplanes and roads, schools and television bring remarkable cultural similarity even to remote regions. They overpower the old separateness. Sameness spreads. The elders, however, remember the last of the old days and have lived the transition from past into present. They can give us insight into what earlier Indian life was like. For example, the late Chief Bill Scow of Alert Bay taped his memories of childhood and youth for the Provincial Archives of British Columbia in Victoria:

I've read certain articles about . . . drafty houses with old cedar shakes on the sides. . . . But it wasn't that bad. They had cubby-holes made out of cedar shakes . . . and cedar matting to cover your bedding. You weren't altogether exposed to the draft. You were well protected.

Top. *Nuu-chah-nulth elder Ella Jackson tells archaeologists where Ohiaht villages once stood and where her people went for resources. She speaks in her own language, and a relative interprets.* BRITISH COLUMBIA PROVINCIAL MUSEUM, ARCHAEOLOGY DIVISION

Bottom. *Houses at the Nuxalk village of Talio, photographed in 1913, are typical of Northwest Coast architecture. Planks as much as a metre (3 feet) wide were hand-split from cedar logs.* BRITISH COLUMBIA PROVINCIAL MUSEUM, ETHNOLOGY DIVISION, PN 10978

*Verandas and a walkway at the front of houses provided a convenient place to work on chores or to gather for special occasions, Blunden Harbour, 1901.* BRITISH COLUMBIA PROVINCIAL MUSEUM, ETHNOLOGY DIVISION, PN 256

# From Cedar Bark to Law School

Alice Paul, a Hesquiaht elder, remembers her mother posing early this century for the glass-plate camera of Edward Curtis, famous photographer of Indians. Mrs. Paul told me:

I always see her picture. . . . Every time I look at the books, she's there. But they never use her name, just "Hesquiaht woman." But I know her name. It's Virginia Tom.

At that time, Alice Paul's father had gone to the Bering Sea on a sealing schooner and her mother had moved for the season to work at the Clayoquot cannery. Mrs. Tom was picked to pose "because she could make those bark clothes and the baskets. Make them real fast." Alice Paul said:

She was always working. Get up *real* early and work hard on what she would wear, and that basket on her back. She was in lots of pictures. Digging the roots. Carrying rolls of cedar bark. With canoes. Getting seafoods. She made that little basket for going in the canoe, and the one on her back, and that special little basket you put the seafoods in and then empty them into the big basket.

That man [Edmund Schwinke] that worked for Curtis would take her to the woods where they were going to peel the [cedar] bark. She could prepare the bark. Soak it three days in salt water, pound it and work it back and forth with your hands until it's really soft. That's hard on your nose and throat. Even with a kerchief over your face those fibres get into you. It's outside work, not in the house. . . .

I remember that camera too, and the man all covered up under there with that black cloth.

Three generations later, Marina Tom, great-granddaughter of Virginia Tom, is a graduate of Simon Fraser University and of the University of British Columbia Law School. The route from posing in cedar bark to finishing law school has taken about seventy years.

*Virginia Tom.* PROVINCIAL ARCHIVES OF BRITISH COLUMBIA, 74510

*Marina Tom.* RUTH AND LOUIS KIRK

15

*The 1918 communion class at Christie mission school near Tofino includes today's elders Hesquiaht hereditary chief Ben Andrews (bottom row, right) and Jessie Tom Webster of Ahousat (middle row, right).* MOUNT ANGEL ABBEY ARCHIVES

In a similar vein, Alice Paul, who lives part-time in Victoria and part-time in her home village of Hesquiat, just south of Nootka Sound, once talked to me about entering school:

I *couldn't* speak English. I didn't know it. Nothing, nothing. But we weren't allowed to speak our language. We'd get punished. We'd have to write: "I must not speak Indian." Write it a hundred times. Or they would make us kneel down for a certain number of hours.

Sometimes families didn't want to send their kids to school. The boat would come around picking up kids, but they'd tie their kids in sacks and say, "We don't have any kids. That's just some old stuff there." One place in Kyuquot they put them into sacks, so nobody from that village went to school for one whole year.

Indian people have no monopoly on change; all cultures evolve. But today's elders are a unique bridge between the last of the old days and the onrush of tomorrow.

Commercial jets now fly over the British Columbia coast high enough to turn the topography into a relief map. On clear days you see hundreds of square kilometres at a glance, including the whole, twisting system of salt-water passages and rivers. Relationships and interconnections easily overlooked on a map, and extremely demanding to experience on the ground, suddenly make sense.

You see the feasibility of paddling a canoe almost anywhere within this realm of waterways. You see too that eastern Vancouver Island is far less mountainous than the western mainland or the outer shore of the island. And you also see how much of the coastal rim is standing on end, ill-suited for human habitation.

Inlets gouged by ice-age glaciers open like throats leading for scores of kilometres from the sea into vast mountain hinterlands. They seem to go and go until they disappear in the haze, still going. The side walls of these fiords are astonishingly steep, offering no reefs where fish and seals might feed, no clam beaches or forested benches for village sites.

Flying over the inlets, you see that land is flat only where large rivers empty into salt water, or where occasional side streams have deposited enough rubble to overcome abrupt dropoffs and build deltas. Beyond the inlet mouths, however, long stretches of suitable beach circle harbours, peninsulas and offshore islands.

This is the character of the coastal home belonging for millenia to the Nuu-chah-nulth, Southern Kwakiutl and Nuxalk people. It is a rugged and harsh domain, in places even barren. The bountiful resources commonly described were available only to those who knew precisely when, where and how to gather and store them—and Northwest Coast Indians had developed that knowledge over thousands of years.

Nuu-chah-nulth. Southern Kwakiutl (or Kwa-kwa-ka'wakw). Nuxalk. These are modern terms for three of the many native language groups along the central coast of British Columbia. The three are separate yet have much in common: the Nuu-chah-nulth and Southern Kwakiutl speak related languages; and, although the Nuxalk speak Bella Coola, an entirely different language, they are culturally closer to their Southern Kwakiutl neighbours than to their linguistic cousins, the Salish.

Until 1978 Nuu-chah-nulth Indians were known as the Westcoast People and for decades before that as the Nootka. Nuu-chah-nulth means "Mountains-in-a-Row," which is how the homeland of these people—the outer coast of Vancouver Island—looks when approached from the sea. Before Whites arrived, no single name existed for the various distinct groups within Nuu-chah-nulth culture; today there are fifteen officially recognized bands with two languages (Nitinat and Nootka) and several dialects. In addition, the neighbouring Makah people of Washington State are blood relatives who speak a closely related language and share cultural ties.

Because of language differences, anthropologists divided people who lived along the inside coast of northern Vancouver Island and the adjacent inlets and islets of the mainland into two groups: Northern and Southern Kwakiutl. Today the term Northern Kwakiutl is no longer used, and Southern Kwakiutl people increasingly object to the name Kwakiutl because it properly applies to only one of many village groups. In its place the

U'Mista Cultural Society of Alert Bay proposes the name Kwa-kwa-ka'wakw, which translates as "Those-Who-Speak-Kwakwala," and the suggestion is gaining acceptance. These people, whose territory stretches from Cape Mudge to Smith Sound, are linguistically united and speak Kwakwala. This language is one of six within the Wakashan Language Family: Kwakwala, Heiltsuk and Haisla (which are spoken by people from Rivers Inlet and Bella Bella to Kitimat, northern neighbours of those who speak Kwakwala), Nitinat, Nootka and Makah.

Nuxalk Nation (with the *x* pronounced much like an *h*) is the name recently adopted by Indian people in the Bella Coola region. Nuxalk, which means "Caught-in-the-Web (of a net)," is a traditional name for the village at the mouth of the Bella Coola River. There used to be a lagoon where the village is now, but Raven thought a river would be better, so he changed it. When the First People arrived, currents at the mouth of the new river caught and held one of their canoes as if in a net.

People from Talio, Kimsquit and half a dozen other villages in the region regret losing their particular identities to the new name, but at least it is a word in their own language. The old name, Bella Coola, came from the Kwakwala word *bil'hwala*, which early-day white people misinterpreted as the name of all Natives in the region of upper Bentinck Arm. Or, according to Nuxalk elder Margaret Siwallace, maybe it originated with the arrival of explorer Capt. George Vancouver. Mrs. Siwallace told me a tale that is surely apocryphal, yet is typical of the offhand circumstances behind names given to Indian groups by Whites:

Bella Coola is Italian for "beautiful bend." Captain Vancouver had an Italian on his boat *Discovery,* and when he looked up at our place he called it a beautiful bend [in the seaway]. It's not really our name. Nuxalk isn't right for all of us either, but I guess we have to go along with it. Myself, I'm from Kimsquit.

In the days before white people dominated the life of the Northwest Coast, each local group of Natives had its own name, which often came from a

*A floatplane lands at Yuquot (Friendly Cove) in 1973* (this page),
*the same village visited in 1873 by* HMS *Boxer* (facing page,
top) *and drawn in 1778 by John Webber* (facing page, bottom),
*official artist with Capt. James Cook.* RUTH AND LOUIS KIRK;
PROVINCIAL ARCHIVES OF BRITISH COLUMBIA, 33550 AND
PDP 237

place where an ancestor had encountered the
supernatural. White missionaries and officials
could not pronounce these names easily. Besides,
they found it more convenient to lump separate
groups of people who spoke the same language.
Native people today accept this reality, although
they are choosing their own names rather than
continuing to use misnomers originated by Whites.

Native children now grow up learning their
home waters and land according to both geography books and the traditions of their people. For
example, a map of the west coast of Vancouver Island shows Friendly Cove, and history records that
eleven years after Captain Cook anchored there in
1778, Spaniards arrived and built a fort. But Nuu-chah-nulth people know that the real name of the
place is Yuquot, Place-That-Is-Hit-by-Winds-from-All-Directions, and that men were paddling

# Notes on Native Languages

Languages spoken by the Nuu-chah-nulth, Southern Kwakiutl and Nuxalk people cannot be adequately written using ordinary English spelling. Their sounds are too different. People can make about 200 vocal sounds, but most languages use only three or four dozen, and no two languages favour the same selection. Infants learn only the throat and lip positions of their own languages and lose the ability to hear or pronounce others.

Writing native languages accurately requires the special, phonetic alphabet and symbols used by linguists. However, since many printing systems lack the necessary symbols and most people do not know phonetic symbols, native words often are spelled with various substitute sounds.

As one example, anthropologist Wilson Duff wrote in his book *The Indian History of British Columbia Volume 1: The Impact of the White Man:*

The sound used by a Scot when he says "loch" or a German when he says "ach" is very common in the local Indian languages. . . . they also use a more elaborate *l* series than does English: *l* (as in English), *l'* (glottalized, as though forced out through a tightened throat which is suddenly relaxed), ł [unvoiced *l,* which is pronounced like the *thl* in "athlete," except that it is . . . whispered and slurred into a single sound with the tongue held in the *l* position], λ (like *dl* run together), ƛ (*t* and ł run together), and ƛ̓ (glottalized λ, which can be one of the most explosive of human sounds).

There are other differences as well. English has an *r;* the languages of British Columbia Natives do not. Nootka, the language of the northern Nuu-chah-nulth people, has an *n* sound. Nitinat, the language spoken by the southern Nuu-chah-nulth really does not have an *n* sound; *d,* formed in the same part of the mouth, is as near as it comes to *n.* Therefore, these people recently changed the spelling of their name to Ditidaht (although the language continues to be spelled "Nitinat"). The *aht* ending means "people of"—in this case the people of Ditidat. The substitution of *n* for *d* came about because the Native interpreter working with anthropologist Edward Sapir spoke Nootka and so changed *n* to *d* when pronouncing Nitinat words.

Words and grammatical structures also vary from one language to the next, but no language is "primitive" or inherently superior to others. On the contrary, each is as well organized and systematic as the rest and just as potentially capable of expressing any concept. Native languages readily spawned new words and expressions that came from contact with Whites.

To cope with new situations, a language often borrows terms and shifts pronunciation as necessary. For example, the Hesquiat dialect of the Nootka language has nothing like an English *d, l* or *r;* therefore, in pronouncing words borrowed from English, Hesquiat speakers match the sounds as closely as possible by substituting others formed in the same parts of the throat. Thus, "dollar" became "taa-na."

Another way that a language accommodates new terms is to use existing words to describe unfamiliar objects or actions. To illustrate, here are literal meanings of native terms for certain English words:

elevator: in Kwakwala, "thing-that-goes-both-directions"

cup: in Bella Coola, combines the words for "thing-you-dip-in-the-water" with those for "take-it-to-your-lips"

saucer: in Bella Coola, "mat-that-the-thing-you-dip-in-the-water-and-take-to-your-lips-sits-on"

flour: in Hesquiat, "looks-like-sand"

raisins: in Hesquiat, "looks-like-flies"

baking soda: in the dialect spoken by Ohiaht Nuu-chah-nulth, "cow-on-the-side," because that was the trademark on soda boxes stocked by early traders.

out from that village to harpoon whales millenia before pale strangers arrived in their odd "floating houses" to trade for sea otter furs.

Similarly, today's Southern Kwakiutl people crossing by ferry from Port McNeill to Alert Bay are aware that a century before commercial logging created the town of Port McNeill, the Hudson's Bay Company had established Fort Rupert not far from where the ferry dock now stands. Long, long before that, a Giant Halibut, stranded near the mouth of the Nimpkish River, had taken off his cloak and become the first man. In the book *Smoke from Their Fires* written with anthropologist Clellan S. Ford, Southern Kwakiutl chief Charles Nowell tells how the man, starting to build a house, was startled by a Thunderbird, which came and sat beside him. The man had been worrying about raising his roof beams, so he said to the Thunderbird:

"How I wish you were a man to help me put up the beams," and the Thunderbird turned his head and there was a human face showing, and he said, "Why I am a man. I've come just for that reason, to help you with your work." And he put back his head and flew up and caught the beam with his claws and flew up and put it on to this post. And after the work was done he flew back and sat on the log and the man said, "I wish you would not depart. Come and build your house by mine and we will be brothers." So the Thunderbird took off his bird dress and bundled it up and sent it into heaven.

The Indian people's sense of place and personal identity began in this distant past before the world became as it now is. White people think of this as a mythological time; to Indians it was a sacred time of beginnings directly linked to daily life. Stories from this past explain how individual families or entire villages came to be kin with certain early beings. For example, the Nuxalk believed human life began when the First People arrived on earth from the Land Above. In that ancestral time, according to accounts told to anthropologist Thomas MacIlwraith in the 1920s, nobody had seen the sun until after wily Raven asked Ałquntam (a supernatural being) to let him play with it on the floor, then

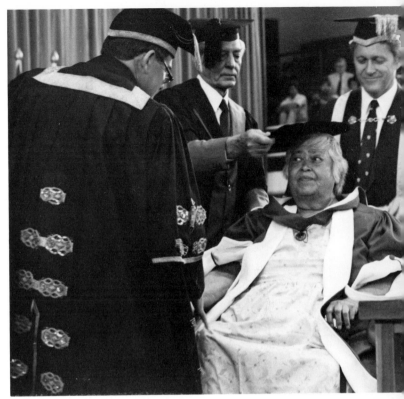

*Margaret Siwallace of Bella Coola receives an academic hood and mortarboard during the 1985 convocation at the University of British Columbia. Awarding the honorary Doctor of Letters degree, the university president spoke of Mrs. Siwallace as "a true scholar and scientist in her own right [who served as] the principal source for many a paper and thesis" in subjects ranging from ethnobotany and archaeology to mythology and linguistics.* RUTH AND LOUIS KIRK

boldly rolled it out the doorway. This happened about the same time that Ałquntam started sending the First People to earth.

In 1967 Nuxalk elder Agnes Davis taped accounts of those origin days for linguists Philip W. Davis and Ross Saunders. Her stories are included in their book *Bella Coola Texts*. This is one:

Okay, I'll tell about the man named Wiyaqa-ay. Wiyaqa-ay didn't like living at the place called Kawac, so he crossed the mountains to the head of the valley here. They say he carried his house on his head. He settled in a clearing at the head of the valley and began to make fish traps. As he was shaping the sticks for the fish trap he made a lot of chips which drifted downriver. The chips were spotted by one of the people who had been dropped down here.

"So we are not the only ones to have been dropped down," said Uniqwatl, who had been the first to have been dropped down here [from the Land Above]. "You all better get dressed," he said to the others. "We'll pole upriver and see for ourselves who it is that is making those chips."

They got all packed up and poled upriver. No one knows how many days it took to reach the head of the valley to the place called Slaxl. Finally they saw Wiyaqa-ay and had a talk with him. It turned out that Wiyaqa-ay was their older brother.

# Chief John Thomas Remembers

One day on the ferry to Victoria, I asked Chief John Thomas, a Nuu-chah-nulth elder from Ditidat, about his early training. He told me:

At age six you begin your training. You go with an uncle, never your father. He's too close to you. There were ten of us little boys. We each were given a stick about two inches long and told: "Keep this in your mouth. Don't cry out. Just bite the stick and don't drop it." . . .

Then I felt a slashing on my back. It was from a spruce bough, and I could feel the blood start to run. But it wasn't too painful; it got numb and I just bit into my stick. Next, I felt the sting of old urine on those cuts. That was like fire. But I still held my stick. After that, I was shoved into the river and told to wash off. . . . That training teaches discipline. Do what you're told and expect the unexpected. Endure pain. . . .

Uncle told us to get spruce roots [to make into a target for use in spearing practice]. So the boys would dig under a spruce and bring him roots. "No. Those aren't the roots of the spruce tree," he'd say. And we'd learn the different appearance of materials, as well as the qualities.

He told us to go hunting, and one boy got a mouse, one a squirrel. I got a snipe. I'd sat so still on the beach that the bird came right under my arm. . . .

When I was ten I started school. Twenty-seven kids from Clo-oose and Whyac went off to residence school at Chilliwack. . . .

[They] took away our clothes from home and gave us school clothes. I was smaller than the rest, so everything was too big. A bell rang and we lined up and went to chapel. Another bell, and it was breakfast. I learned to look around and see what was happening whenever I heard a bell.

I didn't like my shoes, so I'd take them off. But if the teacher sees you have them off, you're punished. You couldn't speak your own language, either. There was punishment for that. So, now when I was teaching linguistics at University of Victoria, I turned that around. On the first day, I wouldn't allow any English in my class until the very end of the lesson.

That gave me a great deal of satisfaction.

Each village and each family within each language group has its own awareness of origins, its own tales of the days when bumbling Mink married Frog who was so noisy he got no rest until he divorced her and married Stone; of when Wren acted as a wise counsellor; of the dire time before Salmon existed; of when the world had no tides and Wolf was without food in winter.

Drive west from Victoria accompanied by an Indian elder—as I once did, taking Nuu-chah-nulth chief John Thomas to visit his mother, Ida Jones—and you travel through places of origin and memory, as well as cutover forest and widespread hamlets. Passing a certain denuded hill, Chief Thomas told about logging there and getting injured, of years as an invalid, and of ultimately studying his own language as part of a university linguistics program. Crossing Jordan River, he mentioned an ancient village on its east bank that grew so crowded three brothers decided to leave. One paddled across Juan de Fuca Strait and established Neah Bay on the northwest tip of Washington State, home of the Makah Indians.

*The Pacheenaht Reserve, across the river from Port Renfrew, is an example of a traditional village site that is still occupied because of its nearness to present-day employment and shopping opportunities.* BRITISH COLUMBIA PROVINCIAL MUSEUM, ARCHAEOLOGY DIVISION

*Ida Jones, wife of 110-year-old Pacheenaht chief Charles Jones, holds a type of basket now made for sale but formerly used to hold deer tallow (for face cream) or powdered mussel shell (for protection from sunburn).* NANCY TURNER

The second brother moved to Whyac and founded the Ditidaht lineage; the third settled at Clo-oose. This happened in ancient times, but people in the villages of Neah Bay, Whyac and Clo-oose still speak closely related languages.

As we drove onto the Pacheenaht Reserve, the silken flow of the San Juan River gleamed faintly rosy with sunset light, and smoke from village chimneys rose wraithlike among the black silhouettes of spruce. Upstream from the bridge, wild swans drifted on the current. Beyond them stretched the bench of land where the village once stood. Near its edge Chief Thomas pointed out a soggy meadow where generations of Pacheenaht women have dug cinquefoil roots to roast communally. In the old days each family wrapped its roots with sword-fern fronds, which they knotted in a distinctive way for identification when the roasting pit was opened and the steaming bundles were lifted out.

Chief Thomas's mother is the wife of Chief Charles Jones, said to be nearly 110 years old—so old that relatives half joke, half worry that the government will cut off his pension. "They say he's used up his share," a niece remarked. We found Mrs. Jones lying ill with a sore throat and loneliness for Chief Charlie, then in a nursing home near Victoria. At the potlatch honouring his one hundredth birthday he had said, "I can't die yet. My wife is too beautiful."

On the wall above where Mrs. Jones lay was the shaft of a whaling harpoon. It was longer than the couch and, at first glance, seemed a structural part of the house rather than a poignant decoration. Apologizing for continuing to lie down, Mrs. Jones said, "You've come so far, I want you to get what you need. I'll just start at the beginning, telling about my life." She spoke of her Ditidaht mother, then continued:

My father was Irish. He went to the Klondike with his brother Gus and was gone a year. Then Gus came back and said my father was dead. I don't know why my mother just couldn't believe he wasn't coming back, but she stayed on there in James Bay [Victoria] right where Saint Joseph Hospital is now. My uncle said, "Don't worry. I'll support you and the kids."

He was a carpenter. And he fell off a roof and died. So after a while my three uncles from Ditidat came paddling down the strait in canoes to get us, and they moved us into a big smokehouse at Ditidat. . . . My grandfather said, "Your white life is over. Now I'll teach you to be Indian." So right away I started learning to talk Indian. I was ten, or maybe nine.

Instead of going to the Pacheenaht Reserve, head north from Victoria to Alert Bay, today the principal village of the Southern Kwakiutl. Rather than swans drifting on the river, you see fishing boats tied to docks and a concrete sea wall, which backs onto the beach that historic photographs show as well-lined with dugout canoes. Today, the boats are modern, and radio transmitting towers and a tall dish-receiver bristle against the skyline, more instantly noticeable than the totem poles of the graveyard or the solitary pole standing near the community Big House. Drumbeats waft from the open windows of homes, coming from tape recorders. Next to the old mission school, a museum holds ceremonial regalia forcefully taken from Kwakiutl families by the government in 1922 and returned half a century later.

Arrive at the Big House by invitation on the day of a ceremonial or come by arrangement as part of a tour group and you sense the linkage between native past and present. While guests take their seats on bleachers, women check huge pots of water set beside an open fire in the middle of the earthen floor. When the water boils, they stir in instant coffee. Chiefs, holding long staffs carved with supernatural crests, take turns speaking into a microphone that rests on a stand nearly as tall as the staffs. In Kwakwala, host chiefs praise visiting chiefs, recount claims to prestigious events, and exhort proper behaviour and remembrance. "We do not invent anything," they say. "We just follow the path . . . laid for us by our ancestors."

Talk with Chief James Sewid, a Southern Kwakiutl elder, and you gain a sense of that path. He has followed traditional ways while living in the modern world; he is a successful and generous fisherman, and also a highly respected hereditary chief who has served as elected chief. The name Sewid combines the Kwakwala words for "pad-dling" with "owner," in the sense of guests paddling to feasts and potlatches given by a great chief. In his autobiography, written in collaboration with James P. Spradley and published as *Guests Never Leave Hungry*, Chief Sewid tells of beginning to fish at age five or six "right along with the older people," using a small gaff hook specially made for him. As a child he enjoyed "swimming among the fish when they were spawning. I guess that's the reason why I love fish [and] would like to live among fish as long as I live."

Traditionally, chiefs controlled fishing rights. After the Whites arrived, canning companies took over, owning and supplying all equipment from nets to boats and holding fishermen in debt. Not until 1923 did the Chief Inspector of Fisheries for British Columbia rule that "salmon and herring and seining licenses similar to those which in the past have been issued to resident whites will in future be available to Canadian Indians in their own names." With this, James Sewid and other native fishermen stepped successfully into the competitive arena of commercial fishing.

However, Chief Sewid has a worry widely shared among chiefs in their sixties and older. He says it is hard today to preserve traditional rank. In his thinking, this matter is crucial, for rank forms the very heart of Northwest Coast Indian social structure:

Each village had a historian in the old days, or maybe ten or twelve of them. They'd talk to the people. My grandmother and grandfather would invite them to come to our house—a big Indian house with a dirt floor and a fire in the middle. And they'd tell us the history of our people; how we're related, and the nobility of the chiefs, and the rank within all the clans. The position. Who is head chief of that village; first clan; second clan.

When the missionaries came . . . the people interpreting for our people were uneducated. That's why the missionaries didn't understand and called even our language heathen. Right through Canada—not just B.C.—the Indians were forbidden to carry on their culture. So, for young people today, there's a big gap. You have to live with your people to understand your culture.

*Helen Peterson, a high-ranking Makah, speaks at the Alert Bay memorial honouring Southern Kwakiutl chief Mungo Martin.*
BRITISH COLUMBIA PROVINCIAL MUSEUM, ETHNOLOGY DIVISION, PN 7964

Being a chief carries great honour. But today there are dilemmas even beyond the responsibility that always has been part of holding high rank. In Alberni, Adam Shewish, head of the Sheshaht Band of the Nuu-chah-nulth, talked about being a chief in today's world. We sat in the Shewish living room. The chief's wife Margaret, recovering from cataract surgery, left her bed to join us briefly, then started teaching a granddaughter how to roll out pie crust. Two preschool great-granddaughters watched television. An adult son came and went. The telephone interrupted us five times. A teenager stepped in to ask what Indian princesses used to wear, a reference to the elaborate hair ornaments that girls wore during their puberty ceremonies. She wanted to dress her hair in a similar way for middle school graduation. Through it all, Adam Shewish spoke of being chief:

It's different being a chief today. In the old days the people served the chief. They respected him and did things for him. But I've turned it around. I serve the people.

There was a big "do" [potlatch] soon after I got the chieftainship and the Ahousahts were there. I was running around serving everybody and when those Ahousahts got home they reported, "They're crazy over there. They've got their chief serving them." But I've found that's how to be close with the people. That way, they're glad to give a hand.

The people come first. I got that lesson from my father. The December that he died there was an important party all scheduled, but then he got sick and I called it off. I went to see him in the hospital and could sense that he wasn't going to last long. But he turned and said to me, "You better go ahead with that party tonight." And I said, "No, I'd sooner be here." He said again, "Put on that party tonight. Remember, you don't count and I don't count. Your people come first and they've been expecting the party. They're ready to sing their songs and put on their dances." So I went home and told my family, "Let's have the party." And late that night the hospital called that he'd died. So my last lesson from my father was, "Your people come first." That was 1950.

Some bands have both elected chiefs and the real, hereditary chiefs. One trouble with elections is that

*The 10-m (32-foot) pole commemorating Mungo Martin is off-loaded at Alert Bay. It was carved by Henry and Tony Hunt, renowned father-and-son artists.* BRITISH COLUMBIA PROVINCIAL MUSEUM, ETHNOLOGY DIVISION, PN 2958

they come every two years. Everybody is waiting, waiting: Who's to be chief? And of course it takes a year to know the ropes and then in one more year, why you're out. With the hereditary system you know you're in for life. I don't have to be elected to let the people know who I am.

On the wall opposite Chief Shewish was a drawing of the thirteen-generation family crest that had been painted on the house front of his ancestral home on Effingham Island. Leaning against another wall of the living room were several full-size canoe paddles, beautifully carved and painted. These are gifts to be distributed at potlatches. Shelves held baskets, a collection the chief first intended for his den but later put in the living room so that everybody entering the house could enjoy them. Among the baskets stood a huge wooden mask, a face at least a metre (three feet) high. It is a copy of an old, old, family mask lost several years ago to fire.

Such masks are ties to the supernatural experiences of long-ago days "when the world was different" and People and Animals interacted comfortably. In the days of canoe travel, villagers gathered

to witness displays of masks and songs and dances that proclaimed their chiefs' contacts with the supernatural. In the modern world they still gather to honour union with their ancestral past. Tape recorders now ease learning family songs associated with rank. English serves as a common language for speaking with guests who have their own separate languages and dialects. Mail service and telephones, or travel aboard diesel-powered fishboats, may speed invitations. Nonetheless, marriages and birthdays and funeral memorials are still occasions for feasting and potlatching.

Chiefs such as the late Southern Kwakiutl artist Mungo Martin are known and respected up and down the coast, and a gathering to memorialize such a person draws representatives from many language groups. A feeling of pan-Indianism results, an awareness of shared legacy. For instance, Helen Peterson, a Makah living in Neah Bay, told me about going to Alert Bay when the totem pole commemorating Chief Martin was raised:

I got the invitation and I said, "We'll go no matter what." When we got there we went to the Cranmers' house and Mrs. Cranmer said, "You're going to stay

27

right here." One of the girls had a tablet and she assigned everybody a place to stay. The Jimmy Sewids invited us to dinner and you know what they had? Platters of smoked fish with eulachon oil.

In the afternoon they had mourning songs in the Big House and then a dance. We went early because we wanted to take some pictures. So we went in and sat down. We thought it was a log we'd sat on, but that was their drum!

At the pole raising we knew they'd ask us for a speech, and when they called me to the microphone I said that this was our first experience putting up a totem pole as it was done long ago. But that of course we'd heard of Chief Mungo Martin, so we were really happy to be there to honour him.

The dances were fabulous. I really like the *Hamatsa* [Cannibal Dance]. It's peppy. I just feel like dancing when I hear it. Our family are Thunderbirds; we don't belong in the Hamatsa Society. We have it in Neah Bay but we do the dance slower. Well, they pulled us out to dance with them and I'd brought a whole lot of olive-shell necklaces, so when we were through I asked one of the Kwakiutl ladies to stand by me and I gave out those necklaces. I had enough for everybody.

*In the Big House, relatives and guests honour Chief Mungo Martin at a memorial potlatch. A woman wearing a button blanket dances, accompanied by singers seated at a log drum.*
BRITISH COLUMBIA PROVINCIAL MUSEUM, ETHNOLOGY DIVISION, PN 8226-A

# Chief Mungo Martin

Mungo Martin was born, he thought, about 1881 or 1882. His father was Yanukwalas, Nobody-Leaves-this-House-without-a-Gift. Mungo's own boyhood name was Kisuyakilis, Coming-Out-to-Do-Something-for-Everybody. In the Southern Kwakiutl way, he took eight additional, highly respected names as time went on, but this early name proved totally apt because, as much as anybody anywhere, this man gave deeply to two quite different societies—his own Indian society and mainstream white society.

*Chief Mungo Martin, shortly before his death in 1965.*
BRITISH COLUMBIA PROVINCIAL MUSEUM, RYAN COLLECTION, ETHNOLOGY DIVISION, PN 13492

In 1947 Mungo Martin went to the University of British Columbia campus in Vancouver to work as a carver, restoring old totem poles and producing new ones. He also found time and patience to entrust knowledge to his new colleagues at the university and later at the British Columbia Provincial Museum, as well as to members of his family and tribe.

The late Wilson Duff, an anthropologist at both the university and the museum, referred to Chief Martin as his friend and teacher. In May 1959 Duff wrote of him in *Museum Notes,* the journal of the Art, Historical and Scientific Association of Vancouver, that

he has assigned himself the task of preserving all he knows of Kwakiutl culture. Whether it is by knife and adze, paintbrush, on the tape recorder or in the notebooks of his anthropologist friends, he is determined that his knowledge will be recorded for posterity. . . . Mungo Martin has a secure place in the history of British Columbia.

As for the chief himself, in 1953, while rehearsing the dedication ceremony of the Kwakiutl cedar house in Thunderbird Park, he thanked his kin and other helpers:

And you have come to help, you with your famous names, you chiefs. You have strengthened me. Your fame will spread because you are down here, and brought your big names along with you. So you will finish what I want to do. You have strength, for you know everything. Not every person knows what you know. Only you know what you know. You also have been left behind to take up the duties which have been passed on to you.

The movements of dances, the words of songs and their beat, the costumes and regalia, the audience reaction to dramatic performances, all are central to Northwest Coast Indian life. All are intertwined with potlatching, which specifically refers to the distribution of gifts to pay an audience for serving as witnesses. In general usage, however, the term includes the entire ceremonial program that is climaxed by the actual potlatching. Such occasions are sociable, but their fundamental purpose always has been to express relative ranking and group relationships. They publicly "record" social changes such as marriages, births, deaths, and the assumption of chiefs' names and privileges.

Potlatches served as the focal point of native society along the entire Northwest Coast. By proclaiming prerogatives, they made the rights of chiefs clear and held society together. Missionaries recognized this role but, since church doctrine ran counter to Indian concepts of kinship and prestige, they deliberately tried to turn young people against the potlatch, alienating them from their elders. Neither missionaries nor government officials were willing to let native people stay native, with their own systems and rights intact. Consequently, from the 1880s until 1951, official policies in both Canada and the United States forbade potlatches as part of a program "for the improvement and control of the Indians," as the Canadian Superintendent of Indian Affairs put it. Southern Kwakiutl chiefs told anthropologist Franz Boas, who arrived to observe and record customs soon after the potlatch was outlawed:

Do we ask the white man, "Do as the Indian does?" No, we do not. Why then do you ask us, "Do as the white man does?" It is a strict law that bids us dance. It is a strict law that bids us distribute our property among our friends and neighbours. It is a good law. Let the white man observe his law. We shall observe ours.

Regardless of white law, Indian marriages and births still had to be validated, the dead memor-

*A traditional welcome figure stands alone at Kingcome in 1933. It now is at the Denver Art Museum, Colorado.* BRITISH COLUMBIA PROVINCIAL MUSEUM, ETHNOLOGY DIVISION, PN 2422

ialized and traditions honoured. Consequently, chiefs started boldly holding gatherings at remote villages, posting sentries to watch for government boats. Sometimes they even would announce a certain location so that police would go there, then hold the potlatch somewhere else. Makah elder Helen Peterson told me:

The agent used to come right into our house and lift the lid where we were cooking and say, "Oh, you must be going to have a party. You can't do that." So we'd go out to Tatoosh Island where he couldn't catch us. We'd say we were going fishing.

Indian fishboats themselves facilitated a semblance of potlatching: tie up at a village, call people aboard individually and give gifts, then head for the next village. No ceremony. No songs or dances or oratory. Just secret, tenacious obedience to established codes. There was a sad irony in the effort, as Agnes Cranmer, a Southern Kwakiutl elder, commented on a tape now at the Provincial Archives of British Columbia:

If you give something away, you got to be happy, you know. But in those times, you have . . . just three [or] four people in that house. They have to just rush in and give their share and run out again. . . .

Now we really enjoy dancing in that Big House [at Alert Bay] today. I never see anything wrong with that.

When potlatching, a chief needed guests from outside his own group; yet, laws opposing the entire practice of the potlatch led chiefs to delay or disguise their distribution of gifts. Sometimes they scheduled ceremonies at Christmastime and credited the holidays as the reason for gifts. Thus, Daisy Sewid Smith, also a Southern Kwakiutl, wrote in her book *Prosecution or Persecution:*

My grandfather, Moses Alfred, had told us children that he had built us a gymnasium upstairs. It did have some gymnastic equipment but as we grew older we found out that was not the true purpose of this huge room. [My grandmother explained]: "That is where we potlatched, upstairs. . . . They would just borrow [take hold of] their potlatch gifts for a moment, and we

would take it back and wrap them in Christmas wrapping—our potlatch gifts! Because we were afraid."

In the early 1920s jail sentences sometimes were given Natives who continued potlatching. On a tape now held at the Provincial Archives of British Columbia, Nuu-chah-nulth elder Peter Webster commented regarding this period:

The Ahousahts were invited by the Clayoquots, so they went [and] their whole tribe got in jail. . . . Myself, I'd say ridiculous! That didn't seem the right way: to punish people and try to banish all what culture we had.

Government land decisions also were motivated by deliberate efforts at dominance and administrative convenience. Among Indian people, a sense of place includes both practical awareness of resources at various locations and seasons, as well as strong ancestral ties to where Animal People first took off their masks and transformed into humans, and to where later meetings between man and the supernatural took place. People can trace back for generations the rights to a winter village, a eulachon river, a salmon stream, a halibut bank, a clam beach, a whaling site, a sealing site, a cinquefoil meadow, a berry patch, a cedar swamp, a mountain goat hunting ground, or whatever.

Conscious identification with such localities—as well as knowledge of modern land values—still characterizes native thinking. People feel incomplete if separated from their traditional land. Daisy Smith, a Southern Kwakiutl who lives in Campbell River and directs native studies in the public schools there, said:

People are returning to the reserves. They're getting away from the hustle, picking back up on the closeness. In the village you have troubles, but still belong.

We find we reminisce when we get together: what we'd be doing at the village if we were there. We miss our own natural foods that are difficult to get here in town. If we were at Village Island we'd go around the corner and dig; we'd have our clams. We miss clams— and cockles and seaweed and grease [eulachon oil].

Sometimes we say to each other: "Has it ever occurred to you that we're stupid? We're trying to live like Whites—running out of oil, always needing cash. We better go learn our own ways. We may need them to survive!"

My generation was raised packing water. There weren't any faucets and the only heat was from a wood fire. But our own kids have no idea how to survive. The villages where we were raised are empty now. It's sad to see them so overgrown. Sometimes on weekends we ride to Turnour Island or Village Island [by boat] and we stop and reminisce.

Similarly, Ruth Tom, a Hesquiaht Nuu-cha-nulth woman living and working in Victoria, told me:

We had a really big territory and we used every bit, season by season. But then white people put us on one little spot [the present village site]. My people weren't inside the harbour [where today's village is]. We lived where you could look out and see the ocean going forever, without any stop—and of course where you first open your eyes, that's where you want to live.

The government breakwater doesn't do much good. When we used canoes, which are really manoeuvrable, the reserve worked out okay because the men would lift the canoes right up onto the beach. But then they got gas-boats and they had to take them all the way into the boat basin; it'd be a two- or three-hour hike to get back to where the village is. And they had to keep checking their boats, too, so it was hard. A lot of men lost their boats—and that was when we started finding other places to live.

It's forty years since we started moving away. But Hesquiat is a magnet pulling us back. We believed this is home. We never left. It was a big move to have to go to another reserve. It was really strange to do that.

For the most part, British Columbia chiefs never signed agreements accepting changes in the ownership of their traditional lands and waters. Hudson's Bay Company officials negotiated a few treaties covering Coast Salish lands on southern Vancouver Island, and the chiefs of four Southern Kwakiutl groups formally agreed to allow the Company to use land for Fort Rupert. In these cases, Chief Factor James Douglas "paid" for the land with trade goods, as was customary, and he promised native people that

they would not be disturbed in the possession of their Village sites and enclosed fields, which are of small extent, and to carry on their fisheries with the same freedom as when they were the sole occupants of the country.

A few chiefs also signed local agreements allowing the opening of trading stores, churches and mission schools. But, overall, no official land settlement was carried out either through British colonial law or, later, Canadian law.

When British Columbia entered Confederation in 1871, native people were given separate status from all other Canadians and placed under an Indian Affairs department. They became administrative wards of the federal government, legally alienated from control of their own destiny and patronized by federal agents who made all decisions and handled all matters regarding land and resources. As far back as 1763, King George III of Great Britain had issued a proclamation that land in British Colonies could not be taken from native people without their consent, yet in British Columbia such an agreement never was reached. It still is not settled. On the contrary, the issue continues to be tossed among successive and overlapping jurisdictions.

# Part II
## *The World That Was*

CHAPTER TWO
# *Kinship, Rank and Privilege*

Winnifred David, a Nuu-chah-nulth elder living in Alberni, taped descriptions of various events for the Linguistics Division of the British Columbia Provincial Museum. Among them was an account of Capt. James Cook's arrival on the coast of British Columbia:

The Indians didn't know what on earth it was when [Captain Cook's] ship came into the harbour. . . . So the chief, Chief Maquinna, he sent out his warriors . . . in a couple of canoes to see what it was. . . . They were taking a good look at those white people on the deck there.

One white man had a real hooked nose, you know. And one of the men was saying to this other guy, "See, see. He must have been a dog salmon, that guy there. He's got a hooked nose." The other guy was looking at him, and a man came out of the galley and he was a hunchback. And the other one said, "Yes! We're right, we're right. . . . Look at that one. He's a humpback. He's a humpback [salmon]. . . ."

So they went ashore and they told the big chief, "You know what we saw? They've got white skin. But we're pretty sure that those people on the floating thing there, that they must have been fish. But they've come here as people."

What was the world of Northwest Coast Indian people like when European explorers and mariners began to intrude upon it? Who you were depended largely on what ancestors and kinship you could claim.

## Kinship and Ancestry

Basic rights to live in particular household groups and to marry into certain other groups rested on ties of kinship. In fact, a fundamental social principle could be summed up in five words: deal closely only with kin. This was not unduly limiting in practice since quite remote connections—on either side of the family—counted as kin and shared deep bonds of relationship. On ceremonial occasions chiefs virtually "displayed" kin as part of their wealth, for ties between relatives—living and dead—determined rights to ceremonial privileges and crests. Kin could be trusted—usually—whereas nonkin were competitors for status.

Wakashan languages (those spoken by the Nuu-chah-nulth and Southern Kwakiutl) make no distinction between "brother" and "sister" or "cousin," nor do they separate "aunts" and "uncles" from "parents." The sense of family went by generation rather than by specific parentage. Thus, Nuu-chah-nulth chief John Thomas told me that an uncle trained him through childhood and youth; and Jane Sterritt, teaching in the Kwakiutl culture program in Campbell River, said:

One thing I noticed when I left the reserve and came out into white society, I thought grandmothers raised the kids. I came from a home where Grandmother said, "I can take the kids when I want to and go shopping," or whatever. So I was shocked to hear grandmothers say: "I raised my kids. I don't want to go through it all again."

The only discipline native people had was you were ostracized. That was worse than jail or torture, if your relatives didn't accept you the way they did before.

Aside from kinship ties, a person's sex and order of birth into a family largely determined his or her inheritance. Separate terms in Nuu-chah-nulth and Southern Kwakiutl languages distinguish older siblings and cousins from those born subsequently. The first-born dominated as heirs. Women—especially if first-born—directly inherited family wealth, although they received it in trust for their sons. Since women usually lived with their husbands' families, their inheritance tended to be transportable, such as honoured names, songs, dances and ceremonial regalia. Hunting grounds and locations for fish traps generally were inherited by men. All such property—tangible and intangible—belonged to high-ranking families. Commoners owned few rights. Slaves had none.

From birth—and even before—the children of chiefs received their legacies a bit at a time, always with formality and display. By maturity, they usually had come into their full inheritance, and an aging chief would retire, although he might still continue to direct rituals and aspects of livelihood until young kinsmen gained experience.

*Wearing a frontlet that proclaims chiefly rank, Ada Williams of Yuquot prepares to dance at a potlatch.* RUTH AND LOUIS KIRK

# Owning Songs

Most songs were privately owned. They came in a dream or while seeking ritual purity. Some, specially composed for ceremonial occasions, belonged to whoever had commissioned them or was given the right to sing them. Families value their songs and bitterly resent all unauthorized use of them.

Reminiscing, Winnifred David of Port Alberni told me:

My mother's mother must have composed thirty songs—and I don't know a one! She used to sing them one after another, and I never learned. . . . Some people got songs by sitting by a brook [or] the ocean. Some, way in the mountains. The wind rustling in trees. From birds. They'd listen to a bird singing and claim that bird was telling them something. Even the little animals too.

Peter Webster of Ahousat, born in 1908, also spoke of songs while taping early memories for the Provincial Archives of British Columbia:

I used to hear parents and grandparents [singing their songs]. I wish there was tape recording machines at that time. I just had to use my brains to remember what I remember now.

There's potlatch songs. . . . Quite a few different ways of singing a song for potlatches. And there are lullaby songs; and there's prayer songs; and there's what I didn't learn, the funeral songs. And another thing I never learned was a love song. And there's bone game [songs] . . . and songs for to make the weather good, and I don't know whether we have songs to make the weather bad—like rain. No, I never heard of it. . . . And what I left out would be our doctors' songs. . . .

Us native Indians, we can't sing somebody else's songs unless they give us permission.

Certain categories of songs, such as welcoming songs, belong to everyone; but questions about the ownership of others causes considerable tension even today. Unfortunately, misunderstandings are inevitable. For decades Natives were told they were "savages" and their customs were "superstitions." The young had little heart to learn from the old, and the old had little heart to teach. Therefore much has been lost. People who want to know their family background but have gaps in their knowledge sometimes overstep propriety and claim songs—and therefore status—not really theirs.

Concern with safeguarding private rights was exemplified recently at Kyuquot, when the band council decided to employ selected high school students to work closely with each band official. Most appointments worked well, but one failed immediately. This was the girl assigned as Cultural Secretary, instructed to contact elders and tape their songs and reminiscences. She resigned the first week. Nobody would co-operate, least of all her grandmother, who explained that the last place on earth she would leave recordings was at the band office where there was no telling who might listen to them and steal them.

*Hesquiaht elders Mary and Alex Amos, Mike Tom and Ben Andrews sing a set of four welcoming songs. Their round "tambourine" drum is a style brought to the West Coast in the nineteenth century as part of the* lahal, *or "bone game." Box drums and specially hollowed-out logs were earlier styles.* RUTH AND LOUIS KIRK

Each person traced descent from all four grandparents, slightly favouring the paternal line in most matters, including residence. Typically, each immediate family lived with three others, forming a self-sufficient household of thirty to forty people. Dwellings often measured 12 m to 30 m (40 to 100 feet) long, 12 m (40 feet) wide, and 3 m to 4 m (10 to 14 feet) high from floor to rafters. "I used to lie there and wonder how they got those big beams up there," Indian elders today sometimes say.

Daily life centred on the house group. Its highest-ranking chief directed practically all activities. He owned the house and its ancestral crests, which were painted and carved onto wall planks, screens, roof support posts and, in some cases, totem poles. His space was the back right corner, as figured from inside the house while facing the door. The chief next in rank lived in the other back corner. In *Smoke from Their Fires*, Chief Charles Nowell reminisced that he lived with his parents and a brother in one back corner; his eldest brother and wife lived in the other. That brother's mother-in-law was given one front corner, his aunt's family the other.

Usually, each set of parents and children, plus perhaps grandparents or other close relatives, had an individual cooking hearth with surrounding work space, sleeping benches and storage areas. Commoners lived along the central walls of a house belonging to a chief with whom they claimed kinship. They were "under his arm," as Nuu-chah-nulth people express it. Low-ranking kin who temporarily joined a household might cook and spread their sleeping mats near the door, sharing undesirable space with slaves, who had no choice but to live exposed to drafts and the possibility of rain blowing in.

Nuxalk and Southern Kwakiutl people traced their ancestry to supernatural beings who took off their masks and became humans when the world began. The Nuxalk believed that when the powerful, supernatural Aɬquntam sent the First People to earth, they each built a river weir for catching salmon or an ocean fish trap. Then they raised the roof poles of a house. Where these things happened determined the primary sense of place for descendants. Furthermore, the closer a chief's kin-

*Only high-ranking individuals are allowed to use crests such as this Raven, which combines painting with carving. The house, built on Gilford Island in 1915, belonged to Chief John Scow.*
BRITISH COLUMBIA PROVINCIAL MUSEUM, ETHNOLOGY DIVISION, PN 2452

ship with these ancestors, the higher his or her rank. All Nuxalk people belonged to one or another ancestral family, or *minmint*. These groups owned the names, fishing grounds, hunting grounds and plant collecting grounds of the First People from whom they had descended.

All Southern Kwakiutl who were descended from a particular supernatural ancestor also shared ownership of economic rights and the use of certain names, songs, dances and crests. People were ranked from high to low depending on their degree of relationship to that ancestor. Together, these kin formed units called *namima*, which in Kwakwala means "one kind." Each of a person's four grandparents served as a potential doorway to membership, and relatives chose which namima a young person should join. Brothers and sisters might belong to different groups. Namima formed a system within a system, an extra bond inside the network of kinship.

# Nuxalk Universe

Nuxalk organization was based on *minmint,* the groups of people descended from the original ancestral families. Minmint territories coincided with the hunting, fishing and gathering grounds granted to the First People by the spirit Alquntam. Until he sent these beings to earth, all people and animals had lived together in the Land Above.

The Nuxalk believed that *siut,* supernatural beings of various sorts, still dwelt there and also in a land below the earth. Previously, these beings travelled to earth and often met people. However, such appearances grew rare after young men and women became careless about purifying themselves. Also, hunters began depending on canneries for a living rather than wandering in the mountains, where men commonly met spirits; and as the unpleasant sound of muskets became frequent, it offended supernatural beings.

Elders told anthropologist Thomas McIlwraith in the 1920s that they traditionally regard the earth as a flat, circular expanse, much like an island. It is steadied by Sninia, a supernatural being who lives in the northern ice and keeps tension on a rope tied to the earth. The Land Above is also flat and warmed by a sun; the sky seen by humans is the underside of this upper realm. Beneath the Bella Coola Valley lies an additional land, or perhaps two. Ghosts live there. So do supernatural ocean animals and fish in human form. Shamans can reach this underworld during their rituals.

Alquntam derives his name from the word for foreman or chief. He is also known as the Wise-One, Father, Adviser, Light-Giver and The-Story-Maker (since he created ancestral myths at the same time he created mankind). Yet another name stems from the word for sun, appropriate because Alquntam uses the sun as a

canoe while wearing a cloak lined with salmon. When he turns this garment inside-out, the rivers of earth flash with myriads of swimming salmon.

Alquntam's house, named Nusmat-a, The-Place-of-Myths, is like houses on earth except for being endless in size. In it, supernatural beings perform the equivalent of the sacred *kusiut* dances known on earth. They do this while awaiting the arrival of Alquntam at winter solstice. It is he who established the order of things. He created the original Carpenters who carved the forefathers of mankind from pieces of wood. Various groups of Indian people, differing in language and custom, were carved in separate rooms of his house. This explains the human diversity known on earth.

The Carpenters also made birds, animals, fishes, trees, rivers, mountains and everything else, even supernatural beings. They shaped and painted each according to instructions from Alquntam, who then gave out tools, names and food, and assigned everything its place within the universe. Some beings reached earth by climbing down poles from the Land Above. Others flew. Each selected a cloak—Raven, Eagle, Whale, Grizzly Bear or whatever—from the wall of Alquntam's house before departing. After landing on a mountaintop, they sent back these cloaks to the Land Above and assumed their present forms.

The birthright of all who are descended from the First People includes three types of knowledge: the names given their ancestors by Alquntam; the cloaked form of those ancestors on arrival in the world, and their place of landing. At death, the spirit of a Nuxalk person travels back to that spot, dons the ancestral bird or animal cloak, and ascends to Nusmat-a, there to live forever.

*Representatives of Southern Kwakiutl families gather at Campbell River in 1974 for the Peter Smith memorial. They include,* left to right: *Jim Dick, James Sewid, George Hunt Jr., Thomas Hunt, Jack Peters, James King and Fred Williams.* CAMPBELL RIVER AND DISTRICT MUSEUM, 9018

## Chiefs

Ideally, the highest-ranking chief of each household was the eldest son of an eldest son, who also was the eldest son of an eldest son, and so on back through time to the group's supernatural ancestor. Lesser chiefs were younger brothers or their descendants, and those who had inherited rank through maternal lines instead of from fathers and grandfathers. Although among the Southern Kwakiutl and Nuxalk the namima and minmint owned the actual resources, chiefs administered their uses, receiving a portion of whatever was caught, killed, gathered or made. Franz Boas, a pioneering anthropologist, recorded that Kwakiutl chiefs received half the yearly salmon catch from their territory, half of the mountain goats killed by hunters, all of the long cinquefoil roots (commoners kept the short ones), a third of whatever shellfish were harvested, and a fifth of the dried berry cakes prepared by women.

Among the Nuu-chah-nulth, only chiefs could claim ancestral ties to beings from before the world became as it now is. Therefore, individual head chiefs directly owned the ceremonial and economic resources established by supernatural ancestors— offshore and river fishing places, village and camp locations, medicines, rituals, songs, names and crests. Nuu-chah-nulth concepts of rank date from the time of their most ancient ancestors. For example, a Mowachaht story tells how Raven, a chief, stole the sun from another chief and announced, "I will not return to my village. The people shall pay me to bring light into the world." All the Animal Chiefs gathered to discuss this problem. At length, Wren suggested, "I think if we promise our chief that when any of us catch fish or clams or game, we will give him one of each kind before we take ours out of the canoes, I think he ought to be pleased with this and will let us see the sun." And ever afterward people gave the first products of each season to their chief.

According to Nuu-chah-nulth chief John Thomas, "The head chief was a *tyee*, an elder brother. He wasn't a ruler in the sense of a monarch, although he had very real authority and power." A head chief had charge of his group's

*Nuu-chah-nulth elder Jessie Webster of Ahousat twines a knobbed-top hat of the type traditionally worn only by chiefs. Similar hats nearly 3000 years old have been found archaeologically, evidence of the length of time rank may have characterized coast culture.*
PROVINCIAL ARCHIVES OF BRITISH COLUMBIA, SOUND AND MOVING IMAGES DIVISION

43

THE WORLD THAT WAS

economic and ceremonial resources; he directed day-to-day use and made long-range plans. Various duties occupied his younger brothers and cousins. Those close to him in rank planned and led raids, gave orations and acted as his "tally men," overseeing the distribution of potlatch gifts.

Low-ranking chiefs and occasionally even commoners who had the proper talent or skills might become clowns, who are important performers even today at potlatches. Their repertoire ranges from buffoonery to satire. Anthropologist Philip Drucker records an account of clowns who danced about with a long narrow board crudely carved at each end with the head of a bird. The clowns claimed it as a display privilege, but when members of the audience asked about its supernatural origin or how they got it, the men could not answer—not even by calling out to their wives for help. At this, everyone laughed uproariously. The very idea of showing a privilege without knowing its full pedigree was hilarious.

## Commoners and Slaves

Nuu-chah-nulth commoners could claim no supernatural ancestor, own no property, hold no rank or ceremonial name that could be passed on to their children. For this reason they did not belong rigidly within the household of any particular chief but could move fairly readily wherever they had blood kin. They might seek optimum economic prospects. Indeed, Nuu-chah-nulth commoners with specific skills could expect not only a welcome but to be courted. Chiefs often granted such persons certain rights and privileges, in effect binding them to that particular household. Today's elders say that other relatives sometimes became jealous when this happened. They felt neglected. The flexibility was distinctly Nuu-chah-nulth; Southern Kwakiutl and Nuxalk commoners had less freedom to seek favourable arrangements. For them, ties to supernatural ancestors determined the place of commoners almost as firmly as that of chiefs.

Special skills generally were handed down within families. This gave young people access to learning

the secret rituals necessary for success, as well as the practicalities and techniques of hunting fur seals or making canoes, knowing where to peel cedar bark, or whatever. Low-ranking people, at least theoretically, always deferred to those of higher rank, and younger people deferred to elders.

Slaves had neither rights nor rank and received no legacy. They were property. Most were taken as booty in raids or were the descendants of such captives. Even today, people are aware of family members lost to slavery generations ago. Thus, Ruth Tom, a Hesquiaht in her forties, once told me that she hopes someday to visit the Quileute, who live on the Washington coast just south of Makah territory. She wants to ask if anybody remembers the name Tu-tee-sa-lip. It belonged to a high-ranking relative who "was taken slave somewhere into that country." Similarly, an elderly woman in Neah Bay spoke of her awareness of tainted ancestry: "Can I help it if slave blood is in my veins?" she asked. And a young Makah woman remarked, "I know who the slave families are and someday my baby daughter will know too." Another commented, "I'm tired of all this about who is slave and who is chief. That kind of talk divides us, and we need to all pull together. We have bigger problems."

Getting captured was the one sure way of changing social position. It was a calamitous downgrading that could strike chief and commoner alike. In fact, nobly-born children and young adults—and even famous chiefs themselves—often were sought as slaves. Their kin would ransom them handsomely or they could be traded for a high price. Or, held by their captor, they gave satisfaction by serving as a deliberate taunt against the group from which they came. One disadvantage of such noble persons was that they had no experience as labourers. A Hudson's Bay Company trader observed this in 1837 while calling at the Stikine River, in Tlingit Indian territory. He happened upon the daughter of a chief who had been taken captive and traded north. She was being taught to unload boxes from a canoe, and obviously was unaccustomed to such labour and still inept.

Chiefs usually quickly traded slaves to a distant

area, thus eliminating easy rescue or escape. What price they got fluctuated according to the reputation of individual captives and the overall supply-demand situation. There are accounts of 43 m (140 feet) of strung dentalia shells, 10 sea otter skins or 100 or more woollen blankets being exchanged for a healthy slave. Perhaps 20 to 25 per cent of Southern Kwakiutl and Nuu-chah-nulth society was slave, to judge from early written documents. A journal kept by John Jewitt, a seaman who was captured and enslaved in 1803, states that twelve was an average number of slaves among Nuu-chah-nulth chiefs, and one had fifty.

Nuxalk chiefs seem to have had a proportionately greater number of slaves than did chiefs of other groups, at least periodically. Elders told anthropologist Thomas MacIlwraith that their abundant salmon supply assured ample "capital" for buying captives from other groups, although during periods of oversupply, such as immediately following a series of successful raids, the price sometimes fell as low as twenty to thirty fish per slave. At these times, up to 30 to 40 per cent of a village's population might be slaves, either purchased or received at potlatches.

In Nuxalk origin tales, no slaves came to earth with the First People. This group may have adopted slavery from neighbours for, at least by the time Europeans arrived, the practice was typical along the Northwest Coast. Slavery's beginnings may never be known; however, some Southern Kwakiutl accounts of mythical times mention slaves, as do tales of a few other groups.

All slaves could be used or given away, discarded or destroyed just like any other property; most were treated fairly well, and their lot was not sharply different from that of low-ranking commoners. Early written accounts and traditions recalled by elders mention slaves as labourers who fetched wood and water, rocked the cradles of crying babies, paddled canoes, laid and tended fires. While in their prime, slave men helped build houses, canoes, fish weirs, drying racks and deadfalls. Women slaves cleaned fish and readied them for smoking or sun drying. They provided the labour absolutely essential to process winter supplies, for getting enough food seldom was a serious

*Chief Maquinna was one of the most famous chiefs on the Northwest Coast during the maritime fur trade era. Here, fifth- and sixth-generation descendants Chiefs Ambrose and Mike Maquinna stand beside their illustrious ancestor's portrait, drawn by the Spaniard Tomas de Suria.* BRITISH COLUMBIA PROVINCIAL MUSEUM, ETHNOLOGY DIVISION, PN 16351

problem; preserving it was. Slaves served as a basic part of the economic foundation on which Northwest Coast culture was built.

A few years ago, at the age of a hundred, Nuu-chah-nulth elder Charles Jones talked to writer Stephen Bosustow, who was compiling the chief's biography, published using his name as the title: *Queesto*. Chief Jones told Bosustow that in his grandfather's time slaves usually were purchased for six hundred to seven hundred blankets and that previously they had been paid for with various goods, from canoes to timber for house planks and uprights. Chief Jones's grandfather had owned sixteen slaves, who represented about 10 000 blankets, a huge investment. He recalled it had been painful to simply watch such wealth vanish when Whites insisted on freeing the captives.

# Tom Sayachapis Gives Advice to His Grandson

*As a young man, Sheshaht chief Alex Thomas was trained by linguist Edward Sapir, then helped gather information from his grandfather and other elders. Over the next decade, he sent a thousand pages of text to the National Museum of Man in Ottawa.* NATIONAL MUSEUMS OF CANADA, 26545

Living properly as a member of a large, multifamily household required listening carefully to one's elders. Alex Thomas, a Nuu-chah-nulth who learned phonetic writing, recorded the advice his grandfather, Chief Tom Sayachapis, gave him in the late nineteenth century. This advice, translated into English, was quoted by linguists Edward Sapir and Morris Swadesh in a book called *Nootka Texts:*

Don't sleep all the time. Go to bed only after having drunk water, so that you will wake up when you need to urinate. Eat once at midday, then go to sleep with [only] that much food in you so that you will not sleep soundly. As soon as everybody goes to sleep, go out and bathe [and observe rituals]. . . .

Sit against the wall in the house working your mind, handling it in such a way as not to forget even one thing, that you may not wish to do evil, that you may not mock an old man, that you may not mock an old woman. Take up the orphan child who has no mother or father and say, "Dear little fellow!" Take him to your home and feed him well so that he will think highly of you. The children to whom you do so, remember you when they grow up. Then they will help you; if you come to the beach with a canoe-load of wood, they will start unloading it for you and they will help pull the canoe up on the beach. . . . Do not make yourself important. Anyone who makes himself important is not manly. . . .

Further, let me bring to you advice as to men's things. Be a carpenter, be a maker of canoes, for you would not be manly if you had to go about the beach seeking to borrow something in which to go out to sea. Be a maker of spears and paddles; be a maker of bows and arrows; be a maker of bailers; be a maker of herring-rakes and scoop-nets for herring, for it would not be manly to lack them when you came to need things of that sort. . . .

I would say in advising her, if I had a girl, that she

should also be willing to pick all kinds of berries and fruit, so that you may say to the old people "Come and eat!" ... If a person enters your house while you are weaving, let your work basket go. Take a good mat and have him sit on it. Don't hesitate because you happen to have clean hands. Say that you will wash your hands when you are through cooking; let him eat. When you marry into a family, look after them, so that you will likewise be looked after.

*In 1934 Alex Thomas worked at Yale University helping linguist Sapir with the publication of the book* Nootka Texts; *in the 1960s he joined anthropologist Eugene Arima in Ottawa to help with a dictionary of the Nootka language. There he was photographed shortly before his death in 1968.* NATIONAL MUSEUMS OF CANADA, J-21201

*Chief Sayachapis, born in 1842, was elderly when first interviewed in 1910, but his memory was clear. His experiences of childhood training, making seasonal rounds to gather resources, names, rights, giving potlatches, trading and so forth are representative of his era, and much of today's understanding of the past rests on information he gave to linguist Sapir and to his grandson Alex Thomas.* NATIONAL MUSEUMS OF CANADA, 26543

## Rank and Privilege

Each house group had a head chief whose rank put him in charge of its economic and ceremonial resources. Among the Southern Kwakiutl, all the namima within a village were ranked in relation to each other, and the chief of each house group within a namima was ranked in relation to the other chiefs. Everywhere along the Northwest Coast, inheritance determined rank, and chiefs of all levels sought to enhance their stature by adding to the legacy they would pass on to successors. Effective exploitation of resources, clever trading, raids, shrewd marriage alliances and effective potlatch displays were the hallmarks of a chief's stewardship.

House groups amounted to extended families. Since the system of kinship included both maternal

*Ceremonial occasions among the Southern Kwakiutl include a dance representing peace, which is performed by host chiefs—here, those of the Hunt Family of Fort Rupert. The men wear fringed Chilkat blankets; their headdresses have trailing ermine skins and a crown of sea-lion whiskers from which fluffy white down floats with each nod of a dancer's head. The down symbolizes peace.*
RUTH AND LOUIS KIRK

and paternal lines and accepted remote relationships, each household could claim a sizable reservoir of potential membership. Chiefs usually welcomed suitable additions, for what good were rights to resources without manpower to make use of them? Everything from a stranded whale to a patch of ripe berries had value only if there were enough hands for cutting and picking and carrying.

Also, the more privileges a chief owned, the more singers and dancers he needed to display them. A chief therefore might try attracting lowly kin to live with him and, through generosity and good treatment, give them reason to stay. Furthermore, rather than risk angering—and losing—successful fishermen or skilled woodworkers or basketmakers, he might even tolerate lazy members of their families as tenants. A large household was an asset.

Chiefs owned the houses and the rights to select and schedule ceremonies. They owned or had charge of all resources within their territories; decided when the time was right for making seasonal rounds; directed the building of fish traps and drying racks; planned the particulars of First Salmon Ceremonies to assure a bountiful catch, and, among the Nuu-chah-nulth, led the spring whale hunts. Advised by a council of elders, chiefs had the final say in all group decisions.

Even when a chief gave a relative or retainer rights to use a salmon stream or halibut bank, a clover meadow or salmonberry hillside, the first fish caught, roots dug or sprouts and berries picked continued to belong to him. He formally opened the season of fishing, hunting, picking and gathering. After that his people could use his lands and waters as they wished and keep what they produced.

Chiefs wore the most elaborate clothing and held the rights to commission complex paintings and carvings of crests, which served as visual statements of ancestry. All such art was more than decorative. It expressed how the culture viewed itself and the invisible forces that shaped the world and human destiny. Nobody used motifs that did not belong to him or her; that would be stealing at a profound level. Crests were displayed so the public would

know a chief's ancestry, rights and privileges. Depictions of spirit helpers and art associated with most rituals expressed private relations between individuals or families and the supernatural. Even today Indian elders are uncomfortable if asked the meaning of such art. "Each family had their own

*Chief Joseph of Opitsat, Clayoquot Sound, here wears a Thunderbird headdress. Among the illustrious names he owned was Wickanninish, which had also belonged to his warrior-chief ancestor who was prominent during the sea-otter fur trade.*
PUBLIC ARCHIVES OF CANADA, PA 140976

*This screen with Thunderbird catching Whale, and Wolf and Lightning Snake at the upper corners, depicts an Opetchesaht chief's encounter with the supernatural while checking his sockeye trap at Sproat Falls. On ceremonial occasions, such screens were prominently displayed. This one is now in New York at the American Museum of Natural History.* BRITISH COLUMBIA PROVINCIAL MUSEUM, ETHNOLOGY DIVISION, PN 4672

*Facing page. Welcome figures —or, possibly, memorials— photographed when they stood in their original location at Cape Mudge. They are now at the Southern Kwakiutl museum located there.* BRITISH COLUMBIA PROVINCIAL MUSEUM, ETHNOLOGY DIVISION, PN 11705

meanings, their own sources of power," they often say. "I can't speak for them."

Masks and rattles were seldom complete in themselves. Rather, they were integral to particular rites and could not be isolated from the words of accompanying songs, the rhythm of drums and dance steps. Context carried great significance.

Totem poles, probably the most widely recognized art form of the Northwest Coast, also carried specific meaning represented by carved crests and ancestral or mythic beings. There are four main types of such poles: the massive house frontal pole; the free-standing memorial pole; the mortuary pole, in which the remains of a high-ranking chief were placed, and the inside house post.

How far back in time do the origins of these poles reach? No one knows. But early written records and historical sketches prove that carved house posts were already characteristic of the coast from Vancouver Island to Alaska when white men arrived. A doorway cut through the elaborate frontal pole of a Haida house is described as early as 1793, and mortuary poles in Tlingit villages were

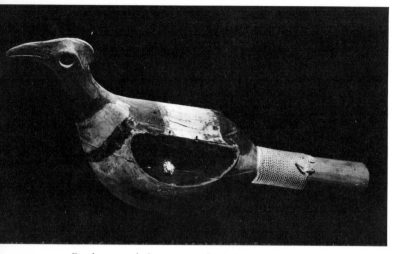

*Rattles were shaken to provide rhythmic accompaniment for the songs of chiefs and also were used by shamans to communicate with the spirit world. Many are carved in the form of a bird, often elaborated with additional figures.* BRITISH COLUMBIA PROVINCIAL MUSEUM, ETHNOLOGY DIVISION, CPN 10247

documented in the late eighteenth century.

Early white mariners saw no "forests" of totem poles like those in later photographs. Indeed, when Whites first arrived on the coast, freestanding memorial poles and house frontal poles evidently were typical only in the north. But after about 1860 to 1870 poles also began appearing in Nuxalk, Southern Kwakiutl and Nuu-chah-nulth territory. Because of access to new wealth, chiefs probably commissioned more totem poles, paintings, dance costumes, regalia and other displays of ceremonial prerogative than previously. The privileges displayed, however, remained inherited rights from a mythic time long before the arrival of white intruders.

The supernatural beings and events depicted by artists are also often the subject of songs or give meaning to prestigious names, which function like noble titles denoting degrees of ceremonial rank. All names had to be formally claimed and validated by appropriate ceremony. Southern Kwakiutl and Nuu-chah-nulth chiefs, while still living, passed their most exalted names on to heirs. Nuxalk titles were more commonly re-established after a chief's death. In each group an oral historian kept a mental list of names, along with knowledge of who had rights to each and the specific ways they could be

## Johnny Moon's Totem Pole

While fishing at Kelsey Bay in the 1950s, a Californian named Eric Sismey discovered a fallen totem pole with a figure that stirred his curiosity. It was obviously that of a white man, wearing a buttoned tunic ornamented with piping, his hands thrust into slash pockets like those on seamen's trousers.

Sismey noticed correspondence from Southern Kwakiutl chief Martin Smith in a newspaper and wrote to him asking about the pole. Back came an answer: Chief Smith had seen the pole raised at a potlatch at Salmon River in 1894 when he was about six years old, and he had often visited in the home of the pole's owner, Chief Weytlakalas, and his son Johnny Moon. The white man on the pole was called Matha Hill, Chief Smith wrote. He added that Johnny Moon had always insisted that this man "wasn't like those white men you see slouching around the coasts but [was] very honourable."

Matha Hill was a crest figure that dated to about the time of Johnny Moon's grandfather. Chief Smith could remember that at feasts the family would demonstrate their rights to the crest by pantomiming the arrival of this white man. They would wear "old fashioned uniforms with frock coats, braid and striped trousers," according to Chief Smith's letter to Sismey, which also mentioned that

the messenger of Matha Hill wore white trousers and white shoes. He appeared bearing a letter, . . . handing it over to the chief in the formal manner of a superior. The chief would scrutinize the paper in the manner of one able to read, then announce, "Matha Hill has arrived." At these words, Johnny Moon's son strode in dressed as Matha Hill, magnificent in early-day white men's uniform and bearing swords.

Chief Smith did not know who this man actually was, but he could identify all the figures on the fallen pole. The Thunderbird at the top was a crest acquired by Johnny Moon's family through marriage with the daughter of a Cape Mudge woman. Next came Matha Hill, then Beaver, a crest also used on Chief Moon's feast dish. Below Beaver were: a bodyguard of Matha Hill's; Wolf, a supernatural ancestor; a second bodyguard; and Dzonoqwa, another crest "which represents the awesomeness of the chief."

Sismey was curious as to who the illustrious white man had been, so he started working back from the pronunciation of the name. Matha Hill proved to be Capt. William Henry McNeill, for whom Port McNeill and also an avenue and a bay in Victoria are named. McNeill came to the coast in 1825 as the young master of a fur-trading brig out of Boston. He was so excellent at his chosen business that the Hudson's Bay Company first tried to stop him, then asked him to join them.

McNeill agreed. In 1837 he accepted command of the *Beaver,* the Company's renowned side-wheel steamer. Captain McNeill married a high-born Kaigani Haida woman, the sort of union encouraged by the Hudson's Bay Company for business reasons, since such marriages led to increased goodwill and understanding between traders and Natives. A granddaughter of McNeill's was a direct forebear of Johnny Moon's father, and the avenue through which Matha Hill became a family crest.

As for how McNeill became known as Matha Hill, the answer lies in differences between English and Kwakwala pronunciation. Sir George Simpson, who headed the western operation of the Hudson's Bay Company, recorded in his journal while aboard the *Beaver:*

The Indians made sad work of Captain McNeill's name, for whenever his head showed itself above the bulwarks, young and old, male and female, vocifer-

ated from every canoe, "Ma-ta-hell? Ma-ta-hell? Ma-ta-hell?" a word which, with the comparative indistinctiveness of the first syllable, sounded like a request on their part that the captain might go a great way beyond the engineer's furnace.

*The head of the McNeill figure from Johnny Moon's pole still survives; it is at the Campbell River Museum. Shown here is a small-scale reproduction of the pole carved by Leslie Nelson.* VANCOUVER MARITIME MUSEUM

*A Southern Kwakiutl chief wears a headdress carved with Loon and Sisiutl. He was photographed by Edward S. Curtis in 1914.* BRITISH COLUMBIA PROVINCIAL MUSEUM, ETHNOLOGY DIVISION, PN 7376

# What's in a Name?

Northwest Coast Indian people considered the names of chiefs as a form of property closely linked with regalia, songs and dances, each one embodying the cumulative honour of all who ever held the name. Thus, prestige from the total number of whales killed by each Nuu-chah-nulth with a particular name stayed with the name itself; and credit for each new potlatch added glory to the name of the host chief rather than to the man. History built not around individuals, but around names.

Typical among highly respected Southern Kwakiutl names are: He-Buries-Them-with-His-Gifts (that is, the people at a potlatch cannot be seen for the piles of gifts surrounding them), Avalanches-Everywhere (avalanches of wealth), and What-You-Get-You-Can't-Store-Up-Because-It-Is-So-Much. Such names were passed from generation to generation.

Occasionally, new names arose. One way this came about is exemplified by the action of a Nuxalk chief. As recorded by anthropologist Thomas F. MacIlwraith in the 1880s, this chief planned a potlatch to give a name to his nephew. While preparations were still underway, fire swept the village and destroyed all houses except the chief's. It was winter and difficult to replace food and goods lost in the fire; therefore, supplies stockpiled for the potlatch took on survival value.

When the chief got ready again to potlatch, he decided to name his nephew Skaml, Charred-Wood, to emphasize that his wealth was so great not even a fire could destroy it. The name carried no glory from past potlatches yet had great honour as a reminder that without the chief's accumulation at the time of the fire, people would have suffered.

Generally speaking, individuals were first given a "baby name," which was followed by a sequence of other names assumed at appropriate chronological stages—child, youth, married adult, elder, or whatever. For generations, this was the way. Then came missionaries, teachers, government officials and employers who insisted on a whole new system of names. These must be "pronounceable," unchanged through life and useful for "properly" identifying children with their parents.

Southern Kwakiutl chief Charles Nowell wrote in *Smoke from Their Fires:*

I got the name Nowell because a Sunday School teacher in England wanted Mr. Hall [the Alert Bay missionary] to give me his name, and they say that he was my godfather . . . and he used to send me presents every Christmas.

Chief James Sewid revealed in *Guests Never Leave Hungry:*

My father's father had taken the name James because he used to work for James Douglas, the first governor of British Columbia, and that was passed on to my father and . . . was given to me.

Sam King of Bella Coola told anthropologist Margaret Stott that he never had liked the name King, given to his family either by a missionary or an employer as acknowledgement of descent from "the last great chief" in the area. In the 1920s Mr. King decided to change his name to that chief's name, Poodlas. To validate his right to do so, he gave $1,000 to the Native Brotherhood of British Columbia. This was a substitute for potlatching, which was illegal at the time.

Stott also recorded that Joe Saunders had been Stikine Joe; George Nelson formerly was Skeena George; and Peter Whitewash got his name when a cannery boss happened along while he was painting a fence.

used. Individual chiefs owned several names, using those that were appropriate for the particular season or activity.

Even slaves, and occasionally pets, had names. Anthropologist Philip Drucker described a Kyuquot chief whose names for dogs included Mouth-Always-Greasy. This was from eating fat, an indication of the chief's great wealth. In many cases, houses, individual carved posts, roof beams, feast dishes and paintings had ritual names. So did large canoes. In fact, a canoe might be called by different names depending on whether a chief was using it for war, a marriage party, travelling to a potlatch or inviting outlying villagers to his potlatch.

Personal names, especially among Southern Kwakiutl and Nuu-chah-nulth people of high rank, came from specific associations. These names changed several times between birth and maturity. At appropriate times from infancy on, parents or other relatives would distribute small gifts and bestow new names chosen from those owned by the family and handed proudly from generation to generation. Each time a name was given, an orator would detail its origin, usually a dream or a meeting with a supernatural being. He also would trace its ownership and the honour added to it through the years. Each new recipient of course tried to live up to and increase this esteem. In time, accumulated glory outshone that of whatever event had inspired the name originally.

Tom Sayachapis, a prominent Nuu-chah-nulth chief of Alberni Inlet, assumed five names beyond his baby name. One of these, Getting-Whale-Skin, was given him at a potlatch mourning his father's death. The next, Having-Chiefs-Behind, became his first boyhood name; and when he was about age ten his grandfather gave him a second boyhood name, Wake-Up, which was associated with an ancestor's dream while preparing for whaling. At a potlatch the chief gave before his marriage, he took the name Come-Here, a command given by a Whale Spirit to another ancestor. At his eldest daughter's puberty potlatch, he took his final name Sayachapis, Stands-Up-High-over-All. This name went back eight generations to an ancestor who had fallen asleep during a whaling ritual, only to have a Sky Chief appear and with typical irony say, "Why are you sleeping, Stands-Up-High-over-All? You are not really desirous of getting wealthy, are you? I was about to make you wealthy and to give you the name Stands-Up-High-over-All."

Today, elders worry about the future of chiefs' names. James Sewid told me what he recently had said to Chief J. J. Wallas of Quatsino Sound:

It's not fair. We're trying to carry on our dances and potlatching. We're trying to continue, but we've learned something from the white people. The person that speaks the loudest, he's the chief! Some people now get up at potlatches—even the ladies—and what they're saying just isn't right. . . . What I'd like to do is get it down which chief belongs ahead of the others, where the names come from, what they mean.

In a similar vein, Chief Wallas told me:

When I was young and the different tribes were talking in the community hall, everybody listened. Everybody wanted to hear what they were going to say and it came from the chief and then down to the common man. I never heard anybody start from the common man and go up to the chief. . . . Always mention the chief's name first. If we didn't, people would say, "What kind of speech is that?"

Elected chief is a job. But hereditary chief is born into that home and trained. You're going to follow your dad's footsteps. You know that all your life.

# CHAPTER THREE
## *Ceremonials and Religion*

A great deal of ceremonial and religious tradition has endured from native past to present—although not without change. For, as Daisy Sewid Smith, a Southern Kwakiutl, told me:

When the Europeans came they lumped our customs. Now we do in one night what used to take the whole winter. Thinking in today's terms doesn't give a full picture of the past.

### Potlatch

Drumbeats coming from the Big House in Alert Bay, and smoke and sparks rising through a roof vent into the night sky, evoke the bond between past and present. Slamming car doors counterpoint the cadence of drums and songs, as latecomers find parking places.

*Matthew Lucas dances at the 1979 memorial for Chief Mike Tom of Hesquiat. He holds a Lightning Snake headdress to be presented to a specially honoured guest.* BRITISH COLUMBIA PROVINCIAL MUSEUM, ETHNOLOGY DIVISION, PN 14514-5A

57

Inside, bleachers or folding chairs accommodate a few hundred people, or a thousand or more, depending on the occasion and location. All have gathered to witness the ceremonial claims of the host chief and his family and kin. These hosts participate as a group—young and old, male and female, those of high rank or lesser rank. The audience also ranges in age and status.

Aprons and sequinned, floor-length dance robes catch the light, their glitter revealing the forms of Whale and Serpent and Thunderbird. Button blankets swirl and flare with the rhythm of dance steps. Masked beings of the land, sky and water appear in the form of dancers. They enter in a strict sequence, determined on each occasion by the particular rights of the host chief or his kin.

As the finale, the entire host family—even babies, held in the arms of mothers and aunts and sisters—circles the fire, each person holding a scarf or towel or some other potlatch gift about to be presented. When they finish, men unfold a huge plastic tarpaulin and spread it onto the dirt floor in front of the drummers and singers. Family mem-

Top. *At Quattishe on northern Vancouver Island, Southern Kwakiutl chief Car-li-te potlatched $500 worth of goods for "his favourite daughter" in 1910.* VANCOUVER PUBLIC LIBRARY, 14049-B

Bottom. *Hesquiaht Larry Paul distributes gifts at the memorial for his uncle, Mike Tom, in 1979.* BRITISH COLUMBIA PROVINCIAL MUSEUM, ETHNOLOGY DIVISION, PN 14516-31A

*Men at Opitsat, the major Clayoquot village on Meares Island, carry guests up the beach in their canoe. This is a traditional honour occasionally still shown to arriving guests. The photograph dates from 1915.* BRITISH COLUMBIA PROVINCIAL MUSEUM, ETHNOLOGY DIVISION, PN 2727

bers carry gifts from behind the painted dance screen to the tarpaulin, piling brightly coloured, hand-crocheted pillows in one corner and new blankets in their transparent wrappings in another. A girl opens a suitcase bulging with crocheted potholders; others stack scores of plastic clothes baskets and dishpans at the remaining corners of the tarpaulin. Spaces between are stacked with cooking pots, glass bowls, metal trays, ceramic cups, drinking glasses, ashtrays, decorative wall plaques, aprons, scarves, towels and yardage. People carry in cardboard cartons filled with apples, oranges and sandwiches in plastic bags.

Several of the chief's relatives begin to circle the hall, carrying the heavy boxes of food and coffee pots to serve the guests. Others in his group distribute gifts to everyone in the audience. People of high rank receive the most goods, of the greatest value, but no one is left out. In fact, everyone receives multiple gifts, multiple servings of food, for all have seen the dances and heard the songs, all have listened to their host's claims and credentials.

They must be paid for their witness; and, by accepting the payment, guests signify their agreement with all that has been claimed. The host or his proxy distributes gifts of cash (in earlier days, Hudson's Bay Company blankets), the amount varying with the rank of each recipient. Helpers too are paid, except for kin, who help without payment. People eat and visit with friends from other villages. They make plans to meet again. Then they file out to their waiting cars.

Potlatches were—and are—occasions for passing on inheritance and ceremonial wealth to oncoming generations. Each was given in honour of a specific person or event, though actual attention focussed largely on the host chief. His purpose in calling people together was to reiterate claims to a specific ancestry and therefore the right to pass on to descendants certain stories, songs, dances, names, crests and other prerogatives.

Potlatching was never an isolated custom, but one that belonged to the entire display network, including the crests on houseposts and feast dishes, and who married whom. The term comes from one of the Nuu-chah-nulth languages via Chinook Jargon, the nineteenth-century argot used by Indians from various groups and the traders, officials and settlers who had come among them. Potlatch means "gift," although Natives often translate it as "Indian business."

Preparations for a potlatch might take years. Hosts had to rehearse dances, compose songs and teach them to singers, commission carvings, plan staging and speeches, devise invitations and send out inviting parties. The ceremonies themselves might last weeks. Guests easily numbered in the hundreds (at least by the time accounts of potlatches started to be written down), and they all had to be housed, sumptuously fed, entertained and extravagantly paid.

The modestly born—and lowly born— figured in the proceedings along with those of high rank; commoners and, to a small degree, even slaves shared the esteem given their chief. Rank determined—and determines—the order of everything done at a potlatch, from the seating of guests to the distribution of gifts.

Formerly, as gifts were presented, individual names were called out and reasons behind them described. Ceremonial and social relationships thus remained clear—more so than is possible now that ceremonies that once took many nights are compressed into a few hours. In previous, more leisurely times, displays dramatically proclaimed the comparative importance of local groups and the status of everyone within them, as well as the ranking of chiefs. Lines of descent and the transmission of titles and privileges were publicly scrutinized, while orators reminded all of the timeless supernatural sanction of rank and the whole social pattern.

Enormous amounts of gifts were given out, at least by the time anthropologists arrived on the coast with their notebooks. Even aside from generosity, chiefs had an incentive to give away as much as possible, for the gifts reflected a family's assessment of the respect due their name. Lavish gifts also showed the high standing of guests invited to grant their respect to the family. Just when overabundance began to be part of potlatching may never be known, but certainly it was true by the late nineteenth century. Photographs from that

---

*Hundred-pound (45-kg) sacks of flour to be given away at an Alert Bay potlatch are stacked in a showy display.* BRITISH COLUMBIA PROVINCIAL MUSEUM, ETHNOLOGY DIVISION, PN 10067

time show thousands of blankets stacked one on top of another, rows of sewing machines and washtubs, scores of calico dress-lengths, hundreds of sacks of flour, boxes and barrels of pilot biscuits and molasses, piles of ceramic and enamelware bowls, plates and cups—all of them goods obtained from white people. These items were wealth acquired, at a high cost in time and energy, in exchange for wages or, earlier, for furs.

In early times, however, not even prominent chiefs are likely to have had a mountainous surplus

*Shield-shaped Coppers, symbols of chiefly wealth, are particularly important among the Southern Kwakiutl. Each carries a specific prestige value that can be expressed in dollars or blankets but is actually derived from how it has been displayed at potlatches. Pieces broken off and given to rivals did not diminish a Copper; on the contrary, each such piece continued to represent its entire history.* UNIVERSITY OF WASHINGTON LIBRARIES, HISTORICAL PHOTOGRAPH COLLECTION

to distribute. Several Kwakiutl families told Boas's assistant George Hunt their histories reaching back many generations, and they listed what each generation had potlatched in order to maintain its social position. Undoubtedly, this record is accurate, for oral historians were scrupulous in their safeguarding of the past. From a time before access to white goods, one family said their ancestors at one potlatch distributed 10 sea otter blankets, 25 marten blankets, 20 black bear blankets, 50 seals and some slaves. At another, a chief gave away 50 cedar bark blankets, 50 elk skins, 8 sea otter blankets, 50 mink blankets and 70 deerskin blankets. "Now the white men had come to Fort Rupert," this family told Boas, and following that year, which was 1849, white trade goods began flooding into the Kwakiutl potlatch system.

Precisely the same thing had happened earlier along the outer coast of Vancouver Island. As soon as maritime fur traders arrived, potlatching soared to new heights. In *A Narrative of the Adventures and Sufferings of John R. Jewitt,* a seaman held captive by Chief Maquinna from 1803 to 1805 describes the potlatching of plunder from his ship "a few days" after it was attacked. According to Jewitt, "Savages from no less than twenty tribes" arrived at Yuquot:

*Most Coppers have black or grey crest figures painted on their surfaces; this drawing on the Copper is probably the work of Chief Willie Seaweed, a renowned Southern Kwakiutl artist.* REDRAWN BY HILARY STEWART

*A pictograph at Kingcome Inlet records a 1927 potlatch. It depicts Coppers and cattle that the host chief brought in by boat.* BRITISH COLUMBIA PROVINCIAL MUSEUM, ARCHAEOLOGY DIVISION

Maquinna invited the strangers to a feast at his house consisting of whale blubber, smoked herring spawn, and dried fish and train-oil [whale oil] of which they ate most plentifully. The feast being over, the trays out of which they ate, were immediately removed to make room for the dance. . . . This dance, with a few intervals of rest, was continued for about two hours, during which the chiefs kept up a constant drumming with sticks about a foot in length on a long hollow plank. . . .

As soon as the dance was finished, Maquinna began to give presents to the strangers, in the name of his son Sat-sat-sak-sis. These were pieces of European cloth, generally of a fathom in length, muskets, powder, shot, etc. Whenever he gave them anything, they had a peculiar manner of snatching it away from him with a very stern and surly look, repeating each time the words, *Wocash Tyee*. . . . On this occasion Maquinna gave away no less than one hundred muskets, the same number of looking glasses, four hundred yards of cloth, and twenty casks of powder, besides other things.

Such goods were valued not for their usefulness but as wealth. They were readily transportable, highly visible owing to their exotic nature and so standardized that outdoing a rival—or one's own previous potlatches—required little more than stockpiling a greater quantity than had been distributed in the past. This infusion of wealth did not affect the underlying purpose of potlatching, but the sheer, swelling mass of goods to be distributed led to unprecedented lavishness.

Written discussion of the potlatch has been largely rooted in this period of historic dislocation. White people's goods had only recently become widely available. Land and water belonging to Natives had been newly lost, their time-honoured social structure and beliefs newly ridiculed, and many ceremonial positions abruptly emptied by disease. Survivors fell into a clamorous attempt to fill the vacuum. No precedents offered guidance. People struggled to hold onto legacies and save the linkage between past the future.

Indeed, the truculent rivalry of potlatches, recorded by Franz Boas and interpreted by later anthropologists as "fighting with property instead of weapons," belongs to this time of trauma and great

*Chiefs valued early trade items like guns, "Spanish blankets" and uniforms for the prestige of owning—and often potlatching—them. The chief shown here, in uniform, is Napoleon Maquinna, grandnephew of the chief who dominated the early fur trade.* BRITISH COLUMBIA PROVINCIAL MUSEUM, ETHNOLOGY DIVISION, PN 11447

*Jessie Maquinna, wife of Napoleon Maquinna, poses wearing a traditional robe of yellow cedar bark edged with fur.* BRITISH COLUMBIA PROVINCIAL MUSEUM, ETHNOLOGY DIVISION, PN 1442

change. Native people were coping with the onslaughts of foreign diseases, missionaries, schools and government officials at the same time that they were switching to a wage economy instead of their traditional role as one part of a balanced ecological whole. Social breakdown fuelled unprecedented competition. In 1895 anthropologist Franz Boas transcribed the words of chiefs attending a Fort Rupert potlatch:

We are the Koskimo, who never have been vanquished by any tribe, neither in wars of blood or in wars of property. . . . Of olden times the Kwakiutl [the four Fort Rupert tribes] ill treated my forefathers and fought them so that the blood ran over the ground. Now we fight with button blankets and other kinds of property.

A responding chief warned his own people:

Friends, I ask you to keep yourselves in readiness, for the Koskimo are like a vast mountain of wealth from which rocks are rolling down all the time. If we do not defend our selves, we shall be buried by their property.

. . . If we do not open our eyes and awake, we shall lose our high rank.

Some chiefs relied on rhetoric, some on flamboyant competition in destroying property such as Coppers, blankets, canoes or slaves. For example, in about 1895, Napoleon Maquinna (the grandnephew of the eighteenth-century Maquinna who had dealt with Vancouver and Bodega y Quadra) felt insulted while visiting at Hesquiat. He returned to Yuquot and sulked. He wanted revenge, but rather than risk punishment by "King George men" for attacking the village with weapons, he asked his retainers to gather all their sea-otter pelts. Since there was a rookery nearby, this amounted to a large quantity.

With the pelts aboard, a flotilla of canoes headed north and drew into line off the Hesquiat beach. Maquinna called to his rival and, holding up one prime sea otter skin after another, slashed them with his knife and threw the pieces overboard. The Hesquiaht chief followed suit but ran out of sea-otter skins. Instead, he shredded a bearskin robe and broke a war canoe. This drew only jeers from

65

the Mowachaht, for Maquinna continued to destroy and discard sea-otter pelts. All present knew that he had bested the Hesquiaht chief. The insult avenged, Maquinna's honour was restored.

"Grease" feasts also seem to have intensified during this period. Flames from an oil fire might leap up to the rafters, at times even igniting roof planks, yet all present maintained unflinching composure, sweat glistening on their faces while they listened to their host taunt his rivals with a song that bragged of how much oil he could afford to burn:

I am the only one on earth;
the only one in the world
who makes thick smoke rise
from the beginning of the year to the end,
for the invited tribes.

A complicated system of loans to be repaid at high interest launched those born of chiefs into these various forms of potlatching while barely beyond infancy. Southern Kwakiutl chief Charles Nowell tells in *Smoke from Their Fires*, his autobiog-

*Chief Charles Nowell displays potlatch bracelets probably made of hammered silver coins. He kept records for his brother, applying a new skill—writing—to the ancient custom of potlatching.* BRITISH COLUMBIA PROVINCIAL MUSEUM, ETHNOLOGY DIVISION, PN 1071

raphy written with Clellan S. Ford, that some of his earliest memories are of his father instructing him in the loan system:

"In giving potlatches is the only good name you'll have when you grow up, but if you are careless and spend your money foolishly, then you'll be no more good. You'll be one of the common people without any rank."

Those chiefs who gave many potlatches and enhanced their reputations were understandably proud of the fact. They had held their names high. For example, Nuu-chah-nulth chief Tom Sayachapis listed for linguist Edward Sapir the twelve potlatches he gave around the turn of the century. The first eight had come fairly close together:

1. A potlatch to "wash away" a child's taint from the low-ranking birth of his father (the boy belonged to Sayachapis's niece)
2. A Wolf Ritual (the primary ceremonial rite of the Nuu-chah-nulth)
3. A bridal purchase at the time of Sayachapis's wedding (of course repaid by the bride's family)
4. A puberty potlatch for his younger sister
5. The birth of his first child (a son)
6. A distribution of gifts to dismiss the shame of his slave's escape
7. Giving his son his first name
8. Giving a new name to his son.

Chief Sayachapis regarded his ninth potlatch as the most important. It announced the puberty of his eldest daughter, and therefore her readiness for marriage. His last potlatch ranked second in importance; it was a Wolf Ritual he gave for an unborn grandchild. Between those two potlatches were two small ones.

Of his greatest achievement, Chief Sayachapis told Sapir: "I was going to invite many tribes to my daughter's puberty potlatch." Because of this, preparations started soon after her birth. First, the chief had to build a house big enough to accommodate all the guests he planned to invite:

I started looking for beams. . . . I started falling a great many cedars, getting house beams. I brought down a score of cedars. [Most] would break and could not be [made into beams] as long as those of the house at Tsiha whose beams were fifteen fathoms [more than 27 m or 90 feet] long. I started collecting wealth. I started collecting blankets. I started saving money. I bought four cauldrons of this size. I got them to use when I would be giving the puberty potlatch and when I would have food cooking to feed the tribes which would be in my big house.

Eventually, Chief Sayachapis took $2,000 in gold to Victoria and bargained four days and nights with a trader who specialized in supplying potlatch gifts. The chief bought 20 bales of blankets, 80 boxes of pilot biscuits and 10 barrels of sugar at $10 each, then haggled for two additional boxes of pilot biscuits as a bonus for each bale of blankets. The trader insisted on giving only one; finally, the chief laid his gold temptingly on the counter and told the trader:

"You are treating my money like a fur-seal . . . because the fur-seals always come back. I shan't return. You have let this money get away." I used [my] hands to gather up my money. "Don't! Don't! Don't!" said Jack. "Take two boxes to boot with each bale," he said. Jack made it two boxes. I had overcome Jack.

Next, Chief Sayachapis dispatched messengers with invitations to the potlatch, so many that

there were no people left; they went to get the Machahlaath, the Clayoquot, the Ucluelet, the Tokwaath, the Hochoktlisath, the Hoiath, the Nitinat, the Pachena, the Makah, the Shinanohath, the Victoria, the Saanitch, the Cowichan. I went to the Nanaimo, the Comox, the Kikwihltaach.

While Chief Sayachapis was still out inviting guests, he got word that the beach in front of his village was so full of people no space was left for canoes. Hearing this, he "rejoiced because that was why I had invited so many tribes, called out so many names."

# Ida Jones's Puberty Seclusion

Through marriage, the young people of high-ranking families formed valuable alliances by which chiefs could enhance their wealth and status, and therefore that of their descendants. Marriages secured the political and economic position of a household, as well as its position within the ceremonial hierarchy. A girl's puberty signalled her readiness to assume this role.

Pacheenaht elder Ida Jones, who belongs to a prominent chief's family, told me about her puberty seclusion early this century. She thought she probably was the last of her people to observe the occasion in the traditional way. At the time, her family was living near Tacoma, in Washington State, where her uncle was digging and selling clams. Mrs. Jones said:

I was in boarding school in the town and learning how to crochet. Then I got sick [her first menses began]. But Auntie said, "You're not sick," and she made me go through it in the Indian way. She sent a note to my teacher not to be looking for me for two weeks. Then she told me to take off my clothes and she put oil on me and put Hudson's Bay Company blankets around me. And she put up a screen right there in the house for me to stay behind. She cut balsam branches and that's what I was sitting on. They were real nice smelling.

They plucked my eyebrows and the front of my hair, right here where you have those short little hairs. And then they criss-crossed over a strand of my hair and fixed it with mountain goat wool. They made ten rows that way. And they took cedar bark six inches wide, folded back and forth so it's wavy [and softened], and they bound me around the middle and told me not to scratch, even though something kept sticking me. Then for four days they didn't let me drink any water; just use a clam shell dipped into water when I was thirsty; just wet my lips.

After that, every day they'd take off one of the mountain goat wool wrappings, and finally there was only one left. I wasn't supposed to eat anything soft—anything that melts—so I'd have a long life. Not eat watermelon or orange, they're too soft. Just dried fish is what I ate and I got so tired of that. But otherwise, if you eat something soft, when your babies come they die soon.

They took that last wool off at daybreak, and we had to cross the road in front of the house, and I was afraid a car would come [which would be embarrassing]. They gave me a container with forty rocks, and I'd drop one where we walked, and I made them reach all the way to where we were going to wash. They made me go in that cold water of the creek there by the beach. It was December. But that was for my long life.

When I got that [cedar bark] belt off, I looked and there was a small little bow and arrow, a *chabood* [halibut hook] made out of yew wood, and a little canoe, and a little spear for salmon, and a little canoe bailer. I never had touched that belt but now I knew what was sticking me. . . . Those little things were so my firstborn would be a boy; to make sure of that prestige.

When I got back to the house from the ritual bathing, I washed all over with soap and hot water and it felt good to get really clean. And the next day I dressed in my Christmas outfit and went to school. My schoolmates asked what was wrong, and I said, "I was just sick." My teacher was real mad about it.

Remarkably—despite disruptive changes and government bans, even the jailing of participants—the custom of potlatching endured and is still the right way to mark birth or death, puberty or marriage, initiation into a secret society or the bestowal of names, the raising of a totem pole or the recovery of a venerable mask or other ceremonial regalia. Potlatching validates major steps within individual lives and thereby integrates native society.

## Feasting and Ceremonial Dancing

A chief's first step in putting on a potlatch was to assemble his own group to enlist support. For example, a Nuu-chah-nulth chief gave a small feast where he danced, displaying a quartz crystal imbued with supernatural power. At the climax of the dance he "threw" the crystal, "sending" it to let guests know that an invitation would be forthcoming in a year or two. A Southern Kwakiutl chief used similar sleight-of-hand to "send" his intended guests a small, doll-like figure representing a spirit.

Next, the chief described how an ancestor had obtained the crystal or spirit effigy and said that it was flying to those he would invite once preparations were complete; then he named these groups and their chiefs. By using his crystal or effigy, a chief announced his intention to hold a potlatch and galvanized his group to provide the necessary assistance. Meeting kin, they spread word of the plans so that intended guests knew to expect a formal invitation in due course.

Feasts were the atmosphere in which to announce and formulate plans for any major undertaking from holding a potlatch to building a new house or taking a new wife. Feasts were also occasions for marking a successful catch or yield, especially of foods like sockeye or salmonberries, neither of which preserved well; or the taking of certain animals such as seals, sea lions or whales.

*At Queen's Cove, an Ehattesaht girl newly entering womanhood poses with her hair ceremonially coiffed. The comb pinned to her robe is for scratching her head without violating ritual restrictions.* BRITISH COLUMBIA PROVINCIAL MUSEUM, ETHNOLOGY DIVISION, PN 4712

Expectations and events alike were shared. Not to do so would insult kin by implying their opinions were of no consequence. And according to custom, feasts were the setting for such sharing.

Feasts reflected the ranked structure of the society. Huge, elaborate feast dishes held the food, and speakers ceremoniously called chiefs to eat from each, seating them by rank. Songs were sung; the names of chiefs—and of feast dishes—announced; origin tales were recounted. How much pomp there was varied with the occasion, but invariably rank determined each chief's treatment. This was true whether guests were few or had come by the hundreds, and whether guests included exalted chiefs or those of lesser stature. A speaker announced the host's reason for calling people together, and jesters or special entertainment groups might stage skits and pantomines. Usually, guests were given food to take home and share with others, of course crediting the donor and describing his reason for having given the feast.

Feasts punctuated various stages of potlatches and underscored wealthy status but could also be complete occasions within themselves. They did not entail distribution of property beyond the modest gifts required of any ceremonial occasion.

Commoners, lacking the status and wealth necessary for potlatching, marked times of personal change with feasts. There they might formally announce a birth, a marriage or a young son's first successful hunt.

Feasting was probably the forerunner of potlatching. For example, a successful whaler might call people from outside his own group to share his sudden abundance of meat and oil. While they were gathered, his orator would detail the extent and riches of the chief's territory and trace his rights to resources dating from ancestral time. Among the Nuu-chah-nulth—virtually the only British Columbia group to hunt whales—the highest ranking potlatch positions still belong to descendants of chiefs who lived on the outermost coast of Vancouver Island, where the whaling villages were located. Among the Southern Kwakiutl and Nuxalk, seasonal bounty such as salmon or eulachon may have facilitated the first potlatching.

## Winter Ceremonials

Throughout the late nineteenth and early twentieth century, winter was the preferred time for feasts and the renowned ceremonial pageantry that culminated with potlatch distributions. However, comparatively few resources were available and access to those few was complicated by weather that often was cold, wet and wild. Earlier, these events may have occurred during each chief's time of plenty, rather than when he would have to rely on stored foods to feed his guests. But winter was the season with the greatest leisure, and also the time when nineteenth-century coast Indians went home from the hop fields and canneries, their wages and trade acquisitions in hand.

Certainly, the memories of today's elders—and the written records of anthropologists beginning a century ago—agree that secret society "carrying-on" took place in winter, after people had returned to their major villages from hunting and fishing camps and from wage jobs.

Margaret Siwallace, a Nuxalk elder raised in the village of Kimsquit, told me: "In winter when I was

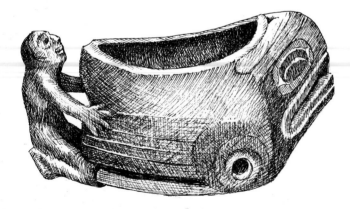

*Chiefs used elaborate feast dishes at potlatches, and their "inviting parties" sometimes took them in their canoes for prospective guests to fill and return as acknowledgement of the invitation. Such dishes might measure a metre (3 feet) or more long; many were named. This one shows an ancestral chief catching the first Kyuquot whale.* DRAWING BY HILARY STEWART

*Spirits gathered close to villages in winter, making it an ideal time for ceremonials.* RUTH AND LOUIS KIRK

*Mr. Roberts, a renowned painter and carver of Ucluelet, wears the headdress of Crawling Wolf, which kidnaps novices during initiation into the* Tlu•kwa•na, *or Wolf Ritual.* PUBLIC ARCHIVES OF CANADA, C 89143

a little girl, we used to hear whistles in the evening and be scared because we didn't know what was going to happen." People believed spirits came close to the village during the short, wet days and long, dark nights of winter. Their presence made that season ideal for ceremonial dancing. The whole order of the world changed. With spirits so near, people dropped their usual names and called each other by a different set of names. They also used special terms for many objects and relationships, and organized themselves outwardly not so much by kinship and rank as by membership in secret societies, which owned various dance privileges. How many societies there were differed from village to village, language group to language group, and doubtless also from time to time. Much depended on the specifics of people's ancestry and on what new dances had been added through marriage and raiding, as well as on particular customs.

In a lifetime a person belonged to several secret societies, each requiring initiation, each with its own rituals and dances portraying supernatural beings or events.

For Nuu-chah-nulth people, the Wolf Ritual, or *Tlu·kwa·na,* led all others in importance. Participation was not restricted by age or sex or rank. The only real requirement was a sponsor wealthy enough to distribute gifts to witnesses. The underlying pattern of the ritual can be summarized as a group drama in which initiates were first captured and then brought back to dance as Wolves and other beings depicted by masks and costumes. Everybody entered into the spirit of the occasion, as Nuu-chah-nulth elder Winnifred David told me:

They used to pretend that the Wolves came and took them [novices to be initiated] into the woods. But really they took them to a certain person's house for four days and they weren't allowed to go outside during that time. You can be taken at any age—a baby, or any age. It all depends on what your parents think of you and if they can afford it; have the money to give away.

It was planned, every bit of it. The parents ask the Wolf to come and take their child and the potlatch had to be after the fourth day. The parents would take turns giving away money when the kids first came into view and were being taken into the Big House where

Top. *Whistles carry high ceremonial value. Chief Mungo Martin told anthropologist Wilson Duff about the theft of one, which led the Kwakiutl to attack the Nuxalk, and also of how his grandmother saved another from destruction by carrying it into the forest when she fled a Royal Navy bombardment of her village. The whistle shown here was collected for a museum in Berlin during the nineteenth century.* MUSEUM FÜR VÖLKERKUNDE, BERLIN, IVA 1721B

Bottom. *The Wolf Ritual formed the very heart of Nuu-chah-nulth and Makah ceremonial life. Anyone could be initiated at any age, but usually in their teenaged years.* BRITISH MUSEUM, LONDON, P5 070204

the potlatch was to be. Each had his own dance, pretending to be a bird or some kind of animal or fish—anything so long as it's nature. Parents go to the Wolf's house in the evening and teach their kids what to do; and they had songs to sing while coming into the Big House.

They felt afraid. Afraid a real wolf would take them. It really was men dressed in a blanket and blowing their whistles and wearing their headdress. I remember hearing the whistles. My, the kids would be scared and the grandparents would tell them, "It's Wolves."

Among the Southern Kwakiutl, two dance series dominate the ritual season, the *t'seka* and the *tla'sala*. Foremost is the t'seka, characterized by cedar bark dyed red and worn as part of the dancer's regalia and also attached to masks.

In *Smoke from Their Fires*, Chief Charles Nowell described a rehearsal for the drama of the t'seka, the "red cedar bark" ceremonial:

Then Omhede stands up and holds a rattle and red [cedar] bark in his hand and says, "o-o-o-o-o-o-i" four times, using the rattle all the time. His face is painted with black charcoal, and he begins to sing his song by himself, shaking his rattle all the time. Then he stops still and everybody keeps quiet—even the children. The song is supposed to give more power to the red bark. Then the red bark is given around. . . . [It] has been beaten very fine so it becomes almost like wool, and this was given around to everybody. They wiped their faces with it, which means that they are wiping away all the ordinary human being. . . .

The next night . . . is the first time all the masks that they use in the winter dance shows. First of all they call a man to carry a box and take it up to where the singers are. He goes around the house four times before he puts this box down amongst the singers. When he puts it down he presses it down and the box makes a squeaky noise which means that the box has magic in it.

After that they call another man that will come and begin to strike at this box. All the singers begin to strike it and beat the board. Then he beckons to them to stop

*Dancers photographed near Fort Rupert in 1914 represent various supernatural beings of the Southern Kwakiutl red cedar bark ceremonial. Through pageantry, people celebrate the spirit-filled world and re-enact ancestral encounters with the supernatural.*
BRITISH COLUMBIA PROVINCIAL MUSEUM, ETHNOLOGY DIVISION, PN 10072

beating the box. Then all the noises for the different masks are heard by all the people in the house. They make each noise that they make in the winter dance, and at the fourth time they beat the box, the screen behind the singers comes down and right on the back of the screen all kinds of masks is shown in one time—all

*Crooked Beak, one of the three Cannibal Birds of the Hamatsa, pauses in a corner of Mungo Martin's ceremonial house in Victoria. Such headdresses are so heavy that helpers must assist dancers to rise from the floor.* RUTH AND LOUIS KIRK

the masks owned by all the Fort Ruperts. . . . After that the singers begin to sing to quiet these masks, so they won't show up without the consent of their owners. They have a special song for that saying that the masks are mad from the beating, and now they should be quiet.

The *Hamatsa*, or "Cannibal Dance," ranks first within the t'seka series. Previously, rigorous training for novice dancers included lengthy seclusion,

but by early this century the time for this was greatly shortened; and instead of remaining outside the village, a Hamatsa novice might stay hidden in a house or attic, secretly meeting his trainers at night. Today the seclusion is little more than symbolic.

A Hamatsa dancer was supposedly held by a Cannibal spirit, whose name Baxwbakwalanuksiwe means literally Becoming-Progressively-More-Human. Wild, cannibalistic hunger still possessed the novice when he reappeared among people after escaping from this spirit. While dancing, he "bit" members of the audience, who actually had been forewarned and were paid for their role. A small, sharp blade hidden in the Hamatsa dancer's palm drew a convincing show of blood; a bladder of seal blood could be burst for an even more dramatic show. Today this supposed bloodthirstiness is rarely performed.

Four times the new Hamatsa circled the floor, while relatives tried to calm his frenzy with the rhythm of their rattles, drumming and chanting. Fearsome Cannibal Birds appeared: Raven, the "food taster," who pecks out and devours the eyes of his master's victims; Galugwaduwis, the Crooked-Beak-of-Heaven, a huge bird "from the upper world" with a distinctive, often elaborate protuberance on its bill; and Hokhokw, who crushes skulls in his beak. Dancers wearing these masks high-stepped around the floor, counter-clockwise, stopping in each corner, squatting with heads swaying and beaks loudly clacking. Then they left. The quieted Hamatsa reappeared, dancing with a proud vigour, while a woman who was closely related circled the floor backward, facing him and holding out her arms. She calmed the novice and eased his return to human society.

Various additional dances and masks followed the Hamatsa, depending on the particular ceremonial prerogatives of the family that was performing. Each dance was ranked in relation to all the others, with the Hamatsa carrying the greatest prestige and requiring the greatest preparation. Novices had to be initiated into seven other societies before being allowed to join the Hamatsa.

The second Southern Kwakiutl dance series is the tla'sala, generally translated as the "chief's

*Participants in an 1894 Hamatsa ceremonial at Fort Rupert. They wear cedar-bark neckrings, their faces are blackened and their hair is covered with feathers.*
SMITHSONIAN INSTITUTION, 3946

*Hokhokw appears during a Hamatsa performance by the Hunt Family Fort Rupert Dancers in 1982. The huge bird comes from the world of the Cannibal Spirit, where Hamatsa initiates receive such power that they must be calmed before rejoining the human realm.* RUTH AND LOUIS KIRK

dance" or "peace dance." During this performance, the tla'sala dancers vanish, supposedly spirited away. Soon afterward, a sound is heard outside the house, and the creature that captured the performer appears and dances. Southern Kwakiutl people still strictly separate the two dance series, with those of the tla'sala always coming after the t'seka. Previously, each series might last for several nights, but now they often occur on the same evening in the same dance house, although there is a clear break between them to symbolically "take off the red cedar bark" of the t'seka.

The Nuxalk also have two series of dances, the *sisaok* and *kisiut*. Elders remember that the sisaok

season began in October, when supplies of stored food were still sure to be ample. Kisiut dances took place from November through February.

For the Nuu-chah-nulth, Nuxalk and Southern Kwakiutl, the most important ritual centred on the crisis of separation from family and village, followed by return and acceptance back into normal life. Only society members had full knowledge of the ritual, and revealing secret symbolism to non-members was punished, even by death. Furthermore, any uninitiated person who watched forbidden rites, whether deliberately or by accident, could expect a dire outcome. Often this meant an immediate, forced induction into the secret

## Social Clubs

Nuu-chah-nulth and Southern Kwakiutl people had social clubs for entertainment. During interludes between potlatch events, club members parodied solemn customs and performed irreverent dances and songs. In the 1930s elders told anthropologist Philip Drucker that part of the special character of these clubs lay in their lack of customary formalities. Anybody—even if lowly born—could be a leader in a social club. Furthermore, neither joining nor switching from one club to another required any special procedure. A person simply started spending more time with the people of a particular club.

Performances were imitative, with club members costuming themselves a certain way and then mimicking the behaviour of what or who they represented. At Yuquot, middle-aged women called "Sea Cucumbers" wrapped themselves in blankets and writhed on the floor; middle-aged men called "Squid" danced with long, hooked poles, which they used like tentacles to drag objects and members of the audience out onto the floor, and "Cormorants" beat their arms rapidly and threw handfuls of flour at spectators, in imitation of bird droppings.

In the 1980s Peter and Jessie Webster told linguist Barbara Efrat about similar performances at Ahousat. For instance, mimicking a potlatch, a club would flamboyantly hand out nickels and pennies instead of dollar bills; or a "chief" would constantly check a book for the particulars of protocol, then insist everybody was making mistakes and the performance must begin again. Such spoofing released tensions surrounding practices central to Northwest Coast Indian culture.

Social clubs also parodied the pomp of other cultures. As an example of this, the Websters told about the staging of a royal coronation at Ahousat. Club members dressed a king and queen in robes made from red curtains; borrowed church vestments for a club member who knew Latin prayers and could act as archbishop, and found a short overcoat and leather gloves—plus cigars and oversize ashtray—for prime ministers Harold Wilson and Winston Churchill. Guards wore green crepe-paper bands diagonally across their chests and paper bags painted black to represent bearskin hats.

No particular culmination concluded the coronation skit. As always, the whole idea was to have fun.

society—a dreaded consequence because of all the powerful unknowns involved.

Members of the audience were themselves made part of a performance without leaving their seats, because their role as public witnesses was indispensable and because of the way dances were staged. For instance, during the Nuxalk Thunderbird dance, a masked figure, holding a perforated rattle filled with smouldering bark, circled the floor. He shook sparks and smoke onto everyone seated within reach. Next, Rain appeared and sprayed the audience with water from concealed bladders. "After thunder comes rain, you know," people today will laughingly explain to a startled outsider seeing the dance for the first time.

Theatrical effects included performers who walked on fire with the aid of an unseen plank laid onto a bed of coals or who walked on water by stepping on a platform resting on a submerged canoe. During a Hamatsa ceremonial, Southern

*Oil shoots from the claws of this Thunderbird after it is lowered to grasp the Whale. The action represents a supernatural encounter that was the source of ceremonial power for the name Maquinna. A replica of this sculpture was carved by Calvin Hunt (whose mother is a Mowachaht), and it is now at the University of British Columbia's Museum of Anthropology.* BRITISH COLUMBIA PROVINCIAL MUSEUM, ETHNOLOGY DIVISION, PN 4662

79

Kwakiutl villagers might watch an initiate fall out of a canoe and drown, yet later see him enter the dance house. Actually, it was a man-sized dummy that "drowned," while the novice surfaced unseen on the far side of the canoe.

One Nuu-chah-nulth chief owned a Thunderbird that rose from the floor and soared around the room. Another displayed a flat board with a Wolf head carved at each end. This device mysteriously elongated then contracted, while the chief sang. Chief Maquinna owned a wooden Whale that floated in a tank of water, while a Thunderbird with movable wings descended onto it by means of ropes.

*Chief Charles Nowell demonstrates the Southern Kwakiutl war dance at the 1893 Chicago World Fair. The dance symbolizes an event from ancestral times, when people had to restrain a great warrior in order to have peace. They tied him to their roof beams, but there, unable to reach others, he bloodied himself with his*

*Sisiutl knife. Villagers quieted him with songs, then took him down. Each time he returned from a war expedition, however, they tied him to a Sisiutl "harness" and again hoisted him up into the rafters.* FIELD MUSEUM OF NATURAL HISTORY, CHICAGO, 13593 AND 13594

With a nod of the head and a pull of a string, masks changed from bird into human. Dancers climbed into boxes to be "cremated," then reappeared after escaping through a false bottom into a pit dug beneath the box. Voices came from underground and from the roof, their sound carried through kelp speaking tubes laid discreetly out of sight. Carved birds flew across rafters, manipulated on strings that linked one dark recess with the next.

Among the Southern Kwakiutl, frogs, huge feathers or the horns of the two-headed serpent known as Sisiutl might come out of the floor and move about the house. Such beings could pull a dancer after them when they sank back underground. In one dance a man known for his strength grasped a woman who was being pulled below. He hung onto her and attempted "rescue"; but, first his hands, then his forearms and elbows, disappeared into the ground, as he was pulled across the floor by the mysterious force dragging the woman. Finally, the would-be rescuer fell into a faint; the woman was lost—although of course scheduled to reappear. A shallow ditch dug into the floor, with a rope laid in it and a light backfilling of dirt, let the man pull himself along while acting the part of being dragged. A tunnel connecting two pits allowed the woman to disappear and return.

Anthropologist Franz Boas described in his book *Ethnology of the Kwakiutl* the tumult of a Hamatsa held in 1894:

Then the ha-mshamst!Es [one particular society] began to cry, "*wip, wip,*" and the Bears [another society] began to growl. Now [the chief] sang out again, "*ho;*" and the people beat boards and responded by the cry, "*he.*" The ham'mshamtsEs began to cry, "*wip,*" and the Bears began to growl, "*who ha,*" and the Fool dancers cried "*wihi.*" After a short interval [the] chief sang "*ho*" for the third time, and the people and the dancers responded in the same manner. Then while the men were still beating time and while the various cries were being uttered . . . the chief Cannibal dancer rushed out of the woods, followed by his six attendants, and crying "*hap, hap, hap, hap.*"

## The Spirit World

The natural, physical world was the one in which people moved and had their daily being, but there was also a world of spirits, which were largely unpredictable yet could be controlled through ritual. Northwest Coast Indians viewed animals and plants—and sometimes even cliffs and mountains—as belonging to both the physical and supernatural realms. They deeply revered the spirits of them all and made every effort to gain their co-operation and avoid annoying them. After all, deer can easily outrun men; therefore, surely, humans could succeed in hunting them only when Deer allowed it. Seals and whales swim far and fast and dive deep; for all the excellence of canoes, spears and harpoons, people would be a poor match for them unless Seal and Whale willingly surrendered to hunters. Salmon purposely filled streams so that people might feast. Cedar trees wore valuable robes as an invitation to weave bark into clothing.

Humans had body, soul, spirit, abilities and feelings—as did Animal People, plants, places and all the phenomena that make up the world. Man is one among many, a small part of a great whole. In the dreamlike time of the ancestors, animals and humans were more closely related than now. They readily transformed back and forth from one realm to the other, and they also could reverse time—living, dying, then living again.

This was true throughout the period when various supernatural beings were actively shaping the world we know. But since then, men and women have lost the power to see animals in their human forms except on rare occasions, such as when at sea alone or far off in the mountains or deep forest, or when sick. Salmon People, Wolf People, Whale People, Seal People, Deer People and the others still live in their own houses, however, and still know joy and sorrow, sickness and health. Their villages are variously located, which explains the separate arrival times of individual salmon runs and migrating whales and waterfowl. Some have farther to come than others.

When they enter their homes, Animal People

# Why Salmon Bones Are Returned to the River

People living in the Bella Coola region say that at the beginning of time there were no sockeye in their rivers. So Raven decided to make some. He carved wooden fish and threw them in the water, but they jumped only a few times, then died. Discouraged, Raven decided to visit the Salmon People's village beyond the western ocean. He invited Mouse to go too, and together they travelled by canoe until they reached a flat land where Salmon lived.

On the beach in front of the village were scores of canoes, each really the skin of a sockeye salmon. Seeing guests, the sockeye chief invited them to his house. But Raven told Mouse to wait

*Bella Coola River.* RUTH AND LOUIS KIRK

on the beach and to nibble holes in all of the canoes.

In the chief's house everyone sat down to eat, and Raven was served a salmon, which actually was the sockeye chief's daughter. While eating, Raven carefully examined the bones so as to learn what was omitted from the salmon he had made. The chief said not to eat any bones, but Raven nonetheless held one against the roof of his mouth.

When the meal ended, the host ordered surplus food tied into a mat for Raven to take home, and then someone gathered the salmon bones left from the meal and threw them into the river. They immediately turned back into a live fish that started swimming to shore but then began circling and jumping madly. Everyone agreed a bone must be missing. They searched the house. Finding nothing, they searched Raven, even checking his mouth. Of course they found the bone. But Raven just said, "Oh, I didn't know that was there." And he decided on a new plan.

He asked the chief to have his daughter carry the bundle of surplus food to his canoe. As she approached, Raven stepped into the canoe, shoving it out a little before he reached for the bundle. The chief's daughter waded out, and Raven shoved the canoe still more. She followed until she was standing waist-deep in the water—which was just what Raven had planned. He hauled her aboard. Salmon People leapt into their canoes to follow, but the canoes sank. Mouse had carried out Raven's instructions and gnawed holes in each one.

Raven returned to North Bentinck Arm and released the chief's daughter. Ever since, sockeye have come to the Bella Coola River, and people have been scrupulous about returning bones to the water whenever they eat salmon.

take off their cloaks and resume human form. They know about earthly people, and some feel they understand the speech of humans and can read their thoughts. All realize their own animal bodies supply men with food, furs and other materials, but they take no offence at this since, after their flesh is eaten, Animal People simply return home. They can put on another cloak of flesh and re-enter the human world whenever they choose. Unless well treated, however, they feel no obligation to let their bodies be taken.

Successful hunting depended on the correct treatment of Animal People as much as on the excellence of a hunter's equipment or his skill in using it. Nuxalk tradition describes how a Mountain Goat long, long, long ago told a shaman he and his friends like to see soot; and so ever afterward, hunters streaked two bands of charcoal across their faces. Similarly, Bear once told a hunter that neither he nor his relatives wanted to be killed by an arrow fletched with owl feathers; so men used arrows with mallard feathers whenever they went after bear. Furthermore, as soon as they killed and skinned a bear, they draped the hide back over the carcass and, patting it, called out: "Please don't linger. Go home and return. . . . Tell your brothers, your sisters, your uncles, your aunts, and your other relatives to come to us."

Salmon received perhaps the greatest ritual care of all: people returned bones to the river so that they could float back to Salmon People's house. If any were missing, the fish would be deformed when they came again, or they might be too annoyed to come at all. Among the Nuu-chah-nulth, the first salmon caught each year were placed on new mats in the chief's house. Fluffy white down, a symbol of peace, dotted the silvery bodies, and Salmon Spirit listened for words of welcome. "We are glad you came to visit us," the chief would say. "We had waited a long time. We hope you will come again soon." Some families changed certain words to special forms, at least during runs of dog salmon. They gave up chewing spruce gum or making loud noises or carrying fire along the beach. Even after white traders and settlers arrived, many Indians lifted salmon only by the tail, used only mussel-shell knives for butchering and avoided eating freshly caught fish at the same meal with any "white-man grub."

All such ritual won favour and virtually guaranteed humans the help of Animal People. Men and women went about even routine tasks "all prayed up and ready," as Indian elders today express it. Luck played no part in success: care with ritual was what counted. Nobody questioned *how* a Nuu-chah-nulth specialist could call drift whales ashore or *what* made childbirth easy for a Southern Kwakiutl woman who dropped four pebbles from beneath her clothing. Certain actions simply got certain results.

Each person's rites were a carefully guarded form of wealth with secret particulars of which

plants to use, when to sing or how to gesture. Since spirits detested the smell of warm, sweaty humans, people bathed privately somewhere down the beach from a village, or at a stream or lake in the woods. Cold water and seaweed or hemlock twigs rubbed vigorously over the skin destroyed human stench; subsequent rubbing with sweet-smelling plants replaced offence with appeal. "Cleanse your body. Cleanse your mind. And then you can find meaning," a Nuu-chah-nulth woman explained to me.

Nuu-chah-nulth elder Winnifred David described how her great-grandmother never ate breakfast until she had walked down the beach to bathe and pray:

*A petroglyph beside Thorsen Creek, at Bella Coola, records specific winter dance events such as the transfer of rights to certain masks, songs and names. Perhaps chiefs carved the designs into rock while preparing for ceremonials, pecking the figures in time with the songs forming in their minds. This association with ceremonials is reported for a nearby petroglyph.* BRITISH COLUMBIA PROVINCIAL MUSEUM, ARCHAEOLOGY DIVISION

*A woman shaman of Clayoquot Sound photographed wearing her regalia early this century. Each such person followed directions given by his or her particular spirit helper.* BRITISH CO-LUMBIA PROVINCIAL MUSEUM, ETHNOLOGY DIVISION, PN 5410

My great-grandmother would pray for care for herself and her family. Keep them safe. She knew it was a spirit up there. Not the sun or the moon. It was a Chief-Above-All, a spirit. It really hurts when I read that Indians prayed to totem poles, or the moon. We were very spiritual.

In his book of reminiscences, *As Far as I Know,* Ahousaht elder Peter Webster emphasizes the same point. He tells of bathing and scrubbing to purify the outside of his body and using "medicine . . . to clean out the internal system." Then, Chief Webster continues:

I was taught the ritual of Oo-simch by my grandfather and father. This consisted of bathing in the sea, scrubbing the body afterwards with tree branches and singing songs of prayer in our native language. Each family had its own Oo-simch. Some carried out the ceremony for a few hours each day for a period of time; others, for a continuous period of as long as 8 days. . . .

Those who were taken to the residential school and taught the English language and the European ways were told that ceremonies such as Oo-simch were "superstitious." I guess this meant that . . . these practices were "savage" or without meaning compared to the customs of the white men. This has always puzzled me.

My parents and grandparents and I offered our prayers to a great, but unseen, Spirit. Is not this the same thing as the God these Christians spoke about? Is there something "savage" about making the body clean inside and outside out of respect for this Spirit? . . . The priests and missionaries talked much about sacrifices and miracles that took place a long, long time ago. But they belittled or condemned those happening in their own time.

Franz Boas records in *Ethnology of the Kwakiutl* the words of a Southern Kwakiutl woman picking berries:

"I have come, Supernatural-Ones, Long-Life-Makers, that I may take you, for that is the reason you have come. . . . Look! I come now dressed in my large basket and my small basket that you may go into it. . . . I mean this that you may not be evilly disposed towards me, friends. That you may treat me well."

All written accounts and memories bear out this deep reverence for the intertwining of the natural and supernatural realms. Thus, Nuu-chah-nulth elder Ida Jones described her grandfather's preparation for whaling to me. The rite demanded enormous physical and spiritual discipline:

He had his own territory so he wouldn't have to meet anybody. He'd have a watchman and two of his own

## Curing Illness

Disease came from special, small, living objects that led their own existence apart from witchcraft or supernatural spirits. These "things" were about half an inch long and black. Their gnawing caused pain. Disease also came from cysts of dark blood, often caused by splinters of bone tied with hair and "thrown" into someone by a witch; or perhaps from meeting an evil spirit, or using the wrong ritual with a spirit that otherwise might have become a helper. The most dire illness of all came from loss of the soul, which, for example, might be taken by Dog Salmon displeased with how they were treated.

The various causes of illness produced different degrees of effect and required different methods of cure. Diseases caused by objects entering the body could be cured by sucking out the offending bit, a procedure requiring a shaman, payment, ceremony and an audience. Getting cured of possession by a supernatural being posed bigger problems. If the offending spirit was riding like an invisible hobgoblin on the patient's back, chances of a cure were promising. If it already had entered the body, hopes fell.

A Kyuquot story tells of a man who saw a Rainbow Bird perched on a whale skeleton

family behind him. He'd be going up and down, up and down, like a whale does. It was at night so nobody would know. And he'd be carrying a little rattle and shaking it real slow. I still have that rattle. . . . He'd be walking all night, praying. Not standing up but walking bent over, like a whale.

Certain meetings with spirits led to power as a shaman, or "medicine man." Youth or elder, man or woman might make the crucial contact, which could happen unexpectedly or through deliberate courting. The power received might call for be-

coming a great shaman or a very limited specialist. Even a commoner could succeed in the right contact and become a shaman, one of the few ways for someone of low rank to gain social standing.

The chances of encountering any particular spirit-person varied from group to group. Among the Nuxalk, any unexplained sound or peculiar action of an animal was a manifestation of the supernatural. So was a thought that came suddenly to mind. Many Nuu-chah-nulth got power from meeting a Ya-ai spirit paddling its supernatural canoe; or seeing a Right Hand sticking up out of

when he went down the beach to bathe. He turned to pick up a stone to throw at the bird—a serious mistake, for when he turned back, the being had flown. The man should have held it with a fixed stare, watched it change form ten times, and then uttered his ritual cry. Instead, he violated proper procedure and therefore fell unconscious. His brother found him and called a shaman, who was unable to diagnose the illness.

Another shaman was called, this time a woman, who arrived commenting that men supposedly are better at curing than women, yet just stepping through the door she could see the patient's problem. She sat close to the sick man and sang four songs, then announced: "You made a bad mistake. You saw something good this morning. That bird could have helped you to become a great shaman but you made a mistake. Probably nobody can cure you now, but I'm going to try to take it from you."

She sang and danced and wiped the man's body, head to foot: front, left side, back, right side. When she was done, he could sit up and use his hands and even say a few words. The shaman told the family to build a hut, and there she and the patient stayed for four days. She hoped that the Rainbow Bird would reappear,

but no spirit came, even though villagers heard singing "all around." During the four days, the sick man seemed to get better. But soon he died.

Lost souls were complicated to get back. Souls were "like a shadow" with no dwelling place other than the body. During sleep, especially a dream, they might leave; or the victim might have a sudden fright and feel the top of the head "moving." That was the soul jumping out, perhaps stolen by a supernatural being. Periods of transition, such as the end of the dog salmon run, were especially worrisome because of increased possibilities for the theft of a soul.

A shaman had to call a lost soul back or fetch it from wherever it had gone, which often was beneath the sea. Accounts tell of shamans returning dripping wet and bloody from battling underwater to regain a soul. Such a shaman would be holding dry eagle-down that was spinning as though powered by a small whirlwind, which was actually the regained soul.

Singing, rubbing and passing sacred cedarbark rings over the patient's body got the soul back into the head. Health then usually returned.

the forest floor shaking a rattle; or coming on Squirrel-Person singing and shaking a rattle beside a punky Log, which was writhing and groaning.

Usually spirits "turned to foam" as they disappeared, leaving behind some physical object, such as Squirrel's rattle. This became a great treasure, for it was a token of the encounter. Wolves, however, never turned to foam. They just trotted off and later returned in a dream to give instructions. There are Nuu-chah-nulth tales of helping a Wolf Person with a fish bone stuck in his throat and receiving gifts as an expression of gratitude; also of men running pell-mell through the forest, ducking logs and colliding with Wolf so hard that both got knocked out. If the man nursed Wolf back to consciousness instead of worrying about himself, he was rewarded by gaining Wolf as a "helper." A certain friendly graciousness almost always worked best when dealing with Wolf-People. Other spirits needed to be treated a bit aggressively: it took a shout, a stare and a stick to command their attention. Not so with Wolf.

Most spirits who became helpers after these encounters uttered a word just before they disappeared. It was the name the new shaman should use when asked to cure someone. Life-Owner or Supernatural-Power-Force or Making-Alive are examples of names belonging to Nuu-chah-nulth shamans. Spirit helpers also indicated paraphernalia to use, rituals to follow, songs to sing, and face paint and cedar-bark ornaments to put on. Instructions detailed bathing procedures and usually called for avoiding certain foods and abstaining from sexual contact for periods involving units of four and/or ten days, or the same number of weeks, months or even years.

Details of encounters with the supernatural of course remained secret, shared at most only within the family. Announcing particulars would not weaken the power or anger the spirit helper, but might help a rival to get the same power. An established shaman assisted a neophyte, strengthening his or her understanding, sharing techniques of curing and overseeing a period of dancing to let villagers know that power had come to the new shaman. "Witches" received power in the same way as shamans, but they manipulated it in evil ways.

No priesthood directed religious practices; indeed, specific beliefs and rituals tended to be individual matters substantially influenced by induction into secret societies, which provided a shared experience. While young, many Nuu-chah-nulth people also prepared through individual ritual for later contact with a lifelong supernatural helper. Usually, this discovery came during a lone vigil well away from the village. Ditidaht elder John Thomas told me he was twenty-one years old at the time of his spirit quest. "It takes a lot of training leading up to that," he commented.

# A Sense of Place and Past

*Elders are a repository of the wisdom from the past, a living bridge across time.*

Ditidaht elder Joshua Edgar.
*British Columbia Provincial Museum, Archaeology Division*

Southern Kwakiutl painting by Mungo Martin: Dzoonokwa (wild woman) of the sea with octopus and sculpin. *British Columbia Provincial Museum, Ethnology Division, CPN 14501*

*Villages scattered along waterways had their own customs, based on ancestral ties with particular locations.*

Elders remember as their homeland much of what today is a wilderness coast. *Ruth and Louis Kirk*

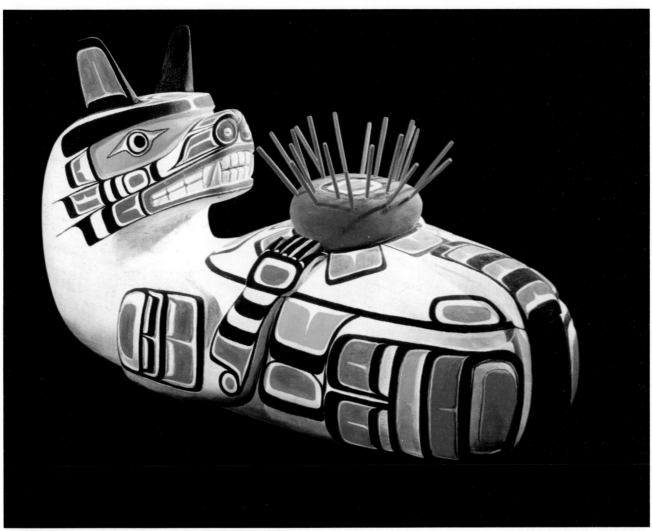

Southern Kwakiutl bowl carved by Henry Hunt: sea otter and sea urchin. *British Columbia Provincial Museum, Ethnology Division, CPN 16613*

Sea otter. *British Columbia Provincial Museum, Aquatic Zoology Division*

*Richly varied resources along the coast nurtured both the physical and spiritual realms of human life.*

Coast forest. *Ruth and Louis Kirk*

*In the days of the ancestors, Animal People
transformed back and forth from earthly form to spirit,
and humans believed that drawing successfully on the
environment depended as much on proper ritual as on
other forms of knowledge.*

Bald eagle. *Ruth and Louis Kirk*

Eagle carving at Bella Coola. *Ruth and Louis Kirk*

Wolf Dance performed by Jeff Hottowe, a Makah. *Ruth and Louis Kirk*

*In the forest fringing the seashores, people found wood, fibre, fruit and other necessities; there also they sought spirit helpers. Dances, songs and names—as well as masks and crests—often refer to contact with such helpers.*

Coast forest. *Ruth and Louis Kirk*

Mountain goats. *Ruth and Louis Kirk*

Chilkat blanket, woven of mountain goat wool, worn only by chiefs. *Ruth and Louis Kirk*

*Animals provided a host of resources for livelihood.*
*Crests, dances and regalia proclaimed a link with the*
*time of the ancestors when Animal People and humans*
*communed easily.*

House remains at old Ohiaht village. *British Columbia Provincial Museum, Archaeology Divison*

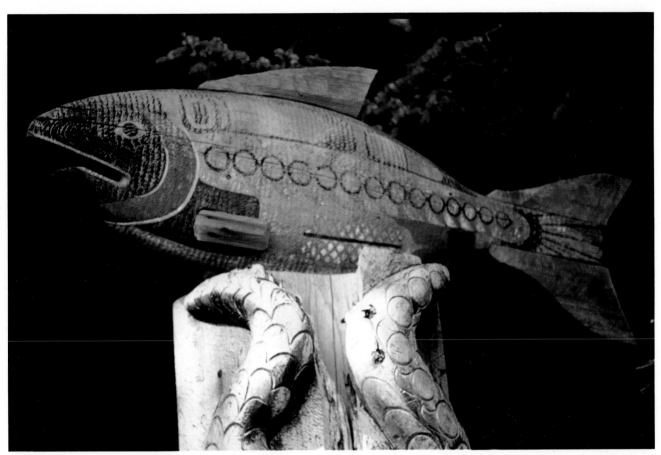

Supernatural fish carving atop a totem pole at Yuquot. *Ruth and Louis Kirk*

*Forests now reclaim remnants of the great houses of
the past, but native continuity with the land and water
is unbroken.*

Roasting salmon. *Ruth and Louis Kirk*

Setting hemlock boughs. *Ruth and Louis Kirk*

Elder Daniel Koon shows how to strip herring roe from seaweed.
*Ruth and Louis Kirk*

*Traditional ways of gathering and preparing food are still practised today. Salmon is often cooked by a traditional method. Archaeologists find roasting sticks that are centuries old yet are identical to those in use today.*

*Herring will spawn on hemlock boughs placed into the water by students of a Campbell River native studies class.*

Harvesting cattail. *Ruth and Louis Kirk*

*Basketry materials come only from certain places, at certain times of the year. Such knowledge, as well as gathering and processing techniques, is as essential to continuation of the art as is that of weaving itself.*

Stripping bark from a cedar tree. *Ruth and Louis Kirk*

Canoe-maker Ted Hudson and grandson. *Ruth and Louis Kirk*

*Tall, sound cedars supply the logs from which to make
the canoes that once enabled people to use the vast network of waterways linking the entire coast.*

# CHAPTER FOUR
## *Daily Life*

Thinking back to her girlhood and her unexpected move, about 1899, from Victoria back into village life at Ditidat, Ida Jones told me about her dismay at seeing the traditional "smokehouse" that was to be her home:

I didn't know how to be comfortable in it—dirt floor. . . . I was ten or maybe nine. My younger sister didn't like to be in that kind of a house either. There were four families in there. . . .

It wasn't smoky. There was lots of places to open in the morning. My sister and me, we'd pull on the ropes and something opened in the ceiling. That let light in and the smoke went out. . . . We made tea from those narrow leaves [Labrador tea?]. You dry the leaves and put them in a basket. It has to be loose [open weave] so those leaves won't get mouldy. And you keep it way up in the rafters. They had a board and . . . you could pull it up; and when you need it, pull it down. Keep dried fish that way too. Get it down and soak it overnight in cedar boxes when you are going to have it the next day, and serve it with oil.

### Yesterday's Big Houses

For centuries, large cedar houses characterized the Northwest Coast. They were big enough to provide shelter, work space and storage space for many families under a single roof and flexible enough to accommodate large numbers of guests for feasts and potlatches. Sturdy corner posts notched at the top supported enormous roof beams and a series of rafters. Over this framework, men placed a sheath of planks split from cedar trees. Stones and logs generally weighted roof boards in place, and during storms men swarmed onto the roof to add still more weights. A slight overlapping of the planks—or channels carved along their edges— controlled rain runoff.

Most groups preferred a gently sloping, gabled roof, although southern Nuu-chah-nulth people built houses with a single, shedlike pitch to the roof. The Nuxalk sometimes lived in a shed-roofed house "as a beginning," in the words of people with whom photographer Edward Curtis spoke in the early twentieth century. They thought of these as

The frame of the Scow Family house at Gwayasdums, photographed in 1955, shows the scale and architectural ingenuity of Northwest Coast houses. Wall planks could be readily removed for use elsewhere, then reattached. This saved needless duplication, for making the planks was a laborious process. BRITISH COLUMBIA PROVINCIAL MUSEUM, ETHNOLOGY DIVISION, PN 2165

The support posts and carved crossbeams of a house photographed in 1934 display crests owned by the Johnson Family of Gilford Island. BRITISH COLUMBIA PROVINCIAL MUSEUM, ETHNOLOGY DIVISION, PN 2442

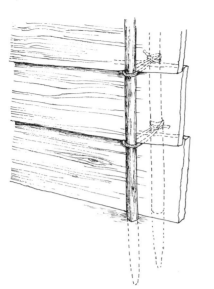

Top. *Wall planks formed an exterior shell. Nuu-chah-nulth people generally tied them horizontally, as shown; the Southern Kwakiutl and Nuxalk set them vertically.* DRAWING BY HILARY STEWART

Bottom. *Blankets are piled high in front of a house at Xumtaspi on Hope Island, and people preparing for a potlatch throng the veranda in this 1899 photograph.* BRITISH COLUMBIA PROVINCIAL MUSEUM, ETHNOLOGY DIVISION, PN 238

"half a house," acceptable until the owner could afford to build the other half and have a "real house."

Wall styles also varied regionally. On the north coast, people placed wall planks vertically. Some Southern Kwakiutl had adopted this style from their neighbours by the late nineteenth century, but previously, they had set wall planks horizontally, as did the Nuu-chah-nulth and Nuxalk. Men tied the boards between pairs of upright poles that had been driven into the ground. This method of attachment, which left each individual plank easy to remove and use elsewhere, was helpful since planks required great skill and time to make. Some boards measured a full 1.5 m (5 feet) wide and were 4.5 to 6 m (15 to 20 feet) long, often painstakingly adzed with a pattern "like ripples on the water." If cracks or lengthwise splits developed, people laced the two sides together, sometimes for the entire length of the board.

The Nuu-chah-nulth and Southern Kwakiutl used a single set of house boards at various seasonal locations, moving them from herring camp to salmon station to winter village, or whatever pattern the particular group's resource rounds called for. They left the frameworks standing permanently; only the planks were taken down for reassembly at the new location. Nuxalk houses were more permanently built; planks could not be easily removed and reassembled.

August Murphy, a Mowachaht Nuu-chah-nulth who could remember back to the 1890s, wrote down his memories about moving the family house:

In the different seasons of the year we were always in a move. . . . My grandfather owned two big canoes and I remember twice that we had to pull down all the cedar boards from our house and load [them] crosswise on the two big canoes and part of our belongings was on the deck made of boards and also in the bottom. . . . When fur traders became more frequent . . . they had nails for sale. So, no more taking down boards. . . . [The] house was nailed together more firmly.

Most Southern Kwakiutl houses were square, about 12 m (40 feet) on each side; Nuxalk and Nuu-chah-nulth houses were two or three times longer than wide. Floors were swept-earth and seldom dug into the ground, although certain Kwakiutl and Nuxalk chiefs owned the right to excavate their floors, a prerogative gained through marriage with northerners. Edward Curtis records that one particular Koskimo Kwakiutl chief had the right to excavate his floor into ten steps, although his house actually had only three such tiers.

The sheer height of roof beams above the floor, as well as their massive size, added to the prestige of the owner of the house. "We heard that the roof was on and that it was very high," Nuu-chah-nulth men told linguist Edward Sapir, speaking of a house built by the renowned chief Becomes-Ten, of Nootka Sound. "One did not hear the rain, the house was so high." When Becomes-Ten potlatched, he gloried in the height of his roof by stacking blankets so that they reached up through an opening in the roof. When the stack was complete, he gave the blankets away. As told to Sapir:

The tribes tried to count [the blankets], but they lost count about halfway up. . . . My! They came near the roof boards as they kept piling on. The blankets went up through the roof. . . .

"O Tribes, do you see now? Becomes-Ten has put things on his rafters to dry."

John Jewitt, taken slave when the Mowachaht of the outer coast captured the trading vessel he was aboard, described Chief Maquinna's house as 4.2 m (14 feet) high, nearly half again that of other houses in the village. Its length was 45 m (150 feet); a single roof beam measured 30 m (100 feet) long and more than 2.5 m (8 feet) in circumference. John Meares, a late eighteenth-century fur trader, reported Chief Wickanninish's house at Clayoquot as 6 m (20 feet) high.

Southern Kwakiutl and Nuxalk houses generally had one door opening in the middle of the wall facing the beach or river; some also had a rear door for bringing in firewood and water. Most Nuu-chah-nulth placed doors at the ends of their houses. Among all three groups, gaps between wall planks provided peepholes; by lifting aside roof planks, light could enter and smoke could leave.

Within the companionable vastness of these houses, each Kwakiutl or Nuu-chah-nulth family usually had its own cooking hearth and used a central fireplace during ceremonials; Nuxalk people used central fireplaces every day. In some cases, mat or board partitions divided house interiors into separate apartments. Ringing the walls were wooden benches for sleeping and working, some of them decorated with carvings or inlaid with shells.

The size of a village ranged from three or four to twenty or more houses set close together in one or two rows that ran parallel to the beach or river bank. Winter villages were the largest; from them, people ranged out to various seasonal camps. How far they went and how many camps they had depended on the diversity of resources and distances within each chief's territory. Some winter village locations offered convenient year-round resources and tended to be occupied at all times. Others provided little more than shelter from storm winds and seas, and people had to move seasonally to gather and preserve the resources they needed for winter.

Even territories with rich fish runs experienced occasional lean periods. Nuxalk elder Margaret Siwallace told me of a famine in the Bella Coola region "maybe four or five hundred years ago." She said:

They had to tell the children, "Here's a half a herring split lengthwise for today, and there's nothing tomorrow." Then on the third day, they gave them another half herring. Everybody saved all the bones they got for boiling into stew, but I guess it wasn't a very good stew. Someone dreamed they saw fish jumping and they went there to fill the water bucket. Use it and feel the presence of the fish, you know.

Three hundred people left by walking through the mountains to the interior. I don't know where they went. They never came back.

## Basketry and Woodworking

Mothers rocked their babies securely tied in wooden or basketry cradles, sometimes hung on

Top. *Makah Mary Butler rocks her daughter Lida the traditional way, which leaves her hands free for other chores.* WASHINGTON STATE HISTORICAL SOCIETY, MORSE 143

Bottom. *Lida Colfax, the baby in the top picture, in the longhouse of the Neah Bay museum. She is reminiscing about whalers in her family. With her are her husband Roger (left) and son John Hottowe.* RUTH AND LOUIS KIRK

109

*A woman of Nootka Sound, sketched by John Webber in 1778, sits on a low, mat-covered bench to weave. Robes of softened cedar bark were the most common type of clothing. Nuxalk and Southern Kwakiutl people also hunted mountain goats for their wool; the Makah, and perhaps also other outer-coast groups, raised small woolly dogs—and traded with Coast Salish—for fleece. Other materials such as feathers, the fluff of cattail or fireweed seedheads sometimes were mixed in during the weaving.* BRITISH COLUMBIA PROVINCIAL MUSEUM, ETHNOLOGY DIVISION, PN 5118

*Women set hot stones into boxes partly filled with water to steam-cook and simmer a great variety of foods. They knew which kinds of rock heated well without cracking and how long each kind held heat. By choosing the size and the number of stones used, they could control the cooking temperature.* DRAWING BY HILARY STEWART

springy poles. The bedding was cedar bark, well pounded and fluffed, or dried moss and lichen. Families slept on mats woven of cedar bark, cattail or tule. They also spread mats as "dinner cloths" when entertaining guests and wore robes woven of cedar bark softened by soaking and pounding. Women twined and wove containers from the bark, often mixing in grasses and sedges. These ranged from small, open baskets for trinkets or berry-picking to soft pouches for a whole set of fish hooks, spare barbs, shanks, twine and a whetstone. Other pouches might hold a ration of dried salmon and a few small implements, yet tuck comfortably into a man's belt as he walked through the forest. Stiff baskets with a coarse mesh were woven from withes or boughs rather than bark. Some huge baskets served as traps for catching salmon. Others were for gathering clams or firewood. Such baskets were useful because they stayed open when set down, and their loose mesh let water and sand drain out. They were carried on the back, supported by a tumpline across the forehead. With them, people could carry a heavy load yet keep their hands free.

Boxes were also used as containers and ranged in size from not more than a hand's breadth per side to several spans long. Some were plain, others

110

displayed family crests. Certain elaborate chests held dance regalia or other items of wealth. A few were made as drums. Women even cooked in boxes, putting water into them, then adding fire-heated stones and food.

Woodworkers made boxes by steaming and bending a board to form the four sides, fastening the corner where the two ends met by sewing or pegging. Next, they attached a bottom and usually also made a beautifully fitted lid. In a documentary film produced in the 1960s, the Southern Kwakiutl master carver Mungo Martin demonstrated the process. To steam the board, he dug three small pits in the house floor and put fire-heated rocks into each, adding water and a layer of shredded cedar bark. Then he laid on the board, which he

*Some wooden boxes held water for cooking, others provided storage. This one probably is a canteen for a canoe.* MUSEUM FÜR VÖLKERKUNDE, BERLIN, IVA 2051

*Baskets made it possible to carry heavy loads without encumbering the hands.* WASHINGTON STATE HISTORICAL SOCIETY, MORSE 503

had grooved where it would be bent, and on top of the board he piled more shredded bark (seaweed would do just as well). A worn mat went on top of everything.

Then, Chief Martin lifted one end of the board and poured more water into each pit. Steam from the hot rocks softened fibres at the grooves so the board could be bent without cracking or splitting. To close the opening where the ends met, Chief Martin fitted pegs into precisely drilled holes, and, as a last step, pegged on a bottom.

A versatile tool kit facilitated woodworking. It included chisels, knives, drills, awls and adzes, plus stone hand mauls used with splitting wedges. Blades were of stone, bone, tooth, shell and sometimes metal (even before the arrival of Europeans). Today's carvers, who work with updated versions of traditional tools, find that small differences in how a blade is hafted affect results. The rebound can help a carver get into the steady rhythm needed to produce a uniform, overall pattern. Roy Hanuse, a carver from Rivers Inlet, says in an article published in the magazine *Fine Woodworking*:

You can go on adzing for hours if you work at the same beat as your heart. But until you get that going for you, you're just hacking all over the place.

Indian woodworkers had a sophisticated knowledge of woods and matched the characteristics of

*Beaver teeth provided curved blades, easily sharpened. This tool, found at Ozette, is 450 to 500 years old.* RUTH AND LOUIS KIRK

*Men used wedges of wood, antler and whalebone to split boards from logs and to rough out everything from arrow shafts to bowls and canoes. Wedge lengths varied from a few centimetres (inches) to a full metre (3 feet) or more.*
DRAWING BY HILARY STEWART

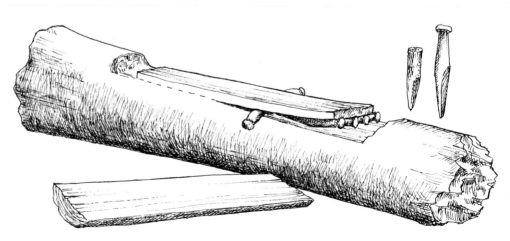

# Woodworking Tools

Archaeologically, wood rarely lasts long; therefore most prehistoric tools and their end products have vanished, except for those of stone, shell, bone and tooth. But at the Ozette archaeological site, in Makah territory, mudslides buried houses from which about thirty thousand wooden artifacts have been recovered. Clearly, wood—especially red cedar— was *the* material people used.

The Ozette houses, which date back to shortly before the arrival of Europeans, held well over two thousand tools. Most seem to have been used for woodworking, although some apparently served other purposes as well. More than forty were knives with iron or steel blades. A few of these blades were so large and broad they probably were used primarily for flensing whale blubber; the rest apparently were for wood carving.

About five hundred knives had blades of mussel shell, useful for cutting and shaving various materials in addition to wood. By working with careful replications, archaeologist Paul Gleeson concluded that all five hundred shell knives probably equalled the total service of the forty metal blades.

In addition to tools as such, the buried houses also held eight hundred sandstone blocks of various sizes, used as whetstones, the largest single implement category. Whetstones are simple objects, yet essential for keeping a sharp edge on everything from knives and drills to fish-hook barbs and harpoon-heads.

Wedges, equally humble but essential tools, also were common in the houses. More than a thousand wedges were made of wood, seventy-five of whalebone, and several dozen of antler and bone other than whale. Splitting wood is an efficient means of reducing it to size, and the wedges ranged from less than 10 cm (4 inches) long to more than 100 cm (40 inches). They were pounded with hand mauls or, probably at times, with beach cobbles. Mauls in the houses were beautifully shaped from black basalt cobbles. This stone is dense, difficult to shape and polish into a desired form, yet its use for mauls is standard for the entire Northwest Coast.

At Ozette and all along the coast, woodworkers used chisels for precision cutting, even into deep, narrow places. Adzes had heavy blades of stone or metal to contribute the necessary weight for dressing wood efficiently, and additional weight came from their handles. The ancestors of today's Nuu-chah-nulth people preferred a D-shaped adze handle, whereas Kwakiutl and Nuxalk woodworkers gained added force from the long handles of their elbow adzes, which had built-in leverage. A third style of adze, present at Ozette and common along the southern coast of Washington, had a heavy, straight handle.

Adzes, drills and knives, along with whetstones, mauls, wedges and chisels formed the basic tool kit. With them, native woodworkers produced the goods needed by their rich and complex society—additional tools, implements, weapons and accoutrements, as well as artwork, shelter and canoes.

*Uses for the wood, bark, branches and roots of cedar were many: house posts and planks, carved poles, dugout canoes, tool handles and weapon shafts, boxes and regalia, clothing, matting and padding, rope and cordage. Archaeologists find cedar baskets and matting 3000 years old, and from the presence of wedges, which are a woodworking tool, they infer that cedar was being used by at least 5000 years ago.* RUTH AND LOUIS KIRK

Facing page. *Old Jim of the Ehattesaht Band built forty-two large canoes during his lifetime, including—at age seventy—this one, which is 13 m (42 feet) long. In 1924 his son gave the canoe to the Lieutenant Governor of British Columbia, who sent a power saw as a return gift. The canoe is now on display at the British Columbia Provincial Museum, Victoria.* PROVINCIAL ARCHIVES OF BRITISH COLUMBIA, 16017

each material to the use intended. They preferred red cedar for monumental artwork and for building houses and canoes, as well as for implements and furnishings from arrows to boxes and benches. Cedar splits easily along the grain, a quality that simplifies working it down to a suitable thickness. Cedar also resists rot, and objects made from it last for fifty years or more even if alternately wet then dry, a situation that speeds deterioration.

The weight and strength of yew made it suitable for clubs, bows and the swordlike beaters that weavers used to prepare wool. The stiff, close grain of wood from the underside of the branches of wind-bent trunks of spruce and hemlock worked well for wedges, which had to withstand pounding, and also for wooden arrow points, which had to penetrate without breaking. Alder carved readily into bowls, cedar into masks. Even shrubs were useful. By removing the pithy centre of elderberry, the stems could be made into valves for inflating the sealskin floats used to slow a harpooned whale. The white wood of devil's club worked well for codfish lures and two-piece hooks for bottom-fish.

So expert were woodworkers that they could split planks from a living cedar by making cuts at top and bottom, then setting wedges to exert pressure as the trunk moved with the wind. When felling a tree for a canoe, men tested it by cutting a tapering hole deep into the trunk; they prized close grain because that meant few knots and less likelihood of splits after the wood was worked. This was a major consideration, for repair required tedious drilling and lacing.

## Canoes

Much care and reverence went into selecting a tree to hollow into a canoe, as Nuu-chah-nulth elder Peter Webster writes in his autobiography, *As Far as I Know:*

I remember watching my father cut down a cedar tree from which he was going to make a large dugout canoe. He carried out his work with great respect for the tree. He would talk to it as though to a fellow

*Whether Northwest Coast people used sails on their canoes before the arrival of Whites is unknown. Certainly, they used canvas sails soon after seeing them on ships, and they may earlier have rigged wide boards or cedar-bark mats to maximize the push of wind against a canoe.* WASHINGTON STATE HISTORICAL SOCIETY

human being. He would ask the tree not to hurt him, as he was going to change it into a beautiful object that was to be useful to him.

Exceptionally large red cedars grew along river drainages and lake systems on the outer coast of Vancouver Island, giving the Nuu-chah-nulth material for canoes renowned throughout the region. Chief Charles Jones—who was raised at Pacheenat, Ditidat and Neah Bay—told anthropologist Eugene Arima that boys began to get the feel of canoe-making while eight or nine years old. They would whittle small canoes out of cedar boards, use leaves from salal bushes as sails and hold races.

At about age nine, Chief Jones's father cut a small log to length and set him to making a child's canoe. He gave no instruction, just said to go ahead and try. "The uglier it is, the better for you," he told the boy. Errors helped a person learn from one attempt to the next.

Coast Indians excelled at seamanship: Whites aboard schooners as much as 65 km (40 miles) offshore reported meeting canoes, sometimes with sealskin bladders lashed along the sides to prevent foundering. Wide travel was an everyday matter for native people, a point of great admiration among newcomers knowledgeable enough to recognize all that was entailed. One of these was Ed Ricketts—the real "Doc" of John Steinbeck's *Cannery Row*—who made a trip along the coast of Vancouver Island in 1945 and described it in his book, *The Outer Shore:*

A revenue man . . . told me they have trouble here all the time because they can't beat it into the heads of the Indians that they mustn't get into their canoes and paddle *60 or 80 miles* over the stormy open ocean to the coast of Washington and buy and sell stuff there, or bring back United States goods here with customs duties unpaid. It ain't right. What people. They're like Gulf [of California] Indians . . . but down there, it's often calm; here, it never is.

Many of today's Indian elders remember canoe travel. How long a journey took depended on wind and current as well as the size of the canoe, the number of paddlers, whether a sail was added, and so on. Chief Charles Jones told anthropologist Eugene Arima that his father travelled in a freight canoe from Port Renfrew to Seattle, about 250 km (155 miles) in a single day, skimming along with two sails raised. Chief Jones himself once sailed a canoe from Jordan River to Victoria in three hours, a distance of nearly 70 km (45 miles), probably something of a record, even allowing for the "free ride" of a favourable current. The usual speed of a Northwest Coast canoe varied with size and conditions but averaged six or seven knots, fast for any vessel before the use of engines. Typical speeds attained by Cook and Vancouver were closer to four or five knots.

James Swan, who taught school at Neah Bay in the mid-nineteenth century and often travelled by canoe, wrote in his book, *The Indians of Cape Flattery:*

If the canoe is large and heavily laden [the Indians] always anchor at night, and for this purpose use a large stone tied to a stout line. Sometimes they moor . . . by tying the canoe to the kelp. When the craft is not heavily burdened it is invariably hauled on the beach whenever the object is to encamp.

Landmarks guided travellers: they knew their location by how certain peaks aligned, or the position of distinctive trees in relation to various points of land, or how islands lined up with each other and with the shoreline. Also, they navigated by the set of ocean swells, which sweep shoreward at a fairly steady angle; and they kept track of how long they had travelled and linked that elapsed time with the direction of the current and the number of rips they had passed, an indication of shoals. Ricketts wrote in *The Outer Shore*, after arriving at Clo-oose aboard a Canadian Pacific Railway steamer:

We came along here very very late at night, I guess 1 or 2 AM; the Indians must have been waiting hours for that whistle. Fog and a heavy sea, you literally couldn't see 100 feet. Anyhow, here they came on out soon as the engines were stopped. Lots of stuff to pick up and deliver. . . .

There were several boatloads and when the first [one] got unloaded of its going-to-the-Indian-boarding-school passengers [and] started back, the steersman hollered up to the Captain—this was I guess 4 miles from shore on a black foggy night—asking him for a point to land. The other Indians just hooted. They shouted him down. They said, "You know from which direction the wind is coming, you know how the waves are hitting, don't be asking the skipper for information self-evident to any boatman." And back he went without it.

Men judged weather by changes in the sound of waves hitting certain rocks or lapping the beach, or by the position of clouds. Harry McCarty, a Makah elder who had gone out whaling, told me:

Southeast [wind], you know, you could hear it down there, kind of loud—little swells going on the beach. That's southeast. Yeah. And then west wind: if you can see them high hills, there'd always be white clouds on this side and that means west wind. East wind, [the clouds] will be on *that* side.

Such knowledge was local. It depended on living closely with the land and sea and knowing every peculiarity. People waited out blows and rough seas, or currents flowing opposite to where they wanted to go. Charles Peterson, another Makah friend, told me of childhood canoe travel:

We were going to LaPush [a Quileute village] for a party . . . and the first stop of course along the way, why we stopped in there to see relatives at Ozette. So we just camped on the beach there, pulled the canoe up and spent the night.

Now in the morning, why of course it's more or less a habit with all Indians to get up at daylight and go out, and everybody has their ideas of what the weather is gonna be like. So they all go down on the beach and . . . sit on a log and take a look at the sky, and see what the stars are doing before it becomes daylight and they disappear; and then as the sun comes up, why then you can pretty much tell what the weather's gonna be like.

I remember they could tell you pretty near which way the wind was gonna blow by the sound of the sea. . . . It made a roaring noise from whichever direction

the wind was gonna blow during the day, and of course the velocity of the wind was governed by how high that roar was.

## Food and Materials

Canoes not only freed people from the limitations of foot travel and from carrying only the small loads they could hold in their arms or on their backs but made far-flung seasonal rounds possible. Without canoes, Northwest Coast culture could not have developed its complexity and richness. No wonder memories of Indian elders often start with travelling to or from a seasonal camp. To illustrate, Hilary Irving, a Neah Bay elder, told me about living at Ozette as a young boy:

Every winter about in February, end of January, we'd move back down there and get ready for the [fur] seal hunting. That's what my grandfather stayed down there for . . . and it was wintertime that they done this. So I moved back and forth till I became school age and then I was more or less forced to come up here and stay. But I didn't do too good in school. It was in my blood too much, I guess: I was a fisherman.

We all had to take part in making a living; like for instance when I started fishing I was seven or eight years old, I guess it was. My grandfather rigged me up so I could pull halibut. . . . After I got to be ten years old, I was almost full time a fisherman. I didn't go to school from January till June. Not always.

J. J. Wallas, a Southern Kwakiutl, told me about canoeing to a herring camp at Winter Harbour, on northern Vancouver Island, when he was at an age "where you remember a little, then lose the rest, like in a dream." He mentioned leaving the winter village in upper Quatsino Sound and canoeing for five or six hours to reach the camp. His father would wait for the tide to be right, then ride its ebb down the inlet:

I remember being under [the drying rack] while my dad was using the hook to get the roe-covered branches up to the top of the rack, maybe fifteen feet high. I was thinking pretty soon I'll be big enough to

help him. The racks had five rows about three feet apart and thirty feet long, depending on how much eggs you want.

Herring arrive early in the year, just as winter storms ease off—a time, in the old days, that coincided with winter food supplies threatening to run out. In some places and some years, herring came at the end of January; elsewhere, not until February or even March. Major winter potlatches and dances were finished by then, and people felt ready for a new year. They paddled out from their villages to the first of the seasonal camps taking their house-boards with them.

*Eggs laid by spawning herring on hemlock boughs or seaweed are a delicacy traditionally preserved by drying in the sun and wind, or by smoking. Today, some families prefer to preserve the eggs by salting.* BRITISH COLUMBIA PROVINCIAL MUSEUM, ETHNOLOGY DIVISION, PN 7226

*Men trolled for salmon holding a kelp line that jerked as they paddled. Stone weights kept the line at a suitable depth; herring attached to a sharpened bone point served as bait.* DRAWING BY HILARY STEWART

Gulls fluttered out over the sea in a noisy congregation of flashing white, calling attention to where herring were schooling. Fishermen could dip their catches from the surface, using a special baglike net, or impale fish by sweeping the water with a rake made of cedar and fitted with thirty to forty sharp points of bone or wood. An experienced fisherman raked herring into the canoe using a smooth, continuous motion.

A few weeks after the fish arrived, spawning began. Occasionally, a false spawning came early when a few herring released eggs ahead of the majority. If men were too eager and placed hemlock boughs in the water to catch this light spawn, they compounded their labour. The roe was too little to be worth drying, yet the boughs could not be left in the water for the real spawning; the embryos in eggs already caught would begin development and spoil the new spawn for human use. Consequently, boughs placed too early had to be cut loose and replaced, a considerable amount of extra work. Reading the signs correctly in the first place was reason for specialists whose ritual and spirit helpers were particularly attuned to herring. Heavy spawning usually lasted four or five days. In a good year, the boughs would be coated with eggs a couple of centimetres or more thick.

Spring salmon arrived with the herring, feeding on them. To make trolling lures, men ran quills through bait herring and set two-piece hooks into them with the points only slightly exposed. Leader was fashioned mostly from nettle fibre. Kelp supplied the line; it was brought ashore by youths specially trained to dive deep. Fresh stems had to be partially dried and then stretched and repeatedly rubbed with oil, a lengthy process. After that, kelp could be used as fishing line, but each wetting meant it had to be again dried, stretched and oiled.

Men trolled by attaching a light sinker well above the hook, then holding onto the line's upper end while they paddled. This gave the bait a jerky, live motion with each stroke. John Jewitt, the seaman held slave at Nootka Sound, wrote in his journal:

The salmon . . . leaps at the herring and is instantly hooked and, by a sudden and dextrous motion of the paddle, drawn on board. I have known some of the natives to take no less than eight or 10 salmon of a morning in this manner, and have seen from 20 to 30 canoes at a time in Friendly Cove thus employed.

Since one kind of fish after another came to the marine shoals and fresh-water streams and lakes of the coast, people moved to a succession of camps according to the rights of their respective chiefs. Southern Kwakiutl elder James Sewid told me:

The great chiefs of the different tribes handled the economy; that was their position to do that. . . . Like right now [March] we'd be getting ready to go up Knight Inlet. There's going to be eulachon and we'd make oil. Then we'd move down behind Malcolm Island to fish for halibut and dry the halibut. Next the salmon would start to come—July, August, and right up through September. So, the people would go to the different rivers to gather the different species of fish.

# Nuxalk Fishing Notes

In Bella Coola, Margaret Siwallace told me she started "being a net woman" in 1934. We were sitting in the living room of her apartment, and she was tying a lead line, completing a fish net for her grandson. Reminiscing, she said:

I didn't like nylon at first. The old people used to use barbed linen and they got one dollar per pound; they'd pay them for [making] the net that way and it'd take all night to make that much. But the money was important to the Indians.

Sometimes I wish the white people hadn't taught us about cash. We had everything, with nature. Now they say we're lazy and give us welfare. But I say, "Who was it that taught us about cash?" It was the white people.

Felicity Walkus also reminisced about Indian women's role in the commercial fishing of the early twentieth century. She spoke of work during the boom days of canneries and of today's dwindling salmon runs:

Even when I was a little girl I used to wash fish [at the cannery]. Sometimes I'd get a dollar. [Later] I filled cans. We'd start real early, about 6:00 A.M. The fish washers, they'd go to work before we got there. There were thirty-five cans on a tray. . . . As soon as you finish a tray, they'd put the lids on. If you were lucky you got seventy-five trays in a day.

From May, we'd start filling. September the cannery closed. We'd work every day there's lots of fish. Sunday too sometimes. Boy, talk about Rivers Inlet! There was canneries all the way from the head [of the inlet]. There used to be a lot of fish in Rivers Inlet till they started logging that lake. The bark of those logs goes down and stays down, and the eggs can't hatch. All covered.

One evening in Bella Coola, after watching a film highlighting present-day Makah Indian fishing problems, Nuxalk elders talked about similar problems at Bella Coola. Willie Hans said:

There used to be all pinks [humpback salmon] in one little place, laying eggs. And you go up another stream and there'd be all cohos spawning, and another it'd be all chums. Each in one place. But then the logger-mens came and they ruined things. Now the fish got no place; they spawn right in the main river. That's why the fish are getting less. The logger-mens ruined it. The limbs sink to the bottom [and choke the spawning gravels].

That reminds me: Up at Four-Mile, the people had high water. Flooded. So the government hired a tractor to dig it down and that tractor belonged to the whole band in the village here. That guy driving the tractor collected us to go to see the eggs, and they were about four feet under the ground. They reported [it] to the Fishery. And they reported to the government. And the government answered: "The human beings is more important that they be saved." And ever since there's no more fish there.

On another occasion, Flora Sewid commented:

I got born on a little island in the [Nimpkish] River, where the bridge is now. It was November. She didn't mean for me to be born on an island but I came a little early. She was going up to where the people smoke fish [dog salmon, the last salmon species of the year, ideal for drying because the flesh is not oily].

Agnes Alfred, sitting next to her daughter Flora in the Sewid living room, then spoke in Kwakwala, and Mrs. Sewid translated:

She says they used to smoke four thousand fish, to last all winter. They'd smoke it real thin [a dry, hard smoke to preserve well] and pile it all together in those baskets. She remembers working on the fish, and it was cold, and she had just a little fire on each side. They'd clean the fish outdoors, then at night take them in and slice them; and in the morning hang them to dry. The girls would hang them.

*Southern Kwakiutl and Nuxalk people net eulachon as the fish enter rivers to spawn. Eulachon oil is used as "butter" and medicine, as well as being sold and traded. Oil-makers are much respected, since the flavour, clarity and colour of their final product varies according to how it is cooked and stored. Great quantities of oil are produced. In 1947 the host of a Kingcome potlatch gave away six hundred cans of oil, each holding about 18 L (4 Imperial gallons).* BRITISH COLUMBIA PROVINCIAL MUSEUM, ETHNOLOGY DIVISION, PN 7704-7

Top. *Men dump eulachon into bins to "ripen" for a week or two; then they transfer the fish to metal-bottomed vats heated over fires.*

Bottom. *Cooks stir the simmering fish and skim off oil.* BRITISH COLUMBIA PROVINCIAL MUSEUM, ETHNOLOGY DIVISION, PN 7707-31 AND PN 7722-30

*When air-dried for one day, then smoked for two weeks, male eulachon will keep a year or two if properly stored. Female fish do not preserve well because of their roe.* BRITISH COLUMBIA PROVINCIAL MUSEUM, ETHNOLOGY DIVISION, PN 7707-35

People went to the right places at the right time for any desirable resource that swam, walked, ran, flew, sprouted or fruited. Salmon alone—spring, sockeye, coho, pink and dog, plus steelhead—were trapped and speared in the rivers, and caught at sea by trolling. Chief Maquinna's men evidently also seined, for John Jewitt noted in his journal:

October 10. Went a fishing with our chief. He had a large seine set in a fortunate place, for it had not been down 10 minutes before it was full with 700 salmon, which we brought home in our canoe.

# The Calendar

Native people viewed time in terms of the scheduling needed to take the best advantage of seasonal weather and resources. Salmonberries ripen when spring has brought renewed warmth to the world; spawning salmon return when autumn rains raise the water level of rivers. There is a time to get ready, and a time to act.

Different groups each had their own ways of monitoring the yearly chain of opportunities, and terms for the seasons varied from language to language and even from dialect to dialect. Most correspond only roughly to the modern calendar, without any overall agreement even within a single culture group as to which month begins the yearly cycle. For example, these calendars (translated into English), used along the outer coast of Vancouver Island, are given by anthropologists Philip Drucker and Eugene Arima:

## Northern and Central Nuu-chah-nulth

| | |
|---|---|
| November | Elder moon (the first month of the year) |
| December | Younger moon |
| January | No food-getting for a long time |
| Early February | Bad weather (John Thomas, Ditidaht linguist, says that a more literal translation of this is "cold weather, but clear.") |
| Late February | False herring spawning |
| March | Herring spawning |
| April | Flying flocks (migrating fowl) |
| May | Stringing berries on grass |
| June | Salmonberries |
| July | Wasps |
| August | Spring salmon |
| September | Dog salmon |
| October | Rough sea |

## Southern Nuu-chah-nulth

| | |
|---|---|
| January | Elder moon (the first month of the year) |
| February | Canoe drifting sideways (John Thomas explains that a canoe drifts sideways during cold weather because the sea is calm and the waves are gentle enough to wash it onto the beach instead of out to sea.) |
| March | Sparkling (i.e., clear and cold) |
| Early April | "Lying" weather (changeable, and therefore deceptive) |
| Late April | Flying flocks (migrating fowl) |
| May | Salmonberry |
| June | Red (tide?) |
| July | Warm |
| August | Salal berry |
| September | Cutting fish |
| Oct/November | "Quarrelling" weather |
| December | Backing up (John Thomas says this refers to the winter solstice, when "the year goes back to the beginning again.") |

A good catch of halibut, which these Makah women are cleaning on the beach, signifies not only the skill of fishermen but also their careful attention to ritual. Men told anthropologist Franz Boas that they prayed to their hooks when catching halibut: "Hold on, hold on, Younger Brother." Stunning a fish, they prayed: "Indeed, this [club] does not sound bad on your head, Old Woman, Flabby-Skin-in-the-Mouth, you Born to be Given [names for the halibut]. . . . Go, go and tell your father, your mother, your uncle, your aunt, your elder brothers, and your youngest brothers that you had good luck because you came to this, my fishing canoe." NORTH OLYMPIC LIBRARY, BERT KELLOGG COLLECTION

November 1. Frosty weather. Our chief went to haul the seine; returned with 50 salmon.

Fishermen caught all types of fish: cod, lingcod, red snapper, eulachon, herring, halibut, salmon and whatever else they found tasty.

From canoes, men also hunted hair seals, fur seals and sea otters. On calm nights they went after porpoises, throwing handfuls of fine gravel onto the water to imitate the sound made by small fish feeding at the surface. This lured the porpoises close to the canoes. Sea lions were not pursued on the water but were clubbed at their rookeries. The meat tasted bitter, Nuu-chah-nulth and Kwakiutl women have told me, but sea-lion hide and gut provided valuable materials, and sea-lion whiskers were used on some dance

*Thinly sliced fish dry in the sun and wind at Neah Bay.* NORTH OLYMPIC LIBRARY, BERT KELLOGG COLLECTION

headdresses. Nuxalk people lived too far from the open coast to get sea-lion products except through trade; indeed, even hair seals were rare for them.

On land, men trapped bear, deer and various fur bearers in deadfalls; and along the coast they also drove deer into the water—generally with dogs—then overtook them by canoe and either clubbed them or held them under the water with paddles to drown. Hunters shot land mammals with the same bows they took in their canoes for shooting sea otter or geese. These bows were over a metre (3 feet) long, held horizontally to shoot 60-cm (2-foot) arrows fletched with gull, duck or eagle feathers. Shell, bone or hardwood served as arrow points. Stone arrowheads were rare.

Nuxalk men, and Southern Kwakiutl with territory at the heads of mainland inlets, speared or snared mountain goats, which they hunted with dogs. They valued the goats for fleece and horn as well as meat. The Nuu-chah-nulth of upper Muchalat Arm relied heavily on elk, pursuing them on simple snowshoes made by lashing branches into circular frames, then crisscrossing them with strips of hide. On these winter hunts men drove elk into snowdrifts where the animals foundered and were easy to spear.

Hunters caught waterfowl by several ingenious methods of netting and snaring or shot them from canoes made into floating blinds by the addition of evergreen boughs. One snaring system involved a submerged latticework with salmon eggs floating beneath it. Reaching for the eggs, ducks stuck their heads into hidden nooses attached to the lattice. A piece of whale baleen or quill from a feather held the nooses open until knocked aside by their heads. Another system was to tie baited slivers of bone onto ropes or short poles, which floated with the tide and remained operable day and night, even while unattended.

On protected waters where ducks, geese and swans spent the winter or took refuge from storms during migration, night-netting was an effective means of capture. Men lit a fire on a sand-covered board, which they set across the stern of a canoe. Sitting just ahead of the fire, the sternman held in his mouth a rod with a small mat attached. This left his hands free for paddling. Trying to escape from the glare of the fire, waterfowl swam into the mat's shadow. When enough birds were

127

*Men shot geese, swans and ducks with arrows and also caught them with nets, both on the wing and in the water.* RUTH AND LOUIS KIRK

concentrated, the bowman dropped a nettle-fibre net over them. The fowl, in panic, poked their heads through the mesh, and the hunters wrung their necks.

Mussels, clams, snails and other marine invertebrates from sea urchins and sea anemones to octopus, crabs, limpets, chitons and barnacles could be gathered at any time of year, although distribution differed greatly from place to place. The lifeforms at wave-pounded headlands were unlike those that burrow into sandy beaches, and species found on rocky reefs were not the same as those on muddy tidal flats. Most of the coast offered at least some kinds of intertidal life, but many stretches had little that particular groups of people relished enough to bother collecting.

Plants contributed richly to the diet of the Northwest Coast. People ate an endless sequence of shoots, fruits and roots, some savoured fresh, others preserved for later use. Women did most of

this gathering. Throughout the year, the first harvest of each seasonal item was ceremoniously celebrated; indeed, at all times, humans expected success only in return for faithfulness to ritual and overall harmony with the spirit world. The result was a satisfyingly varied diet, which elders remember fondly.

In a report on the Southern Kwakiutl, Franz Boas listed 23 ways of gathering specific foods, 33 preservation methods and 155 specific recipes. Yet these represent only a fraction of the actual number of ways people handled food in the past. In his Table of Contents alone, Boas listed procurement methods that range from picking dogwood berries and chokecherries to digging lily roots, lupine roots and bracken, and from gathering seaweed to catching "devil-fish" (octopus). Specifics of preservation include how to care for the pectoral fins of dog salmon, what to do with old sockeye salmon, how to roast fresh backbone

*George Hunt is pictured here with his Kwakiutl wife in about 1930. The son of a Hudson's Bay Company factor who married a Tlingit woman, he taught himself to read from the labels of goods on shelves at Fort Rupert. Later, he learned phonetic writing from anthropologist Franz Boas and used it to record and translate voluminous material ranging from how to prepare food to the rituals of shamans. Hunt's knowledge and help were indispensable to Boas, to collectors such as Adrian Jacobsen and Charles Newcombe, and to photographer Edward Curtis.* BRITISH COLUMBIA PROVINCIAL MUSEUM, ETHNOLOGY DIVISION, PN 9533

and how to cure seaweed. Recipes are for mush of boiled salmon heads, fins and tails; boiled salmon guts; halibut skin (three recipes); fresh herring spawn on cedar branches (or with kelp or salmon-berry shoots); mountain-goat brisket and mountain-goat skin; boiled whale tail; baked sea slugs; four ways to fix clover root; how to clean huckleberries, and how to prepare crabapples and oil.

People had a sense of belonging to the land and waters, a tie that comes only from going to the right place at the right time to gather and process food. Remembering back to the late nineteenth century, Southern Kwakiutl chief Charles Nowell wrote in his book, *Smoke from Their Fires:*

One in our house always gets up early and starts the fire and wakes us up in the morning. Poodlas usually got up first and asked us to have breakfast at his place. He didn't have to; he just liked to get up early. He would . . . boil dried salmon, which was our main food, and serve it to us all with some eulachon grease. After that, there will be something which we call "after-food." That might be rice or bread and molasses, which we got from Mr. Hunt who took the Fort [Rupert] after the Hudson Bay left.

Or sometimes, it would be Indian food—hemlock bark sap. To make this, we cut down the tree and take the bark off during the springtime. We put the bark

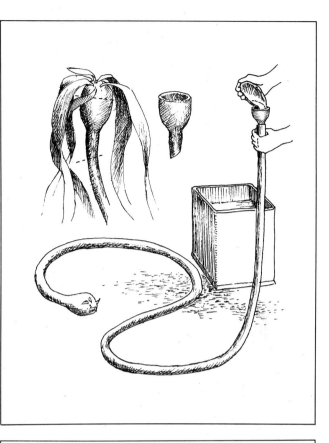

*The importance of plants includes their role in the spirit realm as well as medicinal and economic uses. Each native group—and often each family—had its own customs. Picking trillium (bottom right) might bring fog; rubbing with hemlock boughs would prevent sea mammals from noticing hunters, and prickly devil's club stems warded off disease. Kelp "stems" (top) were useful as oil containers, canteens and fishline. Bracken fern (bottom left) "fiddleheads" were eaten as medicine, the "roots" as a starchy vegetable; and people used the fronds as mats while cleaning fish and as mattresses when sleeping under canoes while travelling.*
**DRAWINGS BY HILARY STEWART**

laying on its back and scrape it and bring home the inner bark and steam it and make balls of it . . . and dry it for the winter, and it keeps a long time.

Sometimes we would have clover root as our after-food. We have sticks on the bottom of the saucepan and put this dried clover root on top of these sticks, and the water under the sticks boils. There is a cover on top to keep the steam in. It is only the steam that cooks it.

Sometimes the after-food will be dried berries which we also boil. We put the berries in boxes and put stones in the fire—only particular kinds of stones that won't break—and, when they are red hot, we put just a little water in to keep [the box] from burning, and put in the hot stones and stir until it all comes to pieces. Then we have long stones which are flat on one end, and mash the berries. . . . We leave it to cool and go out into the woods and get wild [skunk] cabbage leaves and put those on the cedar racks . . . and then put crosspieces so that the berries will be made into cakes. Then we put the berry mash in these blocks and put them out in the sun to dry. At night we put them up close to the fire. . . . The long berry cakes we fold and put away in Indian boxes. These we take out whenever we want to use them for after-food.

Not all foods that were available went into the cooking boxes and roasting pits; Northwest Coast people were choosy. For instance, Chief Nowell reported: "We don't eat seagulls, cormorants and loons. They are too tough and too hard to pluck."

Shifting residence throughout the year took time and effort, but enabled people to escape the problems of enjoying a single lush period, only to find lean pickings the rest of the year. The clear author-

# How Raven Brought Soapberries to the Bella Coola Valley

In 1967 linguists Philip Davis and Ross Saunders worked with Mrs. Agnes Edgar, one of two hundred people who then spoke Bella Coola. She told them a story about soapberries, which was translated into English and published in *Bella Coola Texts*:

Well, I'll tell you now the story about the woman named Simlayxana who was dropped down here at the head of the valley. She came down [from the Land Above] provisioned with soapberries so she would have a means of surviving. After she was here awhile she was approached by someone she took to be a human being. He wanted to make friends with her, but she didn't want to share her soapberries—her food—with anyone so she tried to keep to herself. After a while, however, she took some soapberries from her stores and gave them to the one she thought was a man to soak. He took them and told her he would whip them up as well.

Now the one she thought was a man was really Raven. He came to make friends with Simlayxana just because of the soapberries. We wouldn't have soapberries here in Bella Coola Valley today if it wasn't for Raven. He made friends with her just to get ahold of some soapberries.

Taking some soapberries for himself, Raven started to walk from the head of the valley towards the mouth of the river. He carried the soapberries in his beak while at the same time making his "caw-caw" sound as he walked. This way he scattered the soapberries from the head of the valley to the mouth of the river. And from these soapberries he dropped come all the soapberries we now have in the valley.

ity of chiefs helped by facilitating an organized and timely use of resources. From a native perspective, however, it was not organization or any amount of excellent equipment, bravery, strength or skill that brought success. Ritual preparation was what let a hunter, trapper or fisherman cross the threshold separating the human realm from that of animals and plants. When people told anthropologists about "training," that English word usually meant care with ritual rather than learning particular techniques, which of course were also needed.

Mountain-goat hunters living on mainland inlets described to anthropologist Philip Drucker how well-trained dogs could drive goats into isolated mountain pockets where hunters could kill them. The "training" they referred to consisted of ritual, such as once a day, for four days, pressing a warmed, right forefoot, cut from a kid, against the feet of a puppy. This gave the pup sure-footedness like that of goats themselves; such a dog could climb above a band of goats and turn them downhill towards human hunting parties.

Nuu-chah-nulth elder Chief Tom Sayachapis also explained to Edward Sapir the importance of ritual, as quoted in *Nootka Texts:*

[A man succeeds] only if he has the Wolf Ritual spirit from the start and trains [that is, learns rituals] for various little things while growing up—for trolling spring salmon, for unerring [aim] when spearing tyee salmon . . . for spearing bear along the bank; furthermore, that he perform all sorts of imitative dances when he is a man, that he have land otter swimming on the water when he goes along the bank, that he bring back many raccoons in [his canoe] when he goes clubbing raccoons along the beach, that [his canoe] gets filled to the gunwales when he goes decoy-fishing for cod . . . that he be successful in shooting eagles from behind a screen of branches . . . that his [logs] be closed inside [not rotten] when he fells cedars and adzes them for canoes.

## Whaling

Perhaps no activity matches whale hunting as an example of native ability to draw on all aspects of the environment: eight or so men in a canoe pitted themselves against a leviathan swimming offshore. Powerful ritual, painstaking preparation, courage, patience, skill—plus an ability to design, make and use excellent equipment—these attributes and more went into whaling.

Only people on the outer coast—the Nuu-chah-nulth and probably also the immediately adjoining Southern Kwakiutl, plus the Makah, Quileute and Quinault of Washington—hunted whales at sea. However, most people welcomed whatever dead whales drifted into their territory and even had specialists who "called" them ashore. A single whale represented a huge supply of food and materials: oil, meat, bone and gut.

Humpbacks may have been the main quarry, especially up inlets where they fed each summer, much as is true today along the coast of southeast Alaska. Men told anthropologist Philip Drucker that these whales might be seen almost any month of the year. But as humpbacks got pushed close to oblivion by commercial whaling companies, native whalers were left with little but grey whales to pursue. This species was somewhat less desirable and far more ferocious than humpback. Even so, the arrival of greys in March and April—the Wild-Goose-Moon—seems to have opened the traditional whaling season. More than 5000 L (4400 Imperial quarts) of oil is a typical yield from a single humpback whale, nearly twice as much as from a grey whale.

Right whales, the species preferred by commercial whalers, currently reach the southern limit of their range along Vancouver Island; they may not have been readily available to Nuu-chah-nulth hunters. Sperm whales usually swim far offshore, beyond the reach of men in canoes. Humpback and grey whales, on the other hand, migrate close to shore. Probably two or three per year per village is a reasonable estimate of the kill, in addition to whatever drift whales washed ashore. Some records, however, suggest a much greater number of kills. Alexander Walker, aboard a trading vessel south of Nootka Sound in 1786, wrote:

# When Whales Drifted In

**N**uu-chah-nulth chiefs owned the salvage rights to anything that came ashore, whether it was the carcass of a sea lion or a large drift-log, a runaway slave in a stolen canoe or a dentalium shell.

Alice Paul, a Hesquiaht elder, told me about the whales that washed ashore during her childhood. They came most often when there were storms and always were welcomed as a valuable resource:

A chief used to be in the woods day and night, asking that whale to come to the beach. When the village had no food, he would stay in the woods ten days. Singing and dancing. Asking for that whale to drift onto the shore.

After a long time, he hears a voice: "You can go out now. The whale is drifting onto the shore now." He was talking to human skulls. He kept a dozen of them [to use during the ritual] and when the whale is coming, the skulls fall over. That means, "There's a whale drifting onto the beach. You can go out now." They used to say that they could hear him from the village. He had a big drum to call the whale with, and he's singing and singing. . . .

That first drift whale that I saw myself, I remember a woman clear inside its mouth, cutting the lip. Even that part was divided up: so much on the left side for each person's allotment, and so much measured along the right side. The chief said who got which part and how much. The cutting was done really careful, using a mat to know how much—using it to measure with. Hold it against the whale and then move it along.

The second whale I saw, they started arguing, arguing, arguing [usually in jest, according to what men told anthropologist Drucker]. And they were cutting each other. It was really dangerous because they had steel knives by then. "No! You are cutting it too far." And then the other man said, "No! I know where my son is suppposed to cut. You used your hands to measure with. This is the real measure!" And he held up the mat.

Of course it wasn't the chief doing the cutting himself. It was some of my mother's brother's cousins. A chief always had somebody to speak for him—his uncle or grandfather, a close relative. So that speaker would say who was going to get which part of the whale.

*Detail of a whaling shrine of a Mowachaht chief on the island of a lake inland from the beach. Its contents were collected in 1904 by George Hunt and are now in New York at the American Museum of Natural History. The Nuu-chah-nulth hope to repatriate them.* AMERICAN MUSEUM OF NATURAL HISTORY, 104474

*A Makah harpooner stands in the bow of a canoe, aiming just behind a whale's flipper. This early twentieth-century photograph captures the drama of whaling.* WASHINGTON STATE HISTORICAL SOCIETY

On the beach below the village [probably Ahousat], were entire skeletons of eleven whales, the recent state of which, showed that they had not been killed more than a year previous to our seeing them.

Whale oil was enjoyed much as butter is today, and enormous quantities were traded and consumed. Nuu-chah-nulth elder Ida Jones told me containers of it hung from rafters in Ditidaht houses:

We used to keep the whale oil in sea-lion stomachs—big stomachs. You put a cork in one end, there where it gets that narrow place. You hang the stomach way up high and take what you need in a container when you're going to eat fish. A codfish stomach is good for that little container. You wash it real good in salt water and blow it up like a balloon and hang it outside till it's real thin. Then it's dry. You can even use dog salmons' little stomachs. You get a [salal] leaf and make a funnel for filling the oil.

We always had plenty of whale oil. Tom Parker's father [in Neah Bay] would bring chunks of blubber to my family when he gets a whale. The Ditidahts had

quit whale hunting. My grandfather got old and there was nobody to take over.

To kill a whale, men paddled close alongside their prey and struck with toggling, mussel-shell harpoon heads mounted on heavy shafts of yew, 3 to 4.5 m (10 to 15 feet) long. "As soon as the whale was hit we paddled backwards to get away fast," an elderly whaler once told me, remembering back to his youth. "I was scared the first time I went out."

A Makah elder, examining the shaft from a whaling harpoon found at the Ozette archaeological excavation, south of Neah Bay, explained:

This splice here is for a reason. It's so when you spear the whale [the harpoon] won't bounce back. Even if you had a long pole and made the shaft of it . . . it would bounce right back out if there's no splice.

By making the shaft out of two pieces expertly fitted and bound together, the force of the harpooner's thrust was deadened; the blade stayed in the whale's flesh. Furthermore, the splice let the shaft break if the whale thrashed violently after

*Whaling continued at outer-coast villages until the early twentieth century, although by then it had become sporadic. Here, Makah men float a whale onto the beach at high tide.* WASHINGTON STATE HISTORICAL SOCIETY

being struck. This lessened the danger that the shaft might accidently club the men. To avoid that possibility, hunters paddled backward as soon as the harpoon head penetrated its target.

"I went whaling out there," Harold Ides of Neah Bay told me. "I must have been sixteen, maybe fifteen." He added:

When they get ready for a whaling, they used to soak the [sealskin] floats in a creek during the night. They're going out in the morning and they leave after midnight, and one man had that job blowing them floats up all the way out. . . .

Daybreak, they sized the whale up and the whale has got to be approached not with the sun, 'cause he sees your shadow. . . . And when you go around [the whale], you approached by watching [its] wake. When he's gonna surface, the wake gets closer together . . .

and the man in the bow, he motions his paddlers. Kind of "paddle fast," and that signal for going fast was overhand. Or, if you know he's going to come up just in target range, the motion will be underhand. You hold the same speed paddling. And then when he gets in range for spearing, you spear below the fin. That's where the target is. So, they got him.

One sealskin float was a marker. It was so many yards behind the harpoon, and that was to keep the harpoon in there, you know, kind of tight. That float came out [from the canoe] first, and then the rest of the floats are way back so they don't pull that harpoon out. If they're all together the harpoon comes out. So there had to be just one, to take care of that. And that one was to mark when the whale's getting weak, too. He wouldn't pull that float under no more, you see, when he's getting weak.

So they slide the other floats up closer and closer then, until they can use that barbless spear [the killing lance]. Spear him, you know, just in the right place. And then, well, he can't go anymore. There was one man chosen, when the whale gives up, to dive down

136

*The harpooner keeps the fin from the back of a butchered whale, decorating it and ceremonially honouring the Whale's spirit. He distributes the rest of the carcass among his crew and other villagers.* WASHINGTON STATE HISTORICAL SOCIETY, 15953

there with a piece of rope to tie the mouth closed. It was sewed good. If they don't do that, well, that mouth [comes open] and drags in the water when they tow him to the village.

Whaling was solemn and glorious, directed only by chiefs. They alone had the inherited privilege of whaling, along with the time and wealth needed for ritual preparation and for making and equipping the 12-m (40-foot) canoe. They alone could lead the whaling crews of male relatives or—sometimes—slaves. Secrecy guarded every step right up to the fanfare and communal feasting that welcomed a harpooned whale to the village.

Chief John Thomas recalls hearing that in his family, whalers preparing themselves ritually used the position of the constellation Little Dipper—

which they called the Elk—to tell when dawn approached and it was time to go indoors from a night of bathing and praying. He told me:

My great-grandfather would sprinkle ash from the fire onto his hair and body when he went inside. Then he'd lie down and nobody would think he'd been out all night on that whaling business.

Similarly, in the 1920s, Chief Sayachapis told linguist Edward Sapir:

I was intending to be a whaler when I was growing up. A person bathes for four years if he intends to be a whaler. He goes off for four days at a time to walk around and to bathe. He goes to 10 different rivers to bathe for four days . . . and does not eat for that long. He stays in his house for 10 days, and then goes out again. . . . He bathes in that way for four years.

As a rule the harpooner, a high-ranking chief, performed the major whaling ritual and owned the

137

whaling equipment. He stood in the bow of the canoe and made the actual strike. An older, more experienced relative served as steersman and had charge of readying the canoe and of manoeuvring it into position alongside the whale. Hunters hoped that a harpooned whale would swim shoreward, not to sea. They sang songs and promised the whale great honour and happy times to entice it to head straight for the village, and they did what they could to physically encourage the whale in that direction.

Whalers' wives helped from the shore, although as the late Erna Gunther, University of Washington anthropologist, wrote in *Pacific Northwest Quarterly*, "the wife's position has received little attention." Gunther then told of an old woman who stopped picking strawberries in commercial fields near Seattle long enough to recount her experience while married to a whaler. Of this marriage, she said:

"When I was thirteen years old, my father, Samined, a Klallam of Jamestown [near Port Angeles, on Juan de Fuca Strait], sold me to a rich whaler, Andrew Johnson, a Makah of Neah Bay. I don't know what Johnson paid for me, but my father took me to him at Neah Bay. It was about 1898 when I went there."

The woman was the third wife of the whaler. His other wives and their children all had died, probably owing to epidemics, although it was said that whalers often lost their families; people got so jealous of the power owned by whalers that they used witchcraft to harm them. Also, since whaling rituals demanded the use of human corpses, whalers and their families were constantly suspected of grave-robbing and in danger of retribution. Sometimes a man's own whaling power caused harm simply by being too strong to contain. Because of such potential danger, Johnson gave up whaling after this third wife bore him a son. He wanted to insure the boy's safety.

During the whaling season from May to September, the whaler's widow recalled that her husband stayed constantly ready in case whales should be sighted. He did not sleep with her, and she avoided dressing her hair lest her comb break a few strands, as that might cause his harpoon line to snap.

Usually, the whaling party left at sundown, heading for an overnight camp west of Neah Bay so as to start at dawn for where they expected to find whales. As soon as they left, the whaler's wife went back into the house and lay motionless in a darkened room. Her utter stillness was intended to keep the whale from acting in an unruly manner.

This particular woman, however, told Gunther that she failed the first time:

"When I got up about two o'clock I ate a little dried salmon and I was so thirsty that I drank some tea. When my husband came back he walked up to me and said, 'You drank something when you got up; we got a whale but he is not fat.' This frightened me very much and after that I never drank anything again."

The second time her husband went out, the woman slept, then ate some dried salmon dipped in grease. When the whaler returned he told her, "Well, that whale was fat; I guess you were all right."

Whaling crews sometimes found themselves on the open ocean overnight, despite their care with ritual preparation. Eventually, they might triumph and tow a catch for 40 km (25 miles) or more, approaching the village beach with great ceremony. Each success brought honour to a chief's position, for getting whales demonstrated contact with powerful spirits. And with such helpers, a family could be confident of adding still more respect to their name.

# CHAPTER FIVE
## *Dealing with Others: Trade, Conflict and Marriage*

Reading the cryptic notes John Jewitt of the ship *Boston* entered in his journal while held captive at Yuquot from 1803 to 1805 gives a glimpse of the amount of contact between Indian groups during the days of the maritime fur trade. Jewitt wrote:

Nov. 1 (Tuesday). This month comes in with heavy rains and winds variable. Arrived a canoe from the Wickeningish [sic]. . . . They brought to our chief nine slaves as a present. He gave them in return cloth, muskets, powder, shot, etc.
 Nov 13. Thick and cloudy. Arrived a canoe from Savahina with fresh herring, a present to our chief. . . .
 Nov. 16. Frosty weather. Natives fishing. Arrived a canoe from Chewmadart with a large chest of salmon spawn for our chief. . . .
 Nov. 20. Natives fishing. Arrived a canoe from Aitizarts with infraw [dentalia shells] for our chief. . . .
 Nov. 23. Arrived a canoe from Esquates [Hesquiat] with 600 weight of blubber, being taken from a whale that had been driven ashore in a gale of wind.

## Trade

Jewitt's journal entries also often mention trade parties from other villages arriving at Yuquot with specialties each group was noted for or had recently acquired. The Ehattesaht brought the best dentalia, and the Hesquiaht brought geese and ducks. The Clayoquot and Makah came with many slaves, the best sea otter skins, great quantities of oil, whale sinew, salal-berry cakes, highly ornamented canoes, some dentalia, red ochre, elk hide (valued for armour) and wild onions. Also from the Makah, in Jewitt's words, "was received, though in no great quantity, a cloth manufactured by them from [dog] fur . . . which feels like wool and is of a gray colour."
 By Jewitt's time, the people of Yuquot controlled a supply of exotic goods ransacked from the captured *Boston*. Before that, their village had been a major stopping point for European and American trading ships. As a consequence of such riches, the trade Jewitt records is not characteristic of the coast as a whole, or of the time before white traders

*The first Spanish mariners to sail the Northwest Coast brought abalone from California as trade goods; earlier, native trade networks may have included the shells, which are much larger than Northwest abalone. Shown here as earrings, these squares probably had been sewn onto a button blanket.* BRITISH COLUMBIA PROVINCIAL MUSEUM, ETHNOLOGY DIVISION, PN 7377

140

arrived. Primary access to exotic riches rapidly elevated Maquinna to the status of a great chief controlling trade along the outer coast. Ample evidence exists, however, that for generations Nuu-chah-nulth, Southern Kwakiutl and Nuxalk people traded among themselves. For this reason they also traded with white men as soon as ships crossed the horizon. Exchanging goods was an accepted reason for contact with people from beyond the local group.

Alexander Mackenzie saw trade underway when he arrived at the Bella Coola River after his bold overland crossing of the continent in 1793. He noted in his journal that Indians from Bella Bella visiting the head of the inlet—a long, hard day's canoe journey from their village—were offering cedar bark, fish spawn, copper, iron and beads in exchange for "hemlock-bark" cakes (actually made from the moist, sweet growth layer just under the bark), roasted salmon, dried salmon roe and soapberries.

A few years earlier Manuel Quimper, an eighteenth-century Spanish mariner, wrote that Indians at Pacheenat, which is in Nuu-chah-nulth territory, traded with Salish people near Victoria for camas bulbs; and José Mariano Moziño, who spent the summer of 1792 at the Spanish fort at Yuquot, reported seeing women weave with a yarn of beaten cedar bark mixed with wool from "a quadruped that is not found anywhere on [Vancouver Island]." This may be a reference to mountain goats, whose wool had to be obtained in trade from the mainland, for these animals do not occur on Vancouver Island and were introduced only a few decades ago onto the Olympic Peninsula. Or the reference might be to dogs specially kept for their "wool" along parts of the coast.

The urge to trade for goods otherwise unavailable—and to become middlemen between the Hudson's Bay Company and other Indians—led four Southern Kwakiutl groups to move next to Fort Rupert just three years after it opened. Men told anthropologist Franz Boas how the decision was made:

As soon as he had finished his potlatch, the chief . . . arose and spoke. He said, "O Mamaleleqala! and you Kwag'ul how do you feel about the white people who have come and built a house at Tsaxis? Let us go and see them!" Thus he said. Immediately all agreed to what he said. Then all the Kwag'ul and Mamalelegala and Q!omoyâye and the Walas Kwag'ul went to Tsaxis. Now they believed what was reported to them [that is, they saw the white-men for themselves]. The Kwag'ul and the Mamalelegala went back at once to bring their houses and all their property, and they came to build houses at Fort Rupert.

All of these reports indicate the fundamental role of trade in Northwest Coast Indian life. Some of the exchange involved a variety of specialty goods. Camas bulbs were readily available on the dry slopes of Coast Salish territory but rare on the

*Nuu-chah-nulth and Southern Kwakiutl people traded camas—a member of the lily family—from the Coast Salish. When steamed in a cooking pit, the starchy bulbs become sugary.* RUTH AND LOUIS KIRK

141

*Basketmakers still value beargrass, for its whiteness takes dye well.*
*The plant is not found along the British Columbia coast, so is*
*traded from the Olympic Peninsula.* RUTH AND LOUIS KIRK

outer coast. The exceptionally long beargrass, prized by Nuu-chah-nulth basketmakers, grew in the low country south of Neah Bay, and cattail, useful for mats, was not available at all villages. There were the products of whales and fur seals, and dentalia shells collected from underwater beds off certain Pacific beaches. People living up the inlets of Vancouver Island had groves of prime red cedar. Those at the heads of mainland fiords had access to mountain goats and, through trade, to products from the high plateaus, rivers and lakes of the vast interior region stretching from the Coast Mountains eastward to the Rockies.

Aside from exchanging specialty products, trade also evened out occasional scarcities, such as when a salmon run failed or when prolonged bad weather prevented halibut fishing. It also allowed a conversion of surplus into needed commodities, as exemplified by whaling. A successful season for whalers meant more oil than a village could use, since too much fat in the human diet damages the liver and can prove fatal. Carbohydrates, however, make it safe to eat a much greater quantity of oil—and this ties in with Jewitt's report that people at Yuquot traded oil for camas, wild onions and berry-cakes.

Local trade probably centred on food redistribution in the days before European and American ships arrived and disrupted existing patterns. Across greater distances, trade may have revolved more around matters of prestige. Claims to rank had to be made in the presence of people from beyond a chief's own realm; in itself, this ability to attract audiences and present them with worthy gifts indicated high status. The dentalia shells, slaves and highly ornamented canoes Jewitt listed must have been among wealth items suitable for use when proclaiming rank and upholding prestige. Exceptionally fine or exotic foods and goods surely also figured in: the best smoked herring, the purest oil, the most beautifully made boxes and the most tightly woven baskets.

Canoes turned ocean and rivers into highways, facilitating coastal travel and trade. Additional trade routes crossed overland. The Nuu-chah-nulth at the head of Alberni Canal and on Sproat and Great Central lakes were in contact with Coast

*The Nuu-chah-nulth, and probably also the Makah, used an ingenious system of harvesting dentalia from the sea floor. This made them the only known source of the shells, which were traded inland as far as the plateau and southward at least to California. Dentalia 3000 years old have been found in archaeological excavations. A Wishram girl, photographed near the Columbia River about 1915, wears a dentalia headdress, ear pendants and nose ornament.* UNIVERSITY OF WASHINGTON LIBRARIES, HISTORICAL PHOTOGRAPH COLLECTION

Salish villages on southeast Vancouver Island; and villagers at the upper ends of Nootka and Kyuquot sounds established marriage ties and trade alliances with the Nimpkish Kwakiutl along the inner coast of the island. Aboriginal use of these overland routes may have been less before contact with Europeans, but once native chiefs had the incentive of goods from white men's ships, extensive trade took place across the mountain spine of Vancouver Island. Certain fiords penetrate far enough inland from the Pacific to nearly connect with lakes and rivers that flow to the east coast of Vancouver Island; people could paddle most of the way across the island, greatly minimizing foot travel.

At Bella Coola the topography offered especially strategic access for native trade. People living there had contact with the Southern Kwakiutl on adjacent waterways and with bands of Carrier and Chilcotin Indians, who regularly fished for salmon in the upper Bella Coola Valley, dropping into it from the interior via a precipitous pass. The Nuxalk somewhat disdained these interior people for their lack of ceremony or sense of the dramatic, but nonetheless they welcomed trading with them for exotic items such as dried meat and hides from moose and caribou, dried soapberries to whip into "Indian ice cream," and strong fibres of Indian hemp for cordage and nets.

## Conflict

Sometimes a raid was triggered in response to a trespass into a chief's realm, or a raid was staged in order to seize slaves. Sometimes grief prompted a raid, for by killing others a bereaved chief was not

## Kwiistuh Trades for Oil

In 1916 Chief Tom Sayachapis gave linguist Edward Sapir an account of trade, conveying well the intensity of traditional barter and the satisfaction of publicly outsmarting a trade contact. Kwiistuh, a prominent Ditidaht chief, was planning a potlatch and needed whale oil, which he knew he could get at Usiithl (Ozette).

He set out and went across [Juan de Fuca Strait]. He had only his wives and his slaves with him. . . . He landed. He said he was after oil, that he was going about looking for oil. The seaward tribe [the Ozette people] plotted to set their price up. . . .

My! Kwiistuh got angry at the way he was treated. At night as soon as the tribe went to sleep, he went to bathe and to do ritual for buying. He would make their spirit weaken. All night long he blew spray from his mouth and prayed. At dawn he returned to his vessel. . . . As soon as the people came out in the morning, he told his slaves, "Bring the goods down the beach, so we can set out. It is good that the tribe here wants to keep their oil, because . . . the news will travel quicky that the price has gone up. I will tell them of my bad luck." They brought the goods down the beach [ready to start home]. My! two seaward people [Ozette villagers] came to help him pull his vessel out. "I will take your blankets. I have oil in the house. My price is the same as always. My price hasn't gone up," they told Kwiistuh. . . . He unpacked his bag of blankets. . . . My! down the beach came two full sealion bladders, each worth five blankets. Again those first two who came to sell oil carried blankets up the beach. "Only I have good oil, only I have good oil," said the seaward people. [The chief] did not take notice of the people talking to him. He only bought . . . from two others. He used up forty blankets and got ten bladders of oil.

Then he stopped and loaded in the goods. He returned home. . . . [When time for the potlatch came, guests arrived and entered Kwiistuh's house.] He had a long house with a middle door. Since he had his younger brothers living at both ends, the house

alone in his anguish. If his wife and child drowned when a canoe overturned, a mourning Southern Kwakiutl chief, according to anthropologist Franz Boas, might ask: "Who shall wail? I or someone else?" The death of another gave the first victim an honourable means of "lying face down," sparing a chief the shame of his loss. Killing slaves might also provide such a "pillow"; so did attacking neighbours or slaying wayfarers who happened by. The death of any outsider of sufficiently high rank offset a loss within the group.

Raids could also be a source of gaining new prerogatives, which were normally acquired through astute marriage. Thus, one Southern Kwakiutl group gained the Hamatsa ceremonial. In this case, a ceremonial whistle had been stolen, setting off retaliatory raids and counter raids. On one of these vengeful missions, a war party representing

was very long. Now Kwiistuh poured oil on his fires. "O Tribes, this firewood was obtained at Usiithl," he said. "I went there to fetch wood that you might have fire while in my house. The Usiithl Tribe plotted against me. But I did not seek oil in order to become rich. The whalers of different tribes do not want their oil to drip away. That is what I am now burning while I have you by the fire." Thus he used nothing but oil as fuel as long as they were in the house. He was pouring [whale] oil of the seaward people on the fire as he spoke in that manner. That is why he invited them to be among his guests. My! he distributed many gifts to the invited tribes.

Nuu-chah-nulth chief Charles Jones of Port Renfrew inherited the honoured name Kwiistuh, which is also spelled Queesto. It means Ability-to-Conquer, Never-Failing-Person, He-Who-Outsmarts-Others.

several Southern Kwakiutl villages started for Bella Coola but, en route, chanced upon Heiltsuk (Bella Bella) canoes travelling to a wedding. They attacked these travellers instead of the originally intended victims. Heiltsuk ceremonial goods, meant to be part of the wedding exchange, gave ample restitution for what the Southern Kwakiutl had lost, and killing these "others" offset the earlier Kwakiutl deaths. All purposes were fulfilled. It did not matter who the victims were.

Other raids were calculated from the outset. According to what men told anthropologist Philip Drucker, the Ucluelet chief had no salmon river, so he sent delegates to nearby villages to taste their fish at the feasts required by routine hospitality. These men decided salmon at the Namint village surpassed all others. Consequently, the Ucluelet chief sent war parties there, and after killing everyone, he took over rights to the salmon. This happened before the arrival of white men, although such land grabs were more typical of later disruptions and the ensuing chaos.

Guns of course greatly increased the deadliness of battles. For example, villagers at Ahousat, by the entrance to Clayoquot Sound, used the new weapons to annihilate the people at Otosat. The Ahousaht were well situated for whaling and other open-ocean pursuits, but they lacked a reliable or abundant source of salmon. To get fishing rights, they decided to bring a wife for their second chief from Otosat on Flores Island, which is along the inner waterway. The plan should have worked, but the bride's father craftily did not include rights to dog salmon as part of his daughter's dowry. Furthermore, the new wife quarrelled with her husband and left him. Irritations and insults steadily escalated until eventually all the high-ranking people of Otosat lay dead, and the others had run off. The Ahousaht won the territory and salmon. They had used muskets gained in trade with their kin at Yuquot, who were in direct contact with the first white men to arrive on the coast.

Sporadic violence was an unpleasant reality. No one can say how far back in time it began. However, Barkley Sound alone has at least seven defensive sites where houses were built on inaccessible outcrops that could be readily protected against at-

*House depressions and midden indicate that people lived on top of this abrupt islet in Barkley Sound, most likely using it as a defensive refuge. The rise from the beach to the top is 20 m (65 feet).*
BRITISH COLUMBIA PROVINCIAL MUSEUM, ARCHAEOLOGY DIVISION, 82 B-175

tack by bulwarks of upright logs, sharpened at the top, or stockpiles of rocks, logs and hot oil to pour over the cliff onto an assault party. Certainly by the time of contact with Europeans, warriors held status as subchiefs and high-ranking commoners. They were recognized specialists, although between battles they might hunt and fish as well as tend their rituals and weapons. A Southern Kwakiutl father who wanted his newborn son to be a warrior prepared a special amulet. According to anthropologist Franz Boas, the father held the amulet in his left hand on the baby's fourth day and said:

"The reason I took out your tongues, snake, lizard, toad is that I want my son to be a warrior, for at the points of your tongues you keep a death-bringer. Now you will give this to my son."

The amulet consisted of tongues from these feared creatures, with part of a grizzly bear heart and shavings from a bear's right forepaw. To the grizzly, the father intoned: "Let your heart give my son strength and your claws the power to strike his enemy without mercy." From then on, the child got a daily, predawn bath in cold water. His family fed him boiled grizzly heart, when available, and smeared the blood on his face. He wore a necklace made from the toenails of dead people. When he was grown, the man's father (or the warrior himself) tested the future by running an awl through his lower arm, passing it between the two bones.

146

*Combat typically was hand-to-hand, hence the stone dagger and rope armour of this Southern Kwakiutl warrior. Weapons also included wood or bone clubs; armour was also made from elk hides and wooden slats.*
BRITISH COLUMBIA PROVINCIAL MUSEUM, ETHNOLOGY DIVISION, PN 7369

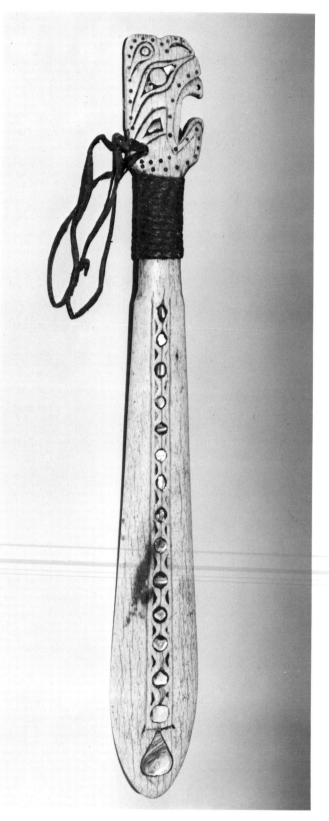

Meeting the pain silently foretold success in coming battle.

The tactics of raids concentrated on secrecy and surprise. Men counselled outdoors so that no hovering women could learn their plans and warn kin of a coming attack. Since slaves and most wives came originally from other villages, having plans overheard was a specific hazard. Late autumn was the best season for fighting. The work of stockpiling food for winter was done, and the major ceremonial season had not yet begun. Seas tended to be calm, and fogs hid raiding parties until prearranged "bird" cries and "wolf" howls signalled the moment for attack. Usually, this came just before dawn.

Raiding parties moved stealthily up a beach,

Left. *Capt. James Cook collected this whalebone club, nearly 0.5 m (20 inches) long. Archaeologists find fragments of similar clubs dating to at least 1000 years ago.* BRITISH MUSEUM, LONDON, P5 056128

Right. *Stone blades set into elaborate handles as "tongues" made efficient weapons, although most battles centred more on capturing slaves than on killing. All taking of life amounted to a ceremonial act involving ritual, hence the artistry and symbolism characteristic of weapons.* BERNE HISTORICAL MUSEUM, BERNE, AL 9

sneaked into houses and attacked everybody they came upon. They particularly enslaved women and children, whom they needed to gather and process the food and materials of a prosperous house-group or village. Men made poorer prospects as slaves, because they were too likely to watch for a chance to avenge themselves or to escape. Victims' heads became trophies strung victoriously on cedar cords or set onto stakes. Once warriors had enough heads for an impressive display, they usually withdrew. If they had attacked only a few people, however—say a canoe party or those at a fish camp—they tried to kill everyone, since survivors might rally kin for retaliation.

## Marriage

People of all social levels valued the sons and daughters of their chiefs, for their marriages could raise family and group prestige, as well as gain partners useful in trade, raids or the settling of various other issues. Close blood relatives never married, but a union—at any social level—often was based on kinship and therefore on shared interest in ceremonial prerogatives. As Southern Kwakiutl chief J. J. Wallas told me:

I used to wonder why they'd chosen my wife instead of me doing the choosing, but I didn't want to turn down my dad and mother. They'd picked a wife that raised our family up some more. When my eldest son was born, my mother came to me and said, "Now you got a son. Now our name isn't going to go downhill. It's still going up." So then I understood.

Marriage ties entailed lifelong responsibilities. Should there be a shortage of food in one area but not in another, or a rumour of a coming raid, kin were expected to help. Such alliances also assured a right to share the bounty of a particularly rich fishing station or other economic resource. Actual ownership of a resource, however, was never transferred through marriage; only rights to come and share the bounty were granted. Nothing could alienate the land itself from the people occupying it.

Marriages were often arranged to end carnage between warring groups. For example, Chief J. J. Wallas said:

My mother was from Hope Island. Her great-great-grandfather was hereditary chief there and the Bella Bella [Heiltsuk], they didn't want to stop fighting with the people. The Hope Island people go to Bella Bella and fight, and the Bella Bellas come down to Hope Island and fight.

So the chief of the Bella Bellas got tired of that and he invited the people into his own big house and explained what he wanted. "I want one of you to paint me a canoe paddle. Nice paddle. When it's finished give it to me." He didn't say what for. Well, when it was done the maker handed it to the chief. "Here's your paddle, nicely made." So the chief invited the people again and he explained, "I'm getting tired of this fighting. We lost a few people with this fighting. I bet Hope Island, they lost some too.

"I'm going to send you to Hope Island to give this paddle to the chief. I presume the chief has a son, and he's going to use that paddle to come marry my daughter. We will have peace."

A brave man set out for Hope Island with the painted paddle and the message "Let's quit fighting." And the plan worked. The Heiltsuk chief's son was Chief J. J. Wallas's great-great-great-grandfather.

Bringing a bride to a Southern Kwakiutl chief's house usually involved sham battles. The groom's family "attacked"; the bride's family "defended." The father of the bride would describe his doorway as a monstrous snapping mouth guarded by fire. On entering, the groom's representative had to run between a row of men holding flaming torches. Or the door might be wreathed with cedar bark soaked in oil and set aflame. The groom's envoys and the young men of the bride's village would pelt each other with stones, sometimes causing actual injury. Eventually, the groom's party was allowed to deliver the bride-price they had brought with them. They were then invited into the house and treated as guests.

After a feast, the bride appeared. With her came a foretaste of the dowry that eventually would be

given to the groom's family. Anthropologist Franz Boas tells of one young woman who went to her husband figuratively "carrying on her back" a ceremonial Copper, 20 boxes of oil, 10 boxes of chokecherries and 4 huge feast dishes, one of them carved as the two-headed serpent Sisiutl, one as Dzoonokwa (a supernatural wild woman who lived in the woods), one as Wolf and one as Seal:

Furthermore [there] were a Dzonoqwa ladle and a grizzly bear ladle, the name Great-Potlatch for [the groom] and the name Place-of-Satiation for his dancer.

These arrays of wealth varied, but every girl's father, of whatever rank, made generous arrangements in order to uphold family prestige. The two families involved exchanged gifts— although "gift" is not quite the right term. The bride-price paid by the groom's father was repaid and outshone, if possible, by final delivery of the entire bridal dowry. Boas recorded that one bride's father "bought his daughter back" with goods that included 120 heavy box lids inlaid with sea otter teeth, 100 abalone shells, 100 copper bracelets, 100 horn bracelets covered with dentalia shells, 100 miniature Coppers, 1000 strings of dentalia each nearly 2 m (6.5 feet) long, 200 dressed deer hides, 500 cedar bark baskets, 200 mats, and a venerable Copper. These items were supplemented by 20 boxes of preserved crabapples, 50 boxes each holding 20 coiled sections of bull-kelp stems filled with oil, 100 baskets of clover roots, 200 boxes of berry cakes, other boxes with horseclams, 50 seals, 100 bundles of 20 dried salmon each, 120 wooden spoons and 100 horn spoons.

The bride's party arranged this resplendent display in front of her father-in-law's house and, with songs and speeches, presented her husband with a Copper and a box holding regalia for various ceremonials. The young man's father then spoke:

*"Come for the bride" reads the caption of this Quatsino Sound photograph from the late nineteenth century. Before stepping ashore at the bride's village, the groom's party sings and performs dances; as accompaniment, the paddlers beat rhythmically against the canoes.* VANCOUVER PUBLIC LIBRARY, 14050

"Now this has come. Now I get what I wished to obtain for my prince through marriage. Although I have many privileges in my house these are different, these which I obtained in war and through the marriage of my prince. Thank you!"

The birth of a first child often became the occasion for completing presentation of a daughter's dowry; the girl's parents then felt content that the marriage was going to work out and assure a proper perpetuation of family status. Preludes of understanding and agreement of course led to

each stage of the marriage arrangement and exchanges continued until this final "repurchase." Afterward, a high-born bride stayed with her husband "for nothing." She was free to leave. If there were no children, her father might even summon her home and start the wealth exchange all over with a different family.

The names and rights to crests included in a dowry went to the new husband in trust for his children. If no children came from a union or there was a divorce, all names and other privileges theoretically went back to the bride's family, al-

*Ditidaht elder John Thomas has worked as a logger, taught linguistics at the University of Victoria and in Neah Bay, acted as an interpreter and helped with countless research projects.* NANCY TURNER

## The Marriage of James Sewid and Flora Alfred

Even within a village, prospective spouses did not necessarily know each other and might be unaware that they were in the process of getting married until the ceremonies culminated. James Sewid tells in *Guests Never Leave Hungry* about his marriage at age fourteen to Flora Alfred. He was lying on the couch one evening when he realized relatives were discussing him. "I think he should get married because we don't want him running around like this," they were saying. When the relatives left, young Jimmy asked his stepfather to go for a walk, and as they passed the Alfred house the stepfather said, "It's the girl that lives in there." Chief Sewid wrote that he "used to see her around the village but didn't know her."

In Alert Bay, Flora Alfred Sewid, who was sixteen at the time of her wedding, told me how she learned of the arrangement. "She's the one who gave the shock," she said, nudging her mother Agnes Alfred, seated next to her. Then she continued:

They were really strict with me. I couldn't walk

down the street by myself. If I smiled when I was out, she really got after me. She tried to make me like people of her time.

The remark drew a comment in Kwakwala from Mrs. Alfred, who was following the English conservation. Flora Sewid translated and added her own thoughts:

She says that's why I'm good. Because she raised me right. Jimmy never did ask for my hand. His oldest relative came and asked. That was the way. They didn't even ask me! I wondered what the old people were talking about. They just kept coming to the room. They wouldn't even let me listen. I didn't know anything about it. But I guess it's all right. We're still together.

My father's first wife came from the west coast [Nuu-chah-nulth]. When he was teenage he was taken to marry a woman there. They put him in a canoe and went up the river. Then they walked. He went to the Mowachaht to marry. The reason he went over there was to get names. But that girl got sick and she died. Later he married my mother.

*By lifting a waterworn beach boulder, William Walkus of Smith Inlet wins a 1955 ceremonial contest. Rock-lifting is sometimes part of potlatch gatherings today, and the boulder is often well greased.*
BRITISH COLUMBIA
PROVINCIAL MUSEUM,
ETHNOLOGY DIVISION,
PN 2239

though this did not always actually happen. Such considerations applied primarily to marriages between the families of chiefs, perhaps 10 per cent of the population. What happened among others had little consequence or interest, for rank, wealth and ownership of territory were concentrated in the hands of the nobility. Commoners—and slaves— might do as they chose in matters such as marriage without consequence for the group.

The elaborate planning and ceremonies surrounding a chief's marriage are apparent in what Nuu-chah-nulth elder John Thomas told me:

Uncle came home one time and said, "There's something wrong with you. You're not walking right."

So I said, "What's the matter with me now?" This was the uncle that gave me all my manhood training.

"You need a wife. Then you'll be complete. A wife connects you with the rest of nature; it's supposed to be like that."

"What am I supposed to do?"

"How much money you got?" So I gave him all I had, and he took it. "We've got a girl picked out for you," he said. "Bundle the money up and we'll put it on a post." [Doing this as part of a marriage negotiation was a *topati*, a ceremonial prerogative belonging to Chief Thomas's family.]

Next Uncle said, "Go out and get four pebbles, one-inch size." He didn't have a rattle for when singing a spiritual song, so he cut a hole in the top of a milk can and put the pebbles in. Then he asked for dried fish.

"What you going to do with that?"

"Don't ask questions."

So we went to the next village just after dark. They're not supposed to see us. There's a big gas lamp shining, no electricity. It looks like something suspicious here. So Uncle gave fish to the dogs, keep them quiet. Somebody opened the door and a beam of light shone right across, and they might see us coming up the hill. So we had to hide till things quieted down. It was nettles there! We'd sneak up some more, and hide some more.

I got a trowel and dug a hole, real fast [close to the house]. Put up the post. Uncle kept saying, "Hurry up. Hurry up. They're going to come out."

He took his rattle and started shaking—but, no sound. He had it upside-down and the pebbles fell out.

So I got more pebbles, and the second time we did that, he started to sing. Insults to me started right away [coming from the bride's house]. "We don't want your son. Take him away. He's not fit to marry my daughter."

But Uncle nudged me. "He likes you."

"It doesn't sound like it," I said.

Next morning we came around in a canoe. Dad had one of our masks and he put one on me. So I went up with the Wolf mask. But, same thing: "We recognize who you are and your good-for-nothing son. He's no good."

Various topati followed, with "the band divided, half on my side, half on the girl's side." The topati were rights to perform specific ceremonial contests owned by individual families and regarded as prized possessions dating from mythical, ancestral times. "The girl's were real hard to do, almost impossible," Chief Thomas told me. "But we managed to win most of them." All topati "gave respect for the family's name" and explained why the girl was almost unattainable because of her high pedigree.

One day's topati included wrestling, a foot race in soft sand, and catching a ball from the midst of the "hollering and tussling mob." Another day, a peeled cedar pole 3.5 to 4.5 m (12 to 15 feet) high was raised with a feather on top, to be retrieved by shinnying up the pole. This was difficult because of the cedar's own sap and also because the pole had been oiled to about its midpoint. Chief Thomas continued:

Everybody kept trying and slipping down. Uncle wasn't tall but he had a solid build. He said, "You run from over there and jump on my shoulder. I'll push you up." So I dashed and jumped onto his shoulder. That's how I got that feather.

Ten days, everything went like that. Contests. And they're still calling me down: "Your son is ugly!" For ten days. But in the meantime, when things quieted down, people in the village would be doing what they always do. Cut wood. Gather food. And we'd go help.
. . .

In the meantime I never saw the girl. Then on the tenth day they told us, late in the afternoon, "You can come in. We'll invite you now to come in and if you're good enough . . ." They weren't quite over it yet.

So they brought us in the house and they came in after us. There was a screen at the end of the house with the girl and her family behind that screen. And we were in the front part of the house. Her supporters danced first. They did their ceremonial stuff and gave us presents and took the money from the pole and divided it among the whole family. Then they started giving it back to me. I didn't get it all back but I got most of it back.

Finally this grand screen [a cloth painted with family crests] opened. All this time we're standing there. They didn't have us sit down. But then they showed the girl.

Her grandfather and grandmother were on each side and they came halfway and stood in the middle of the floor, and asked, "What have you got to show us? How do you think you're fit to marry my daughter? Show us now. Come and get her."

So I danced out toward her, and met them halfway. Then they announced, "You can take my daughter." It was the first good word they'd said to me in ten days.

They put us at the head of the house and sat us together. Then we got all the preaching and advice and family history. What to do. How to behave. What marriage means. How to keep holding the respect of the band, what they put you through. Remember which ones helped you. We sat there for the rest of the night.

Three or four o'clock in the morning, the family showed what came with the girl: the rights to use masks and songs and the kind of songs they use. They weren't hers. She didn't own them, but had the right to use them. Girls didn't inherit topati unless there were no sons in the family.

We sat down. The support people in her family started doing their things, paying us back and all the presents. It takes a long time. She was the oldest daughter of a tyee [chief] at Whyac village and my father was tyee at Clo-oose.

That was 1944, the last of the old-style marriages.

# Part III
## *Time's Flow*

# CHAPTER SIX
## *Seeing the Past from the Present*

In the papers of the late Wilson Duff, anthropologist at the University of British Columbia, this musing appears:

In our thinking about the Indians and their distant past, we are often too much preoccupied with their "origins." The one question everybody seems to ask is: Where did the Indians come from? And the one answer everybody seems to know is, They came from Asia.

That answer is in part true: from time to time what is now the shallow Bering Strait formed a land connection to this continent. So much of the world's water was locked up in glacier ice that the ocean level fell low enough for Siberia to be joined to Alaska. And 14 000 years ago, when the land connection across Bering Strait was most recently available, the ancestors of today's white Europeans and North Americans were living in the forests of western Asia; those of today's Indians were living on the steppes to the east. Duff continues:

White people could claim to come from Asia too. But American Indians are not just transplanted Asiatics. What happened on this continent after its original peopling from Asia is a chronical of thousands of years of developments here. . . .

The genesis of the Indian people and cultures as we know them is essentially a local story.

How early did men begin to trade, hunt whales or potlatch? The record within the ground gives partial answers—and an occasional archaeological site acts as a reminder of how narrowly the window onto the past usually opens.

## What Stone and Bone Can Tell

People probably came to the coast as soon as glaciers had substantially withdrawn. Based on radioactive carbon dating, this would mean they arrived about 13 000 years ago, two millenia before ice sheets melted from the interior of British Columbia. Rates of glacial withdrawal—and effects left as aftermath—are never uniform, however.

Where silt-laden meltwater sluices across the land from lingering ice faces, it may produce channels and oozing deltas that are inhospitable to life, yet nearby streams and lakes fed from other sources may be clear enough for invertebrate life to thrive and salmon to extend their spawning runs. Along the shore, marine plants and animals re-establish themselves as soon as icebergs stop scraping surfaces bare.

The entire process can be seen along the present

*Geologists say that the ice had melted from much of the coast by about 13 000 years ago, leaving it suitable for habitation. Native people say that Raven released the sun, made the trees, painted the birds, brought the fish and berries, arranged the tides and got things ready for people.* RUTH AND LOUIS KIRK

159

*Varied resources are found where one environment meets another. The Northwest Coast combines the riches of ocean, shore, river and forest.* BRITISH COLUMBIA PROVINCIAL MUSEUM, ARCHAEOLOGY DIVISION, 84B-72

coast of southeast Alaska. There, life may reclaim glacial sterility within mere decades at one location, while in an adjoining area ice still thrusts from the mountains into the sea and calves off icebergs. Much of the British Columbia coast must have been suitable for people even while other parts were still dominated by ice. Since early human groups were small and widely scattered, little evidence of their first several thousand years along the coast can be expected.

Archaeology presents objective evidence of how people lived and developed their various cultures. For instance, try to describe Northwest Coast Indian life without discussing watercraft, and you realize the fundamental role of seamanship in the lives of these people. But when did their ancestors learn to make boats?

Finding actual examples more than a few centuries old is not likely since the wood, hide and straw bundles used worldwide for early watercraft are materials that rarely last for long. Even so, archaeologists believe that people began navigating the currents and fogs of this coast at least 10 000 years ago and possibly several millenia earlier. The question may not be when they learned to *make* boats but rather when they *arrived* in boats.

The first people to travel from Siberia to Alaska quite likely not only walked overland, pursuing large mammals and gathering plants, but also paddled along the shore of the land bridging the con-

160

tinents. This is inference: no physical evidence exists, so far as known. But stone tools left at Namu, which is near the mouth of Burke Channel (the inlet with Bella Coola at its head), show that people were living there nearly 10 000 years ago. Access must have been by water, for along much of the coast, steep cliffs plunge straight into the sea, making foot travel on land impossible. Steep mountains also wall off the coast from the interior which, in any case, lay sealed beneath ice-age glaciers until about 11 000 years ago. Nobody can say how many of these early Namu people there were, what their daily routine was like, or how long their forebears had lived in North America. Only the stone they used remains, yet they must also have had tools of bone and shell, perhaps even wood.

At Bear Cove, near Port Hardy on northeastern Vancouver Island, archaeologists have found other evidence of early human activity. They uncovered bones of porpoises and fur seals hunted nearly 6000 years ago; and, by then, people at Namu were also bringing ashore porpoises (or dolphins), seals, sea lions and sea otters.

What do such tiny glimpses of human life imply? The first important answer is that if people were at Namu almost 10 000 years ago, they must also have been at other places along the Northwest Coast. Indeed, tools of that age have been found in southeastern Alaska; and, near Sequim, on Washington's northern Olympic Peninsula, archaeologists found bison bones with evidence of butchering and a mastodon skeleton with what might be a broken spear point protruding from a rib: evidence of hunters nearly 12 000 years ago.

These places must not have been the only ones known to the earliest coast Indians. They simply are those that have been found and studied so far. People that long ago quite surely lived in small groups of two or three families, owned few possessions and travelled from camp to camp rather than staying at settled locations. Such habits leave little evidence, and decay quickly destroys most of what there is. Northwest Coast soils are acidic; organic material rarely lasts long. Wood, perhaps used for boats, cannot be expected to remain from this early period; neither can hide or fibre fashioned into clothing and bedding, bone from tools and fish barbs, nor bone and shell from meals.

Furthermore, the coast along which we drive and boat today is not the same as that known to our earliest human predecessors. Climate and geology constantly reset the stage. Until about 13 000 years ago, ice-age glaciers sheathed most of the coast from Alaska to northern Washington. Their stupendous weight pushed the land down. But as the ice melted and returned water to the ocean, the weight was lifted and the surface of the land rebounded. Sea levels varied several hundred metres owing to alternate glacial expansion and withdrawal. Even today, the coast is rising in places, sinking in others.

The fluctuation means that beaches we see today are not *the* coastline; they are *a* coastline. Now, fish may swim where some of the first Northwesterners paddled ashore and lit their campfires. Other ancient shores known to these people are probably forested benches well above today's tidepools. To find such previous coastlines, archaeologists need to look both beneath the green upholstery of plants and the watery cover of the risen sea—obviously difficult.

Undoubtedly, this coming and going of glacier ice influenced the timetable of life along the Northwest Coast. But, in any case, by Nuxalk tradition it was not until Aɫquntam sent the First People to the upper fiords of Bentinck Arm and Burke Channel that the separation between human ancestors and myth-people became fixed.

Or perhaps, as some Southern Kwakiutl say, man first took up residence on this coast when the Giant Halibut got stranded near the mouth of the Nimpkish River and took off his fins and tail to become a man. And maybe Southern Kwakiutl chief J. J. Wallas was right when he told me about a powerful chief, living in the North, who had one cold shoulder and one warm shoulder. Depending on which way he faced, ice covered the land or melted from it.

What can stone and bone tell? Only a little, but these bits are tangible evidence. For example, two fundamentally different ways of making stone tools are apparent at Namu, although early coastal sites north and south of there have either one style

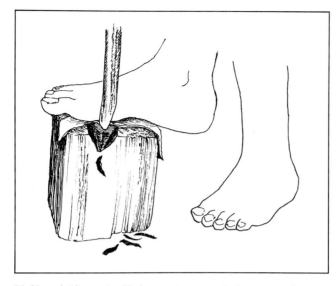

*Making obsidian microblades requires control. A core must be specially shaped, then held steady for the precise removal of flakes. This can be done by using an antler to press blades from a core firmly wedged into a cedar block. Finished tools vary. The simplest may have been single blades tied between cedar slats for use as knives. Obsidian is a naturally occurring glass that breaks with an*

*edge only molecules thick, so the blades made from it are sharper than those made of surgical steel. Under a scanning electron microscope, the edges of surgeons' scalpels look like saws when compared with fine obsidian blades.* DRAWINGS BY HILARY STEWART

*A cobble tool found at Namu represents the flaking technology especially common at early sites to the south of the Bella Coola region.* SIMON FRASER UNIVERSITY

or the other, but not both. To the north, archaeologists find microblades—tiny, sharp, parallel-sided slivers of stone flaked off from precisely prepared cores. These blades may have been hafted singly, or several could have been set side-by-side into wooden or bone handles to make a sharp edge, effective for cutting or piercing.

South of Namu, people made tools an entirely different way. Instead of pressing off microblades, they set pebbles or small cobbles onto rock anvils, then struck them with hammer-stones to break off exact pieces for use as choppers, scrapers and knives. Toolmakers often carefully selected the type of cobble to use and precisely controlled how they broke it. No retouching was needed on such fragments of cobbles for use as tools.

The north-south distribution of these two basic approaches to tool-making from 6000 to 10 000 years ago suggests an overlap of cultural traditions at Namu. The southern approach may represent ancestors of today's Southern Kwakiutl, Nuu-chah-nulth and Salish. The northern may be associated with ancestors of the Haida and Tlingit (and possibly also the Athapaskan, although the ancestors of these people seem to have crossed

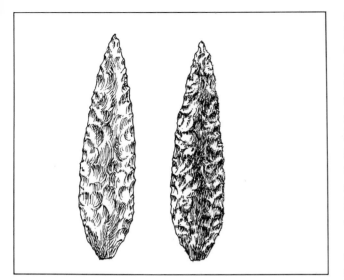

*By working both edges, men could chip implements to whatever size and shape they needed for particular tasks. Chipping techniques—and preferred kinds of stone—differ from those used for microblades or cobble tools.* DRAWINGS BY HILARY STEWART

from Asia in a separate, more recent migration).

Tools of still a third style have been found at dozens of sites along eastern Queen Charlotte Sound and Quatsino Sound. These are chipped to the precise shapes needed for specific tasks. So far they have been found lying in the intertidal zone. Possibly they belong to a time when the sea level was so low that the continental shelf was exposed. Or perhaps at least some of these tools eroded onto the shore from terraces that now stand above sea level but previously were barely beyond the beach. Still another possibility is that men deliberately manufactured tools in the tide zone, which offered a variety of readily accessible stone.

Although most trade items cannot be traced archaeologically, a few at Namu date as far back as 8000 to 9000 years ago. At this and other coastal sites from 4000 to 6000 years ago, archaeologists have found blades and cores of glassy black obsidian. This is a stone from a certain type of lava that cools quickly. Each such flow has its own chemical characteristics, a distinctive "signature" that can be used to trace where pieces of obsidian originated. Surprisingly, the obsidian came from just four regions: the Anahim Peak–Rainbow Mountain area

east of Bella Coola, Mount Edziza south of the Stikine River, northern Vancouver Island and eastern Oregon. People either travelled to these places to quarry obsidian or they obtained it in trade, and considering how widely the stone was used, trade seems more likely. This evidence of trade indicates that for thousands of years people had a wide-ranging awareness of other groups and some contact from one to another. Furthermore, the exchange between them surely included ideas and bloodlines, as well as tangible goods. People had their own areas and outlooks, but also knew of others.

There are roughly two periods of archaeological time along most of the Northwest Coast: earlier than about 3500 to nearly 5500 years ago and since then. Shell middens mark the division in time. Probably this is not because earlier people disliked the taste of mussels and clams or were ignorant of them. Rather, their middens may have already decayed; or, due to changes in sea level, their middens now may be either submerged under the sea or lifted above today's beach and hidden beneath the forest floor.

The oldest shell middens known so far are at Namu beginning about 5500 years ago. A long period without midden is represented there by a surprisingly thin, black deposit. Then—almost suddenly—clam and mussel shells not only appear but remain continuously present right up to recent times. This pattern is typical all along the coast, although usually beginning about 3500 years ago rather than as early as at Namu. Some debris accumulations are at places occupied for thousands of years. Others represent camps used briefly while fishing or hunting, stripping bark or picking berries. A few are on top of small islets or rocky promontories that served as defensive refuges or lookouts. Activities varied from place to place and from time to time and, therefore, evidence also varies.

About 3500 years ago, or a bit earlier, environmental conditions and rates of change became much as they are today. Large red cedar trees, ideal for canoes and house planks, began to flourish, whereas pollen samples from earlier times suggest comparatively sparse cedar; other resources also became much as we now know them.

163

On northern Vancouver Island and the adjacent mainland, Kwakiutl people elongated and narrowed the skulls of babies by binding their heads with tight bandages. The Nuu-chah-nulth and Makah also reshaped heads but to a lesser degree than among the Kwakiutl. BRITISH COLUMBIA PROVINCIAL MUSEUM, ETHNOLOGY DIVISION, PN 10174

The human population of the coast apparently expanded rapidly. This increased the use of food and materials and accelerated the build-up of midden, the main type of deposit studied by archaeologists.

By the time the population increased about 3500 years ago, groups of people were apparently making seasonal rounds within their own familiar areas. Distinctions arose as neighbours started drawing on slightly different resources and developing their own particular techniques. This probably stimulated trade—whale oil from one group exchanged for the dried salmon of another group, for example. Probably there also were social reasons to trade, for the same urge toward the exotic that motivates modern exchanges must have existed then too. Furthermore, access to such items probably helped distinguish persons of wealth from those of lesser status—a basic consideration in view of the social hierarchy of the Northwest Coast.

Gradual changes show within the archaeological record as groups developed individual ways. In the same period that large shell middens became commonplace, antler wedges also became widespread. Presumably, they were used for splitting wood, and this suggests the use of cedar which, in turn, suggests house planks and dugout canoes. By 3500 years ago, they could carve as well as cut, pierce, whittle, chop, split and gouge. And, from at least 1500 years ago, bark shredders, mat creasers and spindle whorls found on the central and southern British Columbia coast indicate the use of fibres for household basketry and weaving, as well as for specialized equipment such as fishing nets. All such objects may have existed earlier but vanished owing to poor preservation. Or they may have been widely present, but not at the particular handful of sites archaeologists have excavated so far.

Perhaps a thousand years later, the basic tool kit changed. In addition to manufacturing microblades and cobble and chipped stone tools, people also made tools by grinding stone or by pecking it with a stone hammer, then polishing; and they made blades from mussel shell, bone and tooth. With these refined tools, craftsmen could engage in increasingly intricate woodworking.

Any of these implements could have arrived as people from outside the region brought in a variety of new techniques and ideas. More likely, however, refinements in existing tools took place generation by generation, as groups developed specific preferences and methods of drawing on the environment. People also bartered for goods from outside their area, and once in a while, they found valuable material drifted ashore, such as wrecked Asian fishing vessels, which were a prime source of iron and steel.

With their blades of shell, bone, stone and sometimes metal, men produced what we today call "art." Native people probably recognized no such distinct category, although early representations of the supernatural found in archaeological sites surely stemmed from the same all-pervasive spiritual quality so eloquently described by today's elders. Designs include geometric patterns and depictions of spirit helpers and ancestral crests. Some stone objects, such as oversize blades and exquisitely shaped and smoothed mauls, have been so superbly and laboriously fashioned that they seem to embody a purpose beyond the strictly utilitarian. Occasionally, a shaman's charm for curing the sick is found; and, at Kwatna (near Bella Coola) a human skull lying apart from any burial suggests witchcraft. It is pierced by seventeen splinters of bone.

Aside from supernatural and spiritual implications, art probably also had ties to wealth and differences in social status. These, in turn, relate to increasingly elaborate ceremonialism, for wealthy families would be able to devote additional time and resources to ritual. This would increase their power and raise their status.

Wealth alone must have carried prestige, and prestige strengthened leadership, which permitted the efficient direction of manpower. Making the best use of spawning runs of salmon depended on enough men working together to build traps and fishing platforms, as well as enough women to slice the daily catches, hang the bright flesh on racks to dry, and faithfully tend the fires that smoked and preserved the fish. Similarly, among the Nuu-chah-nulth, whalers needed to organize the job of towing their prey long distances, beaching it, then

# How Old Is Northwest Coast Art?

The roots of art on the coast date back thousands of years. At a waterlogged site nearly 3000 years old along the Hoko River mouth (traditional Makah territory), archaeologists found a wooden tool decorated with what seems to be a pair of kingfishers. Most likely the tool was a mat creaser, used to crush the fibre of tule or cattail so the stalks would not split when stitched. The kingfishers are the oldest wooden artwork yet discovered on the Northwest Coast, or indeed in all of North America.

At Yuquot, midway along the outer coast of Vancouver Island, Parks Canada archaeologists excavating deposits 3000 to 4300 years old found part of a bird-bone whistle that must have been associated with some sort of ritual. They also found four other equally ancient pieces of artwork too broken to be identified, each with decorative or symbolic patterns incised on the surface.

At Kwatna Bay, off Burke Channel in the Bella Coola region, archaeologists from Simon Fraser University found several bone and antler carvings made sometime between 1800 years ago and the arrival of white men along the British Columbia coast. The earliest of these is an antler or bone figurine of a human wearing a short skirt. It has the elongated head that became fashionable about 3000 years ago among the ancestors of the present Coast Salish, a custom that appeared later in Southern Kwakiutl and Nuu-chah-nulth territory. The shape is achieved by binding a baby's skull for most of the first year.

Perhaps the carving, which is about 20 cm (8 inches) high, was traded up the coast from the Strait of Georgia. The size of the antler it was made from indicates elk, not deer; yet there are no elk in the Bella Coola region. Trade is also

*This mat creaser made of red cedar is nearly 3000 years old. Such tools were used to crush the fibres of cattail or rush stems laid side by side before drawing a twisted cord through them with a long needle. The deliberate crushing prevented splitting.*
RUTH AND LOUIS KIRK

166

*Bone figurines from Bella Coola and northern Puget Sound have elongated heads.* DRAWINGS BY HILARY STEWART

suggested by the fact that five strikingly similar carvings have been found at widely separated places—Kwatna, the Gulf and San Juan islands, northern Puget Sound, and east of the Cascade Mountains near Yakima, Washington.

How old is art along the Northwest Coast? Probably as old as man on the coast, but we are unlikely to see much from those most distant millenia. Time alone augurs against the likelihood, especially in a region where the prime medium for artistic expression was wood, a fragile material usually soon rotted.

efficiently utilizing such a huge carcass. By grouping together, rather than living widely scattered, families could co-ordinate such effort. Differences in status established the roles of each social level.

Gradually, claims to separate territories emerged, and marriage alliances evened out some of the unequal distribution of resources. The richness of one territory compared to another might directly affect rank. For instance, in the Southern Kwakiutl region the yield from individual salmon streams seems to correlate with the rank of the various chiefs who owned them. The more fish a chief had, the more followers and slaves he was likely to have and the higher his status. A large village meant a large labour pool, essential for catching and preserving large quantities of salmon. Enough food stored for winter enabled people not only to survive but to take time for elaborate ceremonies and the manufacture of goods to give to neighbouring villagers at potlatches.

Not every stream provided a silvery horde of salmon every year. Far from it. Furthermore, not every local group had rights at a major spawning stream. Serious shortages of food must have existed at various times and places, as people increasingly divided up the landscape. Limited to a specific territory, each group began depending on specific resources rather than following the ancient pattern of scattering widely and drawing lightly on the coast's full variety. Trade probably became a way of redistributing resources from "haves" to "have-nots." Feasts provided another way. A host chief sent guests home with surplus food to share with their groups. His incentive to do so came from the enhanced prestige that generosity brought— and chiefs could convert prestige to power.

For the last thousand years or more, people along the central coast of British Columbia were evidently living in much the same places and ways as at the opening of the historic era with the arrival of white men. This may also have been true earlier, but poor preservation has largely prevented any detailed archaeological record except at scattered waterlogged sites. Outstanding among these is Ozette (the southernmost land occupied by Makah Indians), where mudslides 400 to 500 years ago flattened several houses in a whaling and fishing

167

village. The wreckage was sealed as effectively as if in a time capsule. Underground water saturated deposits and prevented decay from soil fungi or bacteria.

Thus protected, not only stone, shell and bone stayed intact but so did the cedar posts and planks of the smashed houses and most of the belongings of the families who lived there. Tangled in the wreckage were sleeping benches and bent-corner wooden boxes, wooden spindle whorls and looms. The yew shafts of whaling and fur-sealing harpoons lay still lashed to fallen walls. Harpoon heads, individually packed in folded strips of cedar bark, remained stored in special basketry pouches. Bows and arrows with wooden points littered floors; so did fish-hook kits with whetstones for re-sharpening barbs, and bundles of whale baleen or fibre cordage for use as leader. There were coils of rope twisted from cedar and spruce withes, as well as tools with shell or even metal blades bound into handles of carved wood and bone. Ninety per cent of the objects found within the houses were made of wood or fibre, an indication of the stupendous loss typical at nonwaterlogged sites.

Excavation at Hesquiat Harbour, midway along the west coast of Vancouver Island, shows that people there were settled into distinct territories by at least 1200 years ago. Hesquiaht elders told archaeologists that for generations five separate groups each had their own names and village locations, their own places for getting specific resources. It was a remembered pattern that physical evidence proved to be true. Excavation showed that two Hesquiaht groups had lived along the exposed outer coast and drawn year-round from the range of resources there. Two other groups had been situated on the harbour's protected inner shores, using foods and materials close at hand. A fifth group, barely within the harbour, had drawn from both realms.

Published accounts of Northwest Coast Indian life have usually assumed that stormy weather

*On the earthern floors of houses 400 to 500 years old, Ozette archaeologists find well-preserved wood and fibre artifacts. These include canoe paddles, loom uprights, wooden clubs, boxes, baskets, and hunting and fishing gear.* RUTH AND LOUIS KIRK

made winter life along the outer coast impossible and that only endlessly moving from seasonal camp to camp sustained people. Actually, as the elders knew and as archaeological investigation determined, this really was not the case. Some people lived on the outer coast year-round; others stayed on inner waterways. The human population had expanded enough that available territory was divided to its maximum, and group boundaries were relatively firm.

Inside Hesquiat Harbour people relied on salmon and herring. They seldom hunted sea mammals, not even hair seals; bone preserved in shell middens makes this clear. Composite harpoons, apparently for catching salmon, are preserved in great numbers. There are also shell knives for processing the fish and hundreds of sharpened bone splinters, probably from herring rakes and fishhooks.

In contrast, the middens of people on the outer coast contain the remains of lingcod, greenling, cabezon and other rockfish species. Fishing gear also differed from that of the inner coast. Small harpoons and fish knives were few, but there were a great many hooks attached directly onto stone shanks, which acted as built-in sinkers. Sea-mammal bones and hunting equipment showed that for more than 1000 years people on the outer coast had hunted fur seals, sea lions, sea otters, porpoises and whales—the classic list of marine life, unchanged as far back as the time of Bear Cove and Namu.

Hunting whales and other sea mammals probably was crucially important to people on the outer coast year-round. Living together in winter villages anywhere depended on storing surplus food from other seasons to use during the cold, grey months when fewer resources were available; and since most rivers on the outer coast of Vancouver Island are small—except for those at the heads of inlets—huge salmon catches were not possible. Quantities of other kinds of dried fish would not have been enough to carry outer-coast people through the winter. They must have depended on some other major resource.

According to Nuu-chah-nulth stories, groups at two exposed sites on Nootka Island started hunting

# Elders and Archaeologists: The Hesquiat Example

In 1970, distressed by vandalism in burial caves that had been used for generations, Hesquiaht band members sought help from the British Columbia Provincial Museum. The result has been an ongoing project combining the knowledge of band elders with the scientific skill of archaeologists.

Bio-archaeologist Gay Boehm told me:

The elders could be amazingly specific. Without them, we'd have no hope of understanding the Hesquiat environment from the Hesquiaht standpoint. For instance, they categorize differently than it says in books. They use four different names for fur seals, depending on size and how far at sea they found them. Probably this distance correlates with the seals' sex and age; but, for hunters, what mattered was how big and how far out. Those were the criteria distinguishing one seal from another.

The elders talked about albatrosses too—birds seen only at sea—and they mentioned that the long slender bones were particularly prized. You can't *read* about their taking albatrosses, but—sure enough—we found the bones in the excavations. The elders talked about how to cook raccoon (it tastes like chicken); and they listed four or five kinds of rock fish common at Hesquiat where we classify twenty species.

They also kept asking if I'd found "that grunting, singing fish that lives under rocks." And finally I

came on a midshipman, a fish with an air bladder than makes bubbly, croaking sounds. When sixty-three per cent of the fish bone in one cave turned out to be from this fish, we told the elders and they said, "Of course. Everybody knows about that fish." But we didn't.

The elders *are* the project. They're why it started. They have a firm belief that the culture is worth passing on and they are the key to being sure future generations know anything about their heritage. When today's elders went to school they were told to forget their culture. Now anthropologists say to them: "Please remember. Tell us about traditional life." Auntie Alice [Paul] really laughs at the reversal. She's gone in her life from the days of fishing and hunting by canoe to commuting by floatplane. That's change!

Left. *Hesquiaht band members examine artifacts excavated as part of their archaeology project undertaken with the British Columbia Provincial Museum.* RUTH AND LOUIS KIRK

Right. *Elders Alex Amos and Mike Tom admire a halibut hook from excavations at Hesquiat.* RUTH AND LOUIS KIRK

whales at sea to get enough food for winter. Humpback and grey whales arrived dependably in great numbers before they were overhunted by the commercial whaling industry, and some must always have drifted ashore, a virtual "warehouse" of useful food and raw materials. Just when active whaling came about may never be known, but people on the Broken Islands already had a chief named Has-His-Place-Full-of-Whale-Oil as long ago as the great flood described in Nuu-chah-nulth and Southern Kwakiutl accounts of before the world became as it now is.

Archaeologists have checked places identified by band elders as ancient locations for whaling villages and there have found the largest shell middens of the outer coast. People obviously lived generation after generation at these sites. Fifteen thousand grey whales swim close to shore each year, and an equal number of humpbacks seems to have migrated along the British Columbia coast in the past. The regularity of their migration, as dependable as that of the salmon, let people anticipate enormous quantities of food and materials delivered close to village doorsteps.

Fur seals also migrated offshore and may have had rookeries far south of their present limitation to the Alaska coast. Deposits at Ozette spanning the last 2000 years are consistently dominated by the bones of fur seals, including those of mature males, which no longer come close to shore at the latitude of Washington and southern British Columbia. If rookeries were close by in the past, the ancestors of today's Nuu-chah-nulth and Makah had seasonal access to a rich supply of food, bone, hide and gut.

Whaling called for more skill than sealing and took still greater courage and ritual. The accounts of successful whalers naturally figured into the prestige of outer-coast chiefs, with descriptions of heroic victories passed from generation to generation. Just when reliance on these particular sea mammals may have begun is not known, but a midden 5.5 m (18 feet) deep marks the whaling village site at Yuquot, where Maquinna was chief when European ships started sailing the Northwest Coast. Deposits dated by radioactive carbon represent at least 4300 years of continual occupation.

171

# What a Film of Blood Can Tell

Ordinarily, organic material such as wood or bone has little likelihood of lasting for long unless it is specifically preserved, perhaps buried by chance in a waterlogged deposit or peat, or is frozen or mummified. Yet, traces of blood actually remain for millenia even in acid soils that destroy bone in two or three centuries. Thomas Loy, an archaeologist at the British Columbia Provincial Museum, is pioneering the study of blood left on stone tools, finding out what this "paleo-gunk" can tell. It turns out to be a great deal.

*The quartz blades of Hoko River fish knives are bound between cedar splints about 13 cm (5 inches) long.* WASHINGTON STATE UNIVERSITY, HOKO RIVER ARCHAEOLOGY PROJECT

Loy's study involves extracting and crystallizing the hemoglobin (the red, oxygen-carrying matter of blood) that clings to ancient tools. From this he can identify what kind of animal the blood came from; that knowledge leads to other conclusions. For instance, say that blood from bison turns up on knives and projectile points found in deposits from 6000 years ago, and that the area is presently heavily forested. Since bison live on grasslands, archaeologists could state that environmental conditions had changed substantially: the present forest was previously grassland. And, since grass requires drier conditions than forest, the climate must have changed.

At archaeological sites where bone has disintegrated, blood on tool surfaces may be the only way of discovering previous conditions. Mean temperature within about two months of when the blood got onto the tool can be calculated by analyzing certain oxygen isotopes; and specific carbon, nitrogen and oxygen isotopes may indicate the main types of food that were eaten.

On small, quartz-crystal knives from the Hoko River archaeological site just east of Neah Bay, Loy found red blood cells that indicate fish. On three knives, the precise shape of the cells indicated sand-lances, a small bottom-fish. No sand-lance bones had been found in Hoko River deposits, however. They are tiny and difficult to detect (and most fish bones are troublesome to identify to species, even when found). Yet blood on the little knives clearly showed that nearly 3000 years ago people had been catching sand-lances. Makah elders remember this fish as good eating, and subsequent seining off the river mouth proved that these fish are abundant enough at certain times in spring to form three-quarters of the catch.

*In 1966 Parks Canada archaeologists undertook a major
excavation at Yuquot.* PARKS CANADA, IT-4C

To sample them, archaeologists cut a trench 19
by 4.5 m (64 by 15 feet), cross-sectioning time in the
middle part of the village. Bottom layers—the
oldest—were a greasy black, with rotted and compressed materials that once were food and household goods, fishing and hunting gear. Water-worn
artifacts and animal bones suggest that the sea level
was higher than at present and that winter storms
or unusually high tides occasionally flooded their
homes.

A bone needle lay in the black matrix: four millenia ago someone had sewn with it. A piece broken from the sturdy bone foreshaft of a harpoon

and part of a bone harpoon head belonged to
equipment made and used for taking salmon or
small sea mammals. A smoothly ground basalt
blade probably came from the tool kit of a wood-
worker. Deposits 3000 years old held some
whalebone. Whether this was from drift whales or
from animals hunted at sea nobody can say.

Upper levels of the trench cut through thick
layers of shell and bone, and there archaeologists
found household artifacts, including fragments of
a coarse earthenware jar from Mexico, bits of
glazed English and French china, and part of a
cut-glass tumbler. These date from when the rich

173

*Archaeologists cross-section Yuquot deposits left from a succession of houses dating back for at least 4000 years. Plastic sheeting protects squares not being actively excavated.* PARKS CANADA, IT-6C

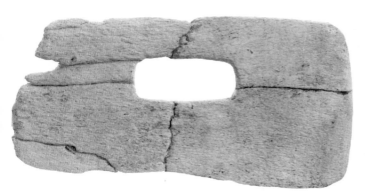

*Yuquot artifacts 1000 to 3000 years old include a shredder of whalebone* (left) *used to soften cedar bark. Yuquot women used this bone awl* (centre) *to pierce and stitched with the needle*

(right). *The awl is from the right ulna of a deer, a shape naturally convenient for a right-handed person to use.* PARKS CANADA, RA-2263B

maritime fur trade was underway and the Spanish had established an outpost at Yuquot. No great change in native household goods or equipment swept aside traditional forms in response to this contact with white men. Artifacts deep within the deposits still were represented in upper layers. New goods, such as ceramics, were simply added to the equipment that had served the local people for thousands of years.

Continuity characterized the deposits. Change came slowly. Villagers absorbed what originated beyond their own area without disrupting their lives and customs. Technology and detailed knowledge had fitted them to a broad range of ecological situations. Storage techniques, efficient transportation and trade evened out inequities from region to region and season to season. Contact beyond the group probably provided stimulus for change, but people directed their own affairs, followed their own pace.

## What Languages Can Tell

Another way of looking at how long people have been on the coast is through the historical development of language. What are similarities and differences in language structure and vocabulary? How did they develop? By tracing the evolution of these, linguists can reach back for scores of genera-

tions. Early relations among groups that today are separate will show up, suggesting probable directions and sequences of human movement, and giving a rough time-frame.

The chance to see through this particular window onto bygone times is fast fading along the Northwest Coast, however. For example, by the 1970s perhaps 1000 Southern Kwakiutl people were fluent in their language, Kwakwala. Several people aged seventy and older could readily understand two or three separate dialects, whereas those from their thirties to sixties had difficulty understanding any dialect other than that of their own childhood village. Few persons younger than age thirty knew the language at all. "The attitude of missionaries and other community workers who came to change Indian life put lots of pressure on us," Robert Joseph, a Southern Kwakiutl man in his early forties, now a district manager for the Department of Indian Affairs, told me in Campbell River:

Language got hurt quite a bit. Young people decided it wasn't important anymore to have a good grasp of Indian language, or to know what the elders were talking about. It didn't seem valuable to learn songs and dances and our history. I lived on Gilford Island, but then my grandfather died and at age seven I was sent to residential school in Alert Bay. That's where lots of kids lost their language, but I didn't. I went home to

175

Kingcome in summer and my grandmother and step-mother didn't speak English. So I kept on speaking Kwakwala.

Bernice Touchie, of Ditidaht heritage, recently headed the Alberni public schools native culture program. She told me:

There was hardly any instruction about our customs or beliefs when I was growing up, except for George

Clutesi teaching dancing to high-school kids at the residential school. Our ways were considered something of the past. Irrelevant. I pursued modern goals—get an education and so on. Then I realized that came at a price. I was severely lacking in my own culture. So now I'm doing what I can to put culture back into education. It used to be taught by the elders, but now education comes mostly through the schools.

Linguists, as archaeologists, use available evidence not merely to describe the past but to *understand* it. Much as incomplete preservation of most physical deposits often distorts the archaeological view of how people lived in the past, so the loss of languages threatens future study of linguistic relationships. Nearly thirty languages are native to British Columbia. Within them are innumerable

*Elders J. J. Wallas and Jim Henderson* (right) *join the language class held for teachers who work in the Campbell River native studies program. The men help with Kwakwala dialect differences, sentence structure and pronunciation. In the front row with the elders are Lisa Wells* (left) *and Jane Sterritt-Jones; in the back row, Donna Lamb and Diane Matilpi.* RUTH AND LOUIS KIRK

dialects, some grading into one another and softening dividing lines. The languages belong to at least five distinct language families, and perhaps as many as seven, close to double the number of European language families. This is true although there were only about a hundred thousand aboriginal speakers in British Columbia, compared with several hundred million in Europe. Within the province, more than half the individual languages and four of the five (or seven) language families, are found along the coast: a disproportionate number considering the land area.

Not surprisingly, the number of languages native to any region is generally related to the number of its habitats. Linguistic and ecological variety go together. Athapaskan speakers, who live from Alaska to the Mexican border, illustrate the point. Their ancestors migrated throughout the continent's vast interior expanse of climate extremes and relatively sparse lifeforms, a region capable of supporting no more than a scattered human population and requiring them to adapt to only a few markedly different ecosystems. Consequently, today's Athapaskan Indians, though widely separated and culturally diverse, speak languages with a common origin; a Carrier or Tahltan

*Linguist Peter Wilson writes Kwakwala during a lesson in pronunciation. The words* (top to bottom) *mean "1000," "noon," "to know" and "sick." Every language holds a view of how its people regard themselves and their landscape, who they accept as kin, what they believe is important, which categories they see as similar and where differences lie. Consequently, studying language reveals much about culture.* RUTH AND LOUIS KIRK

from northern British Columbia can understand some of the words used by an Apache or Navajo from Arizona.

Coast conditions contrast dramatically with the harshness of the British Columbia interior. The coast has ample moisture. It also teems with life, providing perhaps four times the potential human nutrition of the inland region. This richness enabled people to support themselves from comparatively small territories and, when population began pressing the limits of what an area could carry, small groups would bud off.

The particular resources that people drew on, their shared customs and seasonal rhythms, their ways of dressing and pronouncing words gradually set each group apart from others, even those nearby. Indeed, particular language characteristics most likely stimulated feelings of separate identity between adjoining people.

No one can pinpoint just when language differences began. Linguists have nothing comparable to the radioactive carbon dating available to archaeologists. Nonetheless, similarities between the languages of the Kwakiutl and Nuu-chah-nulth indicate that these people share origins despite present differences. All of their languages belong to the linguistic group known as the Wakashan Language Family. The separation must have begun on northern Vancouver Island, where the Brooks Peninsula is still the dividing line between the Southern Kwakiutl people and the Nuu-chah-nulth. Evidently, some Wakashan groups started migrating up the coast from the Brooks Peninsula region and others moved down the coast. Over time, their differing languages—and customs—divided their descendants into the present northern and southern groups.

Where Wakashan people originated nobody knows. No linguistic trace is present in the interior of British Columbia, nor is there evidence they travelled from the interior to the coast or spread out from the Fraser River delta as the Salish seem to have done. Most likely, the early Wakashan

*Life along the coast permits access to resources of ocean, shore, forest, rivers and lakes. Sea lions, elk, salmon—the variety has no end.* RUTH AND LOUIS KIRK

178

# Chinook Jargon

Nuxalk elder Margaret Siwallace told me:

When I was young, I spoke Bella Coola and I learned English too. Then I married a man from Bella Bella and his mother didn't speak Bella Coola or English, so I learned Jargon. I used to talk to her in Chinook Jargon, and to hear it quite a bit. Now you don't hear it anymore and not many people can speak Bella Coola anymore either. Just a very few of us.

The trade pidgin known as Chinook Jargon seems to have developed before Europeans arrived on the Northwest Coast, because linguists find the structure fundamentally Indian, despite the inclusion of French and English words. The name comes from an Indian group living along the lower Columbia River, people strategically located for east-west trade between the interior and the coast, and also for coastal trade north and south. When European fur companies reached the Northwest Coast, Chinook territory was where they established their headquarters.

During the ensuing fur trade period, Chinook Jargon became the lingua franca of the area from northern California to Alaska. With a vocabulary representing various unrelated Wakashan, Salishan, Athapaskan, Penutian and Indo-European languages, the Jargon eased communication among Indian groups, as well as among Indians and American, English and French traders and travellers. Gestures, facial expressions and tone of voice filled gaps in meaning.

Chinook Jargon used only sounds that could be pronounced by all its speakers. Thus, for example, the French *n* lost its nasal quality, the English *j* became *teh,* the Indian *ł* lost its *thl* sound and became *l,* and the many gutturals and explosive combinations of consonants common in Indian languages were dropped. Pronunciation varied, depending on the language background of the individual speaker. Word order stayed fundamentally Indian.

The result never became a true language. It stayed a pidgin, doomed to die as the circumstances it served changed. As Indian people were pressured to learn English, Chinook Jargon lost its niche and vanished.

*Ahousaht elder Peter Webster works with linguist Barbara Efrat of the British Columbia Provincial Museum.* PROVINCIAL ARCHIVES OF BRITISH COLUMBIA, SOUND AND MOVING IMAGES DIVISION

moved down the coast from the north. Their route may now lie underwater or hidden in the forest. Probably, their languages began separating a little at a time among a few hundred people as one group started travelling south for seasonal resources while another chose opportunities to the north. Each group increasingly spoke and interacted within itself. Dialects grew into separate languages.

This happened slowly. Customs change more readily than languages, as the history of the Nuxalk people illustrates particularly well. They speak a Salishan language, although they and the Southern Kwakiutl—a Wakashan group—share similar customs. Linguists find that the Nuxalk split off as their own group earlier than any other

Salishan speakers. Bella Coola, the language of the Nuxalk, has changed the most of any within the Salish language family; it has evolved separately for the longest time. Evidently, the ancestors of the present Nuxalk people expanded northward from the Fraser River delta, moving along the ecologically bountiful inner coast. They eventually reached the mouth of Burke and Dean channels and moved up the inlets. There, they were cut off from contact with other Salishan groups by a northeastward expansion of the Kwakiutl. Later, they were blocked from moving across the Coast Mountains by an expansion of interior people, probably the Chilcotin. The Nuxalk became an enclave of their own.

Differing (or similar) rules of grammar within

181

*By perhaps 3500 years ago, people were distributed along the coast much as they were when the first Europeans arrived. Environments varied from open ocean to sandy beach, rocky headlands, steep-sided fiords and quiet river-mouth estuaries. Such a diverse landscape meant widely varying resources, and resource differences, in turn, reinforced cultural and linguistic differences.* RUTH AND LOUIS KIRK; BRITISH COLUMBIA PROVINCIAL MUSEUM, ARCHAEOLOGY DIVISION

separate languages and certain aspects of vocabulary, such as place names and kinship terms, act as flags to help linguists trace relationships between groups of people. For example, in languages spoken by the Nuu-chah-nulth, nobody would refer simply to a point of land but would break the concept of topography into fine-tuned considerations: the point as it appears from up here above the beach, down there right at beach level, out in the intertidal zone or far at sea. Where you are in relation to the point matters; environmental facts, which are fundamental to outer-coast life, are built into the language itself. Kwakwala makes closely

similar distinctions and belongs to the same language family. The Bella Coola language also is sensitive to environment but follows a different pattern of topographic distinctions. It belongs to a different family.

The three southern Wakashan languages are Nootka, Nitinat and Makah. There are shared elements, but the similarities are not enough for one set of speakers to understand the other.

The northern Wakashan languages are Kwakwala, Heiltsuk and Haisla. Of these, Kwakwala is spoken by the Southern Kwakiutl. It is completely separate from the other northern Wakashan lan-

183

guages, although related. Heiltsuk and Haisla speakers share more customs with their Tsimshian neighbours than with their Southern Kwakiutl language relatives. Linguistic boundaries often do not coincide with cultural boundaries.

Ancestral relationships leave linguistic traces for no more than 6000 to 7000 years and usually are decidedly tenuous at that age. Yet, on the coast, linguists sense the presence of two distinct early human populations. This is an ancient north-south division much like that described by archaeologists for Namu. The linguists cannot give dates, but they know that Wakashan and Salishan speakers have been in close contact for many thousands of years, borrowing not just certain words from each other but entire styles of grammar. This sort of deep relation usually takes a long time to develop. Linguistic evidence thus parallels archaeological evidence at the earliest discernible levels of time.

By about 3500 years ago both lines of investigation come into clearer focus. Time has had less opportunity to take its inevitable toll; also the widespread build-up of huge shell middens greatly improves preservation, for shell is alkaline enough to neutralize soil acids and slow some kinds of deterioration. About the same time that middens became huge, Wakashan speakers separated into northern and southern branches, and the ancestors of today's Coast Salish began moving out from the Fraser River delta.

Differences intensified as various coastal populations reached the limits of their expansion. Groups who were separated from ancestral associations gradually developed their own customs and ways of speaking, even their own origin myths. Archaeological evidence suggests that people 3000 to 4000 years ago had large communal houses like those today's elders remember. Wealth and artwork are apparent. Conflict seems probable. On the north coast archaeological deposits hold skeletons with smashed skulls and broken forearms seemingly raised to fend off blows; people on the south and central coast probably also experienced outbreaks of violence, for archaeologists find heavy whalebone clubs like those used in historic times as battle clubs.

Over thousands of years the human pattern of the coast developed. People settled onto the landscape, picking protected sites where they found a variety of resources. Small, scattered groups drew from the entire marine environment. Then, gradually, populations grew. Territories became restricted and groups developed differences. Uneven access to materials and products led to a system of distribution; acquiring rare items and controlling abundance produced wealth and differences in status. People of high rank could afford trade, which reinforced their prestige—the *best* fish, the *finest* oil, the *rarest* shells and furs.

Then a new era dawned. Foreigners arrived.

# To Carry on the Legacy

Chief LaChester, Neah Bay. *Ruth Kirk*

*Territories and traditions claimed today can be traced
back for generations. This legacy reaching into the
past lives in the memories of elders.*

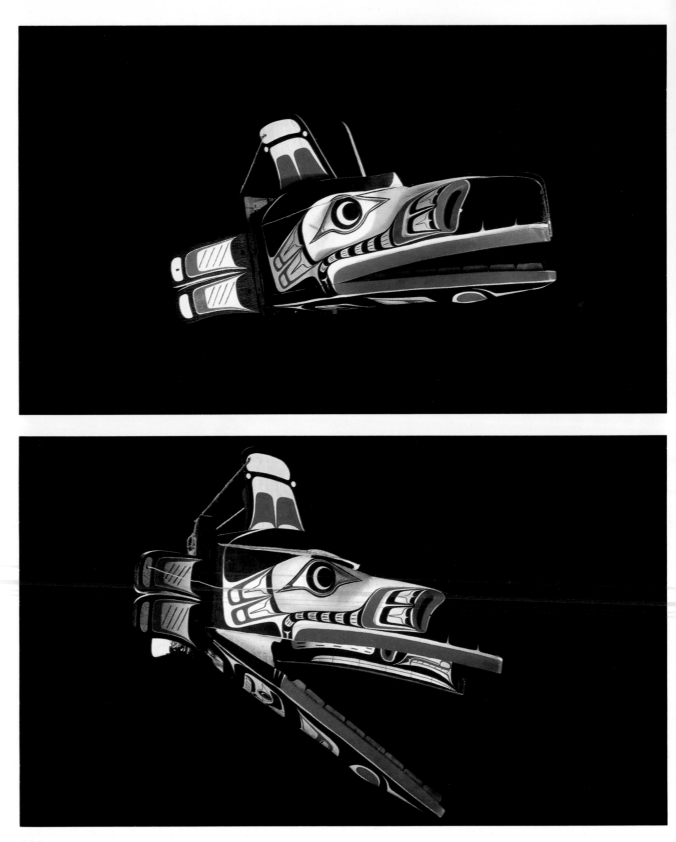

*Another type of unwritten record, of origin and rank, rests in the ownership of regalia. The right to dance with this mask links the family that owns it to the beginnings of mankind.*

Southern Kwakiutl transformation mask carved by Tony Hunt (shown open and closed): Sea Raven and moon. *British Columbia Provincial Museum, Ethnology Division, CPN 13848*

Bone game. *Ruth and Louis Kirk*

Beavertooth dice. *Ruth and Louis Kirk*

*Ceremonies are not the only activities practised today.*
Lahal, *or "bone game"—which is still widely*
*popular—had various counterparts in the past.*
*Beavertooth dice similar to these have been found in*
*archaeological excavations.*

Ahousat. *Ruth and Louis Kirk*

*Only a small number of traditional village and camp
sites survive today, as shown both by the memories of
elders and the work of archaeologists. The village of
Ozette —which was buried, then preserved by
mud —yielded many treasures from the past.*

Ozette house planks. *Ruth and Louis Kirk*

Opening a basket that is 400 to 500 years old at Ozette. *Ruth and Louis Kirk*

Tidal fish trap. *British Columbia Provincial Museum, Archaaeology Division*

*The archaeological record reveals at least 10 000 years of human tenure along the coast. Remnants include hundreds of fish-trap sites, some with rock walls still standing, which penned fish on outgoing tides.*

*Fishing gear ranged from the simple to complex; there was an astonishing array of hooks, lures, lines, weights and floats, each specifically suited to its task.*

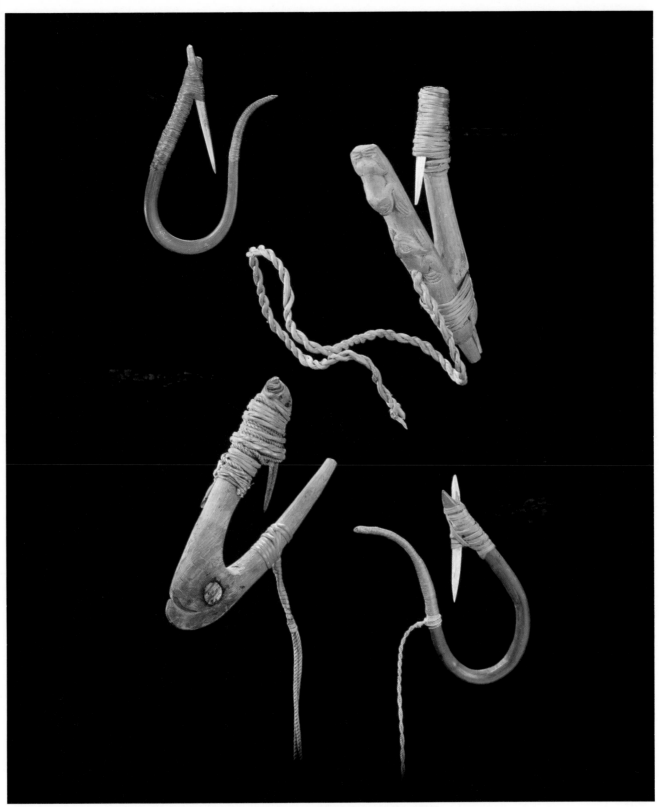

Fish hooks. *British Columbia Provincial Museum, Ethnology Division, CPN 711, 714, 2438, 16415*

Hubert Markishtum, a Makah, landing a salmon. *Ruth and Louis Kirk*

*Although modern methods are often used, the sea and the forest still sustain native people both physically and culturally.*

Fisherman mending his net. *Ruth and Louis Kirk*

Yuquot street scene. *Ruth and Louis Kirk*

*In today's villages, carved poles that proclaim family
rank and lineage still stand alongside modern homes.*

Abandoned cannery at Bella Coola. *Ruth and Louis Kirk*

Richard Hunt, a Southern Kwakiutl, cutting silver for a brooch. *British Columbia Provincial Museum, Ethnology Division, PN 16748*

*Artists continue to depict ancient themes in new media
such as gold and silver jewellery and silkscreen prints.*

Tim Paul, a Hesquiaht, preparing a painting for silkscreening. *British Columbia Provincial Museum, Ethnology Division, PN 16747*

*Yellow Cedar Man,* a print by Art Thompson, a Ditidaht. *British Columbia Provincial Museum, Ethnology Division, CPN 14903-a*

Wearing a button blanket. *Ruth and Louis Kirk*

*For millennia, each generation has played its part in passing on the legacy. The traditions of the past continue on into the present and will live on in the future.*

# CHAPTER SEVEN
## *The Dawn of a New Era*

In 1774, off the mouth of Hesquiat Harbour, which is about midway along the outer coast of Vancouver Island, Indians saw the ship of Juan José Pérez y Hernandez, the first European vessel to enter the waters of what is now British Columbia. Four years later, villagers at Yuquot watched the vessels of the great English mariner Capt. James Cook work their way into Nootka Sound. Oral accounts passed from generation to generation tell of the Nuu-chah-nulth reaction to the pale newcomers, at first believed supernatural. Hesquiaht people thought Pérez's ship was a white bird, its sails the huge outstretched wings. Yuquot men who paddled out to Cook's ships thought the men aboard were Salmon People in the guise of humans.

Leslie John, a Mowachaht elder, told a traditional account of Cook's arrival on a tape that was transcribed and published in *Sound Heritage:*

So they sent four brave men to go and see and investigate what it is, and nothing happened. They were all friendly. The only thing that made it hard for them is that they didn't understand each other. When the white men speak their language, they didn't understand. And when the Indian speak *their* language, *they* didn't understand.

Nuu-chah-nulth elder Winnifred David, of Clayoquot and Alberni, also described Captain Cook's arrival, explaining the origin of names:

So, the Chief told them to go out there again and see, you know. . . . They started making signs and they were talking and they were saying, "*Nu-tka-icim.*" "Nu-tka-icim," they were saying. That means, "You go around the harbour [to find better anchorage]." So Captain Cook said, "Oh. They're telling us the name of this place is Nootka. That's how Nootka got its name. . . . But the Indian name is altogether different. . . .

We call white people "*Muh-muɫ-ni*" because . . . they came in boats that looked high and strange to us, and muh-muɫ-ni means "houses on the water." Those people seemed to be in houses floating on the water.

*John Webber, official artist with Captain Cook, visually documented native reaction to the British arrival at Nootka Sound. Here, canoes circle the* Resolution *while chiefs give ceremonial orations before coming alongside to trade.* BRITISH LIBRARY, LONDON, ADD. 15514.10

In 1792 Chief Maquinna hosted British and Spanish commanders meeting at Nootka Sound to settle their nations' conflicting claims to the Northwest. The chief treated them to a feast in his house at Tahsis, followed by an elaborate performance that included a dance by Maquinna himself. A Spaniard present at the time made this sketch, which was later finished by Mexico City artists.
BRITISH COLUMBIA PROVINCIAL MUSEUM, ETHNOLOGY DIVISION, PN 13501

## The Early Years of Contact

Meetings with Muh-muɬ-ni became pivotal within the long flow of native tenure on the coast, but the first meetings gave no hint of their ultimate outcome. After all, chiefs had been dealing with outsiders for thousands of years. Even so, these new people were stranger and wealthier than any the villagers' fathers or grandfathers or great-great-great-grandfathers had ever told about.

Spain's presence on the Northwest Coast heightened Britain's interest in sending Cook on his third voyage of exploration. He entered the quiet waters off Yuquot and stayed a month. Indians supplied his ships *Resolution* and *Discovery* with foods ranging from herring, halibut, mussels, cockles and whale oil to bracken-fern roots, wild onions and various berries. They traded cedar-bark clothing and hats, masks, rattles, weapons, fishing gear and furs of many kinds, including sea otter. In exchange for these items they accepted mostly metal—anything from knives, chisels and saws to barrel hoops, brass buttons, copper coins and kettles, tin canisters, pewter plates and basins, bars of iron and lead, candlesticks and nails. They valued the metal itself rather than the object it had been made into. Natives also bartered for mirrors, but refused most offers of beads and, at first, cloth.

Among the native people, trade was nothing new. Access to trade wealth that came by ship simply called for an adroit use of tactics already well honed. Yuquot chiefs would not let villagers from

203

*The Spanish schooners* Sutil *and* Mexicana *visited the Southern Kwakiutl village of Maguaa in 1792. José Cardero, on his second voyage to the coast, made the drawing. The exact location of the village is uncertain.* OREGON HISTORICAL SOCIETY, 53428 AND MUSEO DE AMERICA, MADRID

neighbouring territories contact Cook unless their own men were present to act as brokers in case an exchange came about. The chance prize of Muh-muɬ-ni wealth belonged exclusively to local chiefs, as would the rights to a beached whale or a run of spawning fish.

For the first few years after the voyages of Pérez and Cook, trading ships rarely entered waters belonging to the Nuu-chah-nulth, Southern Kwakiutl or Nuxalk. After Cook's log was published in 1784, however, word about the expedition's lucrative sale of sea otter furs in China quickly spread. Between 1785 and 1825 at least 450 ships arrived to trade, and a dozen more came in connection with a political squabble between Spain and England, which centred at Yuquot where the Spanish had built a fort in 1789. While the dispute raged, local chiefs were courted by European emissaries as well as by traders. They could not know that the international politics they so unexpectedly were hosting would ultimately result in the replacement of their own social system with that of British colonial rule.

They could recognize, however, the patchwork of slights and honours received from all newcomers, of whatever flag. Favoured treatment unquestionably helped Maquinna to emerge as the leading chief of Nootka Sound and territory farther north and his brother-in-law, Wickanninish, to become the most powerful chief of Clayoquot Sound. Chiefs in a position to barter with the pale newcomers gained a decided advantage in their rivalry with other chiefs. The wealth created by the new fur trade intensified traits long characteristic of Indian society on the Northwest Coast.

In an early compilation of diaries written by Spanish officials on the coast, José Espinosa y Tello described native rivalry. A certain Nuu-chah-nulth chief, who owned high prerogatives gained through marriage with the daughter of a Southern Kwakiutl chief, told Spaniards at Yuquot that he viewed exchanging goods with Muh-muł-ni as a mutual bestowal of gifts. His names and crests were superior to Maquinna's, he claimed; therefore he should be receiving more goods than his rival. "This vaunting each above the other is the main topic of conversation among the taises [chiefs]," Espinosa y Tello concluded, and he was right. The drive for prestige motivated the whole native social system.

Few trade goods stayed for long at Yuquot. Native people quickly potlatched some for prestige and traded others for furs to carry back to the ships and exchange for still more goods. As early as 1792, Capt. George Vancouver found numerous Spanish muskets at a Southern Kwakiutl village near the Nimpkish River mouth. They had been traded overland from Yuquot. Also present, via Yuquot, was a pewter vessel marked with the name of a French ship, *La Flavie*. Nimpkish of course was not the only village trading for such white goods. For example, when Alexander Mackenzie arrived at Bella Coola in 1793, he noted:

[The chief] presented me with a roasted salmon; he then opened one of his chests, and took out of it a garment of blue cloth, decorated with brass buttons; and another of a flowered cotton, which I supposed were Spanish; it had been trimmed with leather fringe, after the fashion of their cloaks. . . . They also abounded in iron. I saw some of their twisted collars of that metal which weighed upwards of twelve pounds.

As trade increased along the Northwest Coast, vessels usually arrived from Hawaii in spring, anchored in the protected waters of Nootka and Clayoquot sounds, and spent the summer gathering furs. These ships were large—205 t (200 tons) and over—and their captains hesitated to venture through untested passages or lay-to off villages at exposed sites. Chiefs at established trade anchorages on the outer coast did all they could to reinforce these fears. They claimed people in other villages were vicious and described sea monsters that devoured voyagers. They also said there were no furs beyond their particular territory anyway!

Gradually, the two-way monopoly between a few chiefs and the early white traders broke down. By the end of the eighteenth century, American sea captains had joined—and all but taken over—the trade previously dominated by the British. Systematic coastal surveying lifted much of the earlier aura of the unknown, and increasing competition resulted in the use of small vessels able to manoeuvre intricate waterways and gather furs directly. The effect of this was to diminish the status of certain chiefs because they no longer could control the trade networks supplying pelts.

In the eighteenth century, Indians and Muh-muł-ni approached their business exchanges in different ways. Europeans and Americans tried for brisk trade with no delays, little ceremony and standardized equivalences—one sea otter pelt for a set number of chisels or sheets of copper, or whatever. Natives, on the other hand, would not treat an exchange of wealth with such rude abruptness. First, there should be oratory and a mutual presentation of gifts; then each fur should be individually assessed and bargained for. Not all ship captains realized it, but the speeches and crest displays preceding trade had a purpose. Lacking a written language, people used public oratory, dances, songs, carvings and paintings as a specific means of keeping the record straight. Chiefs intending to barter with ship captains were not indulging in routine pleasantries but were making clear statements of who they were and where they came from. Propriety demanded such declarations—which white traders failed to make in response because they were Muh-muł-ni, floating people without the status of certain origin.

Sea otters furnished the first key to trade. They ranged from northern Japan around the Pacific

# Memories of Sea Otter Hunting

Years ago, in the Nanaimo tuberculosis sanitorium, Mowachaht Nuu-chah-nulth elder August Murphy thought back to the sea otter hunting of his youth and wrote out a description. By his time, the great herds were gone, the thriving trade of 1785 and 1825 was long over. Nonetheless, hunters took what skins they could.

Chief Murphy said it was "young men's business." Through the winter, from the second quarter of the moon to full moon, they prayed, "bathing and scourging their bodies with some kind of tree branches." For hunting, they used "the best-made canoes, about 17 or 18 feet in length," charring the bottoms to get off slivers so that the hulls would be as silent as possible in the water. Paddles were "best-made" too. He wrote:

The best time for chase sea otter had to be very calm and smooth sea and no wind at all. The purpose of choosen the calmest weather was for tracing the little bubbles coming up when sea otter is living underwater and they claim that the otter is more lively with brezze [sic] and little ripples on the surface of the sea [and therefore harder to shoot].

There were some very good weather-men to watch the signs for good and bad weather. These men were praying and watching closely for the best calm weather for going out. When they were sure of the calm weather, before dawn they went to all the houses of hunters knocking on sides of their houses to wake them up, and bring the good news of fine weather for their hunt.

About the year of 1896 or 1897, at that time there were 24 small canoes, special made for sea otter hunt. Each canoe had 2 or 3 men. When all were up [awake] and every men went down on the beach and helped each other to lift haul down their canoes to the water's edge [not drag them, which would roughen the bottoms].

The boss We-yak gave orders "We shall go to Wa-ka-ta [Bajo Reef] and work slowly toward west. You all know the rules when you sight a sea otter. Both men shall lift his paddle above his head and wave. All canoes shall in haste pull towards the canoe gaven [sic] signal. When we come to Wa-ka-ta all canoes shall get on line up from shore to off sea, spread approsemately [sic] 200 yards apart from each other. Travel slow, Watch for otter and signal."

My aunt's husband took me along. One of the canoes near the Bajo point reefs gave us the waving of their paddle signal. All canoes turned and paddled towards the gaven signal.

No time lost, the signal canoe was in the middle of a big circle of 23 canoes and the leader We-yak was appointed for watching for the otter's bubble, and when pointing his paddle towards the course of the bubbles, leads, and canoe [in] that direction was then ready with their bows and arrows.

When poor sea otter came up surface to take in his breath, rain of arrows was pouring down at the otter. All the shooters were watching their arrows to see if he hit the otter. When one of the hunters hit it, the steerman stands up and shouts on top his voice, he mentions his hunter's name. His arrows has hit the otter.

In that season, 12 otters was caught. Large size was worth $400.00 medium size, $300.00 Small $200.00 very small $150.00. . . . A person catch one otter he made money.

Rim to the California coast. Both wealthy Chinese lords and Northwest Coast chiefs had prized sea otter fur since time immemorial. It stays prime all year, because the animals live in the fairly uniform conditions of the ocean and do not need separate summer and winter coats. Their pelts are about 2 cm (1 inch) thick with an unusually fine, soft, dense undercoat overlain by long dark guard-hairs—a "survival suit" for the icy waters sea otters call home.

Natives held the upper hand, for white traders were passionate in their urge to get sea otter pelts, the most valuable skin in the history of commercial fur. Fortunes awaited traders carrying this fur to China; therefore, captains wanted to please local chiefs and ensure a continued supply. The chiefs also wanted to please, so that ships would keep coming, but at the same time they were shrewdly capable of protecting their interests. Some would show a great supply of furs, then refuse to barter until their terms seemed sure of acceptance. Or they might offer high-quality furs, then actually supply inferior ones. "A glossy blackness was the criterion of the superior quality of the Furs," wrote Alexander Walker in 1786 while aboard an East India Company ship commanded by James Strange, "and [Chief] Kurrighum . . . contrived to give them a fine colour or to improve it by means of charcoal." Another trick was to insist on trading at dusk, when fur quality was hard to see.

White traders quickly learned to be wary. They also learned to offer items currently in vogue, for native ideas of desirable goods changed by the year and satisfying demand took ingenuity. Some captains sent their blacksmiths, carpenters and sailmakers to set up shop on shore and custom manufacture goods. Josiah Roberts, captain of the *Jefferson*, rented his jolly boat to Chief Wickanninish for three weeks in exchange for furs; another time, a chief liked the carpet of the captain's cabin, so Roberts traded it.

Sometimes nothing seemed acceptable. James Strange wrote of his frustration in offering chiefs at Nootka Sound "a variety of goods such as knives, chisels, axes, swords, etc.," but drawing steady refusal. Then, noticing that the rhythmic beat of Na-

This sketch of rival Nootka Sound chiefs Callicum (left) and Maquinna incorporates a handshake—a European greeting custom that quite surely was added by the artist. The men wear sea-otter robes, owned only by chiefs; large abalone shells, an eighteenth-century trade item, lie at their feet. Chief Callicum was shot by the Spanish in 1789; Chief Maquinna dominated the fur trade for years and lived to an old age. PROVINCIAL ARCHIVES OF BRITISH COLUMBIA

tive songs kept disrupting negotiations, he hit on an idea:

I now recollected that amoungst our various articles which composed our investment there was a considerable number of cymbals. . . . I accordingly produced a pair.

The expression of rapture and delight which the first clash of them excited in the breasts of all present, is not to be described. Displaying the effects of my music, I composed for the occasion a ring-ting tune [which was] encored again and again. It was joined in by a great majority of all present.

The consequence of this exhibition was that I stripped my Gentlemen to the Buff in an hour's time . . . three or four skins for every pair of cymbals.

Furs of all kinds flowed out of villages and onto ships in such numbers that Indians genuinely needed blankets, yardage and clothing for winter use, as well as to astonish rivals who lacked such splendour. Blankets also gained immediate popularity as potlatch goods, perhaps as a substitute for the sea otter and bearskin robes previously favoured for the purpose but now traded onto ships.

Copper and iron pots were another item that fit easily into native life. They could be set directly on a fire, eliminating the cumbersome process of heating rocks in order to boil water and cook food in wooden boxes. Even so, they were not primarily valued for their mundane usefulness. Rather, they were wealth goods to be potlatched, used as raw material, or—sometimes—as ornaments. Alexander Walker noted that the expedition he accompanied traded six small copper pots for thirty sea otter pelts and carefully showed the Indians how to use them, "but they immediately cut them up into Bracelets and Earrings, no doubt thinking that such materials were too costly for cookery."

Two years later the English trader-adventurer John Meares described the awesome appearance of

*Stacks of Hudson's Bay Company blankets—a standardized medium of exchange during the nineteenth century—line the walls of a Fort Rupert house. They are to be distributed at a potlatch.*
AMERICAN MUSEUM OF NATURAL HISTORY, 411813

*Chiefs prized uniforms from the time of earliest contact with Whites. Such clothing obviously was a symbol of authority among the newcomers, and therefore was appropriate to wear while dealing with them.* VANCOUVER PUBLIC LIBRARY, 14087

Maquinna's younger brother Comekela on his return to Nootka Sound from China:

His scarlet coat was decorated with quantities of brass buttons and copper additions of one kind or another. . . . From his ears copper ornaments were suspended, and . . . from his hair . . . so many handles of copper saucepans, that his head was kept back by the weight of them. . . . In such a state he set out for the shore.

The ready availability of metal did not, however, greatly affect native technology in the first decades of the new trade. Cook reported that Yuquot men not only already knew its use but "had several tools and instruments that were made of it." The deposits excavated at Ozette also prove native people already had at least limited access to metal. In buried houses there, archaeologists found about forty woodworking tools with iron or steel blades

either still bound into handles or indicated by rust stains and tiny metal fragments. Wrecked Asian fishing vessels drifted across the Pacific are the probable source of such metal, although some could also have been traded around the Pacific Rim from Asia.

For the first two or three decades of contact with Muh-muɫ-ni, native people were reluctant to use metal instead of traditional materials when making certain implements such as fish hooks, harpoon heads or spears. This is not surprising. No man would set out to hunt or fish without first attuning both himself and his gear into harmony with the supernatural. He knew that all living things have souls and deserve respectful treatment according to their own particular preferences. Pleasing the spirits was a necessary exchange for the human right to kill an animal or take a strip of cedar bark, or any other resource. Animal People had specific expectations of how they should be handled by humans, and these certainly did not include assault by unfamiliar materials. Iron was exotic. It played a role, but offending long-established harmony with fellow creatures was not to be risked.

Read the manifests of ships trading along the coast in the closing two decades of the eighteenth century and you find an astonishing range of Muh-muɫ-ni goods entering Indian life. An arbitrary sample, compiled from the cargo lists of various ships, includes:

18 doz. Carpenters' planes with two Irons to each
18 doz. saws
bar Iron; unwrought Iron
20 doz. yds. Ribbands to string some medals
Muskets no matter how bad if they will but go off
Trunks with brass nails in them
Large blankets
Long coats to reach the ground with two rows of buttons all the way down the front
2 pudding pans
2 large bear traps
60 gross of thimbles
100 doz. small looking glasses.

Such goods poured into outer-coast villages without saturating demand, because they quickly

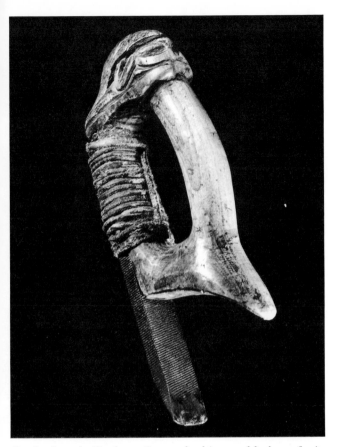

*People along the Northwest Coast valued iron and had uses for it before the arrival of white mariners. Consequently, as the new trade era opened, they eagerly sought the metal as a replacement for certain uses of native materials. Blades for tools, such as this D-adze, are an example.* BRITISH COLUMBIA PROVINCIAL MUSEUM, ETHNOLOGY DIVISION, CPN 9613

became part of the ever-expanding potlatch flow. New goods served old purposes.

## Increasing Tensions

During the first forty years of contact between Indians and Muh-muɬ-ni, more than a quarter million sea otter pelts went from the Northwest Coast to Canton. In exchange, chiefs received, retraded and potlatched a stream of white goods. It was chiefs who controlled the trade, not the Muh-muɬ-ni. The white outsiders could not yet intentionally force changes in the lives of independent, local native groups, though changes had actually begun with the arrival of the first ship.

Political strategy based on chance contact with the first Muh-muɬ-ni had allowed Chief Maquinna to expand his sphere of influence; to cement the new relationships he arranged to marry the daughters and sisters of former rivals, such as Chief Wickanninish. Thus allied, Maquinna could continue to dominate the fur market, controlling a wide network of supply, while local resources diminished because of overhunting. Maintaining position in this way came at a high cost, however, for it required reallocation of manpower. Increasing trade required more people to deal with the Muh-muɬ-ni and more armed men to protect trading harbours from rival Indian groups and to respond to sporadic attacks by Whites. As a result Maquinna was forced to keep three to four hundred men ready to fight at any time. Wickanninish equipped and maintained an even greater force. Group time and energy shifted drastically away from subsistence activities to safeguarding trade possibilities.

Indians feared white men, and fear went the other way, too, leading each side to an occasional "show of force." Ships' crews were overwhelmingly outnumbered and far from home, supplies and reinforcements. Whites had a more advanced technology, but native people were far superior in local knowledge and adaptation to the coast. European and American sea captains knew this and were wary. Dreading "blood-thirsty savages" and "atrocities" like those reported elsewhere, they worried when several large canoes approached at once; at times, they reacted quickly with a paranoid firing of cannon and muskets. They also felt a righteous need to punish Indians who boarded their ships and made off with cutlery or other small items, or removed metal fittings and nails from unattended skiffs drawn up on the beach. Anger at such pilfering sometimes led to seizing hostages—even chiefs—and holding them until the items were returned and the "thieves" had been turned over to the captain. Entire villages might be cannonaded "to teach a lesson."

By Indian custom, too, thievery was unacceptable. The Muh-muɬ-ni and their possessions, however, were outside the native family system and codes of shame and retaliation. Also, legitimate

salvage was altogether different from stealing: chiefs owned rights to whatever drifted in from the sea, and vessels anchored off their beaches came into this category. Punishing "misbehaviour," as Whites occasionally did by heaping indignity onto a chief, utterly ignored rank and was insulting. It demanded revenge—and the newcomers, after all, were basically one more set of nonrelatives to treat with suspicion and take advantage of, or kill, as occasion warranted.

Uncertainties and skirmishes began almost as soon as the first ships paused offshore from coastal villages. For instance, in 1792, the commander of the Spanish fort at Yuquot shot and killed Chief Callicum over a trifling disagreement. In the same year, Chief Wickanninish used his store of guns in a futile effort to capture the *Columbia*, commanded by Robert Gray. Gray, a notorious hothead, was infuriated. In revenge, he sent men to burn the Clayoquot village of Opitsat. John Boit, one of the *Columbia*'s officers, noted that he felt "grieved to think Capt. Gray shou'd let his passions go so far," but carried out orders:

This village was half a mile in Diameter, and contained upwards of 200 Houses, generally well built for Indians. Ev'ry door that you enter'd was in resemblance to an human and Beasts head, the passage being through the mouth, besides which there was much more rude carved work about the dwellings some of which was by no means inelegant. This fine village, the work of ages, was in a short time totally destroy'd.

Tensions flared from place to place without any overall easing. When Spain abandoned the fort at Yuquot, Maquinna's position suffered somewhat, and a still greater blow came as trading ships

212

THE DAWN OF A NEW ERA

bypassed Nootka Sound after Maquinna could no longer offer sea otter pelts. The chief found himself cut off from previous sources of potlatch wealth and lost prestige.

Consequently, when the American ship *Boston* entered Nootka Sound in 1803, Maquinna chose to feel insulted over the loan of a musket and used the incident as an excuse to retaliate for accumulated ill fortune. He attacked the ship and killed all but two of its crew, whom he enslaved. His men then sailed the *Boston* to their village beach, for by that time a few Nuu-chah-nulth had voluntarily and involuntarily travelled aboard Muh-mul-ni ships and literally "learned the ropes."

The assault on the *Boston* was neither the first nor the last instance of battle between Natives and Whites. Often the Royal Navy was involved, as in the well-known case of delayed "punishment" for the sinking of the ship *Tonquin* in 1811. The attack actually happened at Clayoquot Sound but was blamed on Southern Kwakiutl villagers around the northern tip of Vancouver Island at Nawitti.

Forty years later, when Nawitti men were provoked into killing three Hudson's Bay Company sailors, the Whites recalled this supposed offence and dealt harshly with the village after the chief refused to turn over any "culprits." Men from the HMS *Daedalus* went ashore and destroyed several houses "to teach a lesson." Pursuing the matter further, the Royal Navy next sent HMS *Daphnae*. Sixty sailors and officers stormed the stockade of a new, defensive village built by embittered Nawitti on a small island. They burned houses and also smashed canoes, a loss even more devastating than that of houses since, without transportation, the Indians were cut off from access to resources.

"All [Nawitti] property and provisions were captured and destroyed," wrote James Douglas, chief factor of the Hudson's Bay Company in a letter dated 6 August 1851. "The tribe is now completely dispersed and are reported to be somewhere on the West side of [Vancouver] Island." Thus people who had lived for millenia along the coast learned the new rules from men present less than a century.

Hostilities among Indian groups themselves intensified as fresh tensions tore the traditional social fabric—and guns added a potent force to the confusion of the period. Men at the Southern Kwakiutl village of He'gams reported that as early as Vancouver's time they had lost a chief to a single shot from a musket, which Heiltsuk Indians had rented out with only the one charge. The attackers had exchanged four slaves for the "magic stick."

Similarly, Chief Mungo Martin told anthropologist Wilson Duff that his great-great-grandfather had heard the Heiltsuk owned "an abundance of muskets" and, consequently, married a woman there to gain access to guns and ammunition. Then he persuaded his new in-laws to join the chiefs of seven Southern Kwakiutl groups in attacking Kingcome. The resulting armada was "so big that the canoes reached from one side of the river to the other."

In the middle of the nineteenth century guns made warfare increasingly deadly; whole groups were decimated. By the 1830s the Southern Kwakiutl persistently raided as far south as Puget Sound, and as owners of the narrow waterways between Vancouver Island and the mainland, they also freely attacked and plundered parties of northern Indians en route to and from Fort Victoria. Reprisals in the 1840s included what anthropologist Wilson Duff described as a "contest of mutual annihilation" between the Southern Kwakiutl and the Salish of the Strait of Georgia. Each side made ever-widening alliances, "then embarked in greater and greater flotillas bent on the enemy's extermination."

In 1849 and 1850 Salish villagers from Comox to Victoria and from the Fraser River to the southern end of Puget Sound combined forces to attack the Euclataw Kwakiutl. Losses resulted in population shifts on each side, and the territorial line separating Southern Kwakiutl territory from that of the Coast Salish seems to have been redrawn at this time. The Euclataw moved southward into the Campbell River–Cape Mudge area, in what some anthropologists call the final expansion into Salish territory that had begun when ancient Wakashan-speakers cut off the Nuxalk at Bella Coola. By the time of the Euclataw wars, epidemics, alcohol, settlers and government gunboats were causing truly drastic changes.

# CHAPTER EIGHT
## *A Changing World*

The arrival of the Hudson's Bay Company on the Northwest Coast in the 1820s began a new chapter of Indian and Muh-muł-ni relations. The maritime fur trade became mostly memory, and emphasis shifted to a land base. Indians now brought furs to established trading posts rather than waiting for vessels to call at their villages. They still controlled both the fur supply and their own culture, but winds of change were stirring.

### A New Kind of Contact

In 1825 the Hudson's Bay Company opened a western headquarters at Fort Vancouver on the Columbia River near present-day Portland, Oregon. From there the Company began pushing onto the British Columbia coast and tapping the interior. Hudson's Bay Company posts were joined to the outside world first by sailing ships, then by the puffing, clanking *Beaver* and other steamers that plied the coast. The men of these new posts did not leave when the summer trading season

*A petroglyph at Clo-oose depicts the Hudson's Bay Company sidewheeler* Beaver, *a new steam-powered puffing marvel.*
BRITISH COLUMBIA PROVINCIAL MUSEUM, ARCHAEOLOGY DIVISION

ended, as seaborne traders had done. On the contrary, men working with the Company even married Indian women, doing so with much the same awareness of alliances to be gained as the native people themselves.

The Natives' manipulation of the newcomers was masterly. The chiefs still controlled the routing of fur, and therefore its potential supply in the storerooms and on the ships of the Company. Hudson's Bay factors had to offer higher prices for furs not only whenever American ship captains called along the coast but also whenever competing groups of Indians appeared at the forts.

Chiefs of the four Southern Kwakiutl groups that had moved to Fort Rupert quickly took control of incoming furs there, much as chiefs at Yuquot and Clayoquot had done along the outer coast during the previous maritime trade. So strong was their position that, through alliances with Musqueam Salish people, Kwakiutl chiefs could obtain

pelts intended for Fort Langley on the lower Fraser River and divert them all the way north to Fort Rupert or Fort Simpson, depending on where prices were highest.

For a time, Heiltsuk chiefs near Fort McLoughlin also enjoyed a key position, although Company ships occasionally bypassed them and called at villages in the Bella Coola region. This direct seaborne trade was welcomed by the Nuxalk, because it relieved them of the need to act through neighbouring middlemen, who often were enemies. Bella Coola itself was strategically located. Chilcotin and Carrier Indians from the interior often descended into the valley to barter moose and caribou hides for salmon; and from their own stores, the Nuxalk could offer marten, wolverine, black bear and grizzly pelts.

Through this second period of contact, Indian and white traders alike remained largely dependent on the fishing, trapping, hunting and gather-

*The establishment of Fort Victoria in 1843 changed trade relations: instead of traders going to villages, native people began coming to land-based posts.*
PROVINCIAL ARCHIVES OF
BRITISH COLUMBIA, 58566

215

# When Alexander Mackenzie Arrived at Bella Coola

In the 1960s Orden Mack, an elder living at Bella Coola, recorded in English for anthropologist Susanne Storie the account he had heard about explorer Alexander Mackenzie's visit to his ancestors. In 1793 Mackenzie, an agent for the North West Company, travelled up the Peace River, then down the Fraser, until he realized its mouth could not possibly lie near Nootka Sound, where he knew the lucrative sea otter trade was underway. He struck off to the west and arrived in the Bella Coola Valley just six weeks after one of the boats from Capt. George Vancouver's ship *Discovery* had been in the nearby waters of Dean Channel.

This is Chief Mack's account:

Well . . . this story about Alexander Mackenzie . . . was told to me by Joshua Moody, one of the big headmen in Bella Coola that really understood and really knew everything that he was talking about and had a good head and didn't forget anything that he'd seen or what he'd heard. And this is what I heard from him.

When Alexander Mackenzie came [it seemed like he had been] born from the dead. He'd come to life again, because his face was white. He didn't look like the Indians. So the chief said, "Don't touch him."

He was afraid if they killed him maybe the tribe will get. . . . Well, he was superstitious or something like that. So he told the people . . . not to bother [Mackenzie]; not to kill him. Told them to, "Put your arms away." . . .

And then he fed them. They were hungry and they were tired. And when they were fed, and he got his real good canoe-man there and put everything they had in the canoe, and he started their trip down, down to the front—after he made signs that he wanted to . . . taste some salt water. That's what he wanted. That was his goal, to taste it. He went like that to the water—shakes his face [that is, Mackenzie put some water to his lips and made an expression of distaste]—and the chief knew what he wanted. He pointed out to the front there [down the inlet].

He says, "Okay, let's go down."

And when they got to the mouth of the river, they changed their boats. They left the canoe there, the river canoe, and they go in the [big] war canoe and paddled out the inlet. Oh, about three or four miles out, he tried to taste the water. He got disgusted. He thought it was a lake because the flow of this river has got about three inches of fresh water on the surface, which made him disgusted. [Fresh water is lighter than salt water, so rain and runoff float at the surface before mixing.] He thought he was on another lake again.

And he kept pointing out that way and the chief said, "Further out." Then [Mackenzie] tastes it again. Then he starts to get happy then. He goes this way. [He clasped his hands over his head in victory, realizing at a point about 16 km or 10 miles after leaving the river mouth that he had indeed reached salt water.]

That was his goal. He reached the ocean, from the other continent to the other continent [from the Atlantic to the Pacific]. So he says it was okay. "I got it now." And he travelled out, out, further out, out till they reached Elcho Harbour there. That's when he made that mark on the rock. In what year, this I don't know. Maybe you'll find that out. Seventeen hundred something. He wrote that "Alexander Mackenzie across land." . . . They turned around. They came back. . . .

But every, every fish trap they got into, they have to portage. . . . The man that comes from the dead—he was dead once and came to life again, this Mackenzie was. What they believe, if he sees the fish trap, the fish wouldn't come by it. So they wouldn't let him see it. All the way up, another fish trap, they have to portage everything, the baggage and the canoe. When they got by this [last] fish trap, they put the canoe in the river and they continue like that all the way up, right up to Burnt Bridge again [the side creek where Mackenzie had first reached the Bella Coola Valley].

And they start to pack them up. Give them food—dry fish, dry meat, dry berries. And they left again, across Canada again by land.

That's all I know.

ing that took place at traditional locations in traditional ways. The Hudson's Bay Company had no reason to encourage change, for the existing system served its ends remarkably well. This uneventful second chapter of the fur trade gave no warning of the exploitive settlement period soon to begin.

The year 1849 brought a crucial turning point: that year Britain issued a Royal Charter proclaiming Vancouver Island a colony. Nine years later the mainland also dropped from Hudson's Bay Company control. What had been the Company's vast domain of New Caledonia became accountable instead to the British Colonial Office. There was no immediate flood of settlers; indeed, the 1850s brought more gold prospectors than farmers or loggers. Nonetheless, native destiny had veered away from millenia of evolving on its own, and outsiders began to dictate changes. Missionaries said that the old ways were evil. The government denied native people rights to most of their land and granted only small reserves. New economic realities forced many Natives to accept a cash economy, and this meant abandoning traditional territories for much of the year in order to earn wages. Gunboats enforced "good behaviour," which included living only where employed or on officially recognized reserves. Skills and material possessions changed to those of the new, white system.

Most journals kept by early explorers and fur traders along the coast report fairly objectively concerning people and conditions. For instance, Alexander Mackenzie noted ceremonial screens at Bella Coola:

They were made of thick cedar boards, which were joined with so much neatness that I at first thought they were one piece. They were painted with hieroglyphics, and figures of different animals, and with a degree of correctness that was not to be expected from such an uncultivated people.

Later white arrivals rarely expressed admiration. They rationalized their takeover of land by emphasizing what they saw as bizarre or horrifying. Their written accounts all too often reflect the prejudices they brought with them, and also those of the public back home. European readers were fascinated and shocked—and perhaps comforted—to find the "wretched savages" so unlike themselves. Occasionally, they expressed admiration, crediting Indians with "ingenuity" and acknowledging, for example, a surprising woodworking skill for "primitive" people using "crude" tools. But they described Indian ceremonials as "grotesque antics" and claimed native religion was nonexistent or "a childish belief in omens."

Virtually no early account seeks to understand coast culture from the perspective of people living there. Although white men held a romantic notion of "noble redmen" in tune with a primeval world, they did not apply the concept to the "fish eaters" of the Northwest Coast. In 1869 the Victoria *British Colonist* expressed the feeling by saying no one among the "miserable . . . tribes on the seaboard" could compare favourably with the "more noble and warlike redman of the interior, who lives by the chase."

Settlers knew they were destroying local culture; it was sad but unavoidable. In 1869, when Gilbert Malcolm Sproat came to the head of Alberni Canal to oversee the building of a sawmill, he realized that the land had "passed into the unrelaxing English grip as our anchor sank to the bottom." Recalling the period later, Sproat wrote:

In the morning I sent a boat for their chief and explained to him that his tribe must move their encampment, as we had bought all the surrounding land from the Queen of England, and wished to occupy the site of the village for a particular purpose. . . .

Two or three days afterwards . . . I visited the principal house at the new encampment, with a native interpreter. . . . "Yes," [said] an old man, "our families are well, our people have plenty of food; but how long this will last we know not. We see your ships, and hear things that make our hearts grow faint. They say that more King-George-men will soon be here and will take our land, our firewood, our fishing grounds. That we shall be placed on a little spot, and shall have to do everything according to the fancies of the King-George-men."

Although native people continued to dominate

British Columbia's population in t   of numbers until the middle of the nineteenth century they were losing control of their lands and lives.

## Economic Change

By the middle of the nineteenth century obvious and irreversible changes had swept Indian society like a succession of storm waves. The old economic system was fast vanishing. For example, rendering oil from dogfish (a small shark) had developed into a village industry, one of the few instances where a traditional skill fit into the new opportunities and realities of the era.

People on the outer coast of Vancouver Island had traditionally used the rough skins of dogfish as "sandpaper" and oil from the livers as a base for paint and a flavouring for food. By the 1850s, Nuu-chah-nulth groups were supplying trading schooners with the oil, and through the 1860s and 1870s they exchanged it at small outpost stores for food staples and manufactured goods. Dogfish oil greased the skid roads of timber crews and lubricated the machinery of sawmills from the lower Fraser River to Puget Sound. It lit the lamps of homes, mines, industrial plants, ships and lighthouses. When commercial whaling collapsed from overhunting in the 1870s, demand for dogfish oil increased still more, and white men set up processing plants, employing Natives but taking over the previous oil production of scattered villages. People moved to participate directly in the dogfish-oil industry and to be near trading posts.

"I Fred Thornberg took charge of Clayoquot Station in 1874 buying furs, Seals and Dogfish Oil," an issue of *Sound Heritage* quotes an early trader, who went on to say:

I traded through a hole in the End of the Building. It was two feet high and about a foot 6 inches wide and two Indians could just stand and look in with their elbows and breasts leaning on the bottom part of the hole. A small counter was just inside the hole. On the outside was a small veranda so that the Indian would be out of the rain when he came to trade. I could not talk the Indian dialect and very few of the Indians un-

# From Bella Coola to Berlin

An issue of *Der Berliner Tageblatt* in 1886 promoted a forthcoming dance performance by Indians from the coast of British Columbia. The article was written by Franz Boas who, at the time, had been no farther north or west than Baffin Island, where he had studied Inuit people. Boas opened his article by saying it long "had been the fashion for representatives of foreign tribes to be brought to Europe" so that the public could catch a glimpse of their lives and customs.

Arrangements for the Nuxalk appearance had been made in Victoria when Capt. J. Adrian Jacobsen and his brother Fillip happened to meet nine men heading from Bella Coola to the hop fields near Seattle. The nine agreed to switch employment and destination.

The result was a year's tour of fourteen German cities performing dances, shooting with bows and arrows, and demonstrating bone games and potlatching. The public showed little interest. They preferred family groups to a troupe of men only; worse yet, these people did not fit German expectations of what "red Indians" should look like. Their noses were wrong, their skin colour wrong, and they had no tomahawks or feather headdresses, which even then were indispensable to the stereotype of a "true" Indian.

Even so, the exhibition had a noteworthy outcome. Geographer-ethnographer Aurel Krause, who had worked among the Tlingit, asked Franz Boas to help him record details of Nuxalk culture. He pointed out—with totally scrambled

*The Northwest Coast was little known in nineteenth-century Europe, but anthropologists in Berlin were fascinated by the touring Nuxalk dancers.* BRITISH COLUMBIA PROVINCIAL MUSEUM, ETHNOLOGY DIVISION, PN 15505

geography—that Boas's knowledge of the Inuit and his own of the Tlingit might be applied to studying these "neighbouring" people.

Regardless of that illogic, Krause's invitation launched Boas on the Northwest career he had dreamt of, and one month after the dance troupe arrived back in British Columbia, Boas strode down the gangplank and began asking questions and meticulously noting answers.

*Schooners called at Nuu-chah-nulth and Makah villages —and a few Southern Kwakiutl villages —to pick up fur seal hunters. Most vessels belonged to Whites, but several were owned by native captains who sailed them as far north as the Bering Sea. In 1911 an international treaty halted commercial fur sealing. This caused native people great economic loss without their having been consulted or compensated.* BRITISH COLUMBIA PROVINCIAL MUSEUM, ETHNOLOGY DIVISION, PN 7277

derstood the Hudson Bay company giberits called Chenook—but I soon learnet to talk the Indian Dialect.

In 1874 George Blenkinsop, a former Hudson's Bay Company trader, made an extensive trip in the Barkley Sound area, observing Indian "conditions" at these settlements—and elsewhere—and reporting to the Commissioner of Indian Affairs. Of the dogfish trade, Blenkinsop wrote:

About the beginning of December their stock of Salmon is dried and secured and they then go into winter quarters where they give up their time solely to feasting and distributing property, emerging however occa-

*Fur sealers hunted with double-pronged harpoons, as in this photograph of Ohiaht hunter Jackson Jack. Schooner captains stacked ten to fifteen canoes on deck to carry them to distant fur sealing grounds.* ALBERNI VAL-LEY MUSEUM PHOTOGRAPHIC ARCHIVES, 1854

sionally, even when the air is full of snow, to make oil from the dogfish which are at this time very abundant. . . .

An old woman told me that she was willing to dig the ground to plant potatoes provided she was furnished with seed, which I promised her, but she also said that she could earn a bushel of potatoes in an hour or less by making dogfish oil and this appears to be truth.

Commercial sealing began at the same time as the dogfish-oil trade when Indians travelling to Fort Victoria took along fur seal skins to trade. Soon, several independent traders opened posts from Port San Juan to Quatsino Sound, so as to be closer to trade possibilities. In 1867 one of these, Capt. James Christianson, took four sealing canoes and twelve Clayoquot hunters aboard his trading schooner and sailed out to intercept migrating fur seals. This was the first of the "mother-ship" sealing, which was to continue through the next four decades and introduce the outside world to scores of Nuu-chah-nulth and Makah men, as well as a few Nuxalk and Southern Kwakiutl who also signed aboard sealing schooners.

For millenia native sealers had been loading the animals into their canoes; the bones of fur seals make up about 80 per cent of the animal remains at some outer-coast middens, such as Ozette. But the new demand by Whites changed this ancient pattern: mother-ships carried men and canoes far beyond their homes to meet the herds en route to their Arctic breeding grounds. By the 1880s some schooners headed for California in early spring; others sailed for the Bering Sea to await the herds. In one year, 1894, the fleet killed nearly 30 000 fur seals along the British Columbia coast and an even greater number around the Pacific Rim to Japan. Men from widely scattered villages, speaking wholly different languages, began meeting each other at the Bering Sea hunting grounds and occasionally in Japanese teahouses and Hawaiian cafés. Four brothers from Neah Bay who hunted aboard separate schooners came home with four different surnames, each used by Makah descendants even today.

Recalling those commercial sealing days, Kyuquot pioneering settler Charles Moser in 1925 wrote in his *Reminiscences of the West Coast of Van-*

221

*A photograph taken at Quatsino Sound in 1897 captures some of the social change associated with the wage economy of the era. Villages were periodically vacated as people moved to distant areas to take on paid jobs. Photographer Benjamin Leeson wrote that some of the men who worked aboard fur sealing schooners had made two or three trips to Japan.* VANCOUVER PUBLIC LIBRARY, 14082

*couver Island* that in spite of missionary objection, villagers still observed traditional sea-mammal hunting rituals:

When the young men are out [on the sealing schooners], the people at home observe strict old-fashioned rules. So, for instance, the doors of the houses must remain closed and the room be kept as dark as possible; dogs, chickens, and even children are turned outside. I heard a young man say that he missed a seal—or rather saw a small school of seals on which he was gaining stealthily, expecting to throw his spear at one of them and kill it—when all at once they woke and began to fight in the water; and he attributed his ill luck of not killing it—as they can only be speared when they are sleeping—to the fact that at that very time a band of dogs had a row in his house, as he was afterwards informed by the women at home.

The last of the old-time sealers still can tell how

to throw a spear, timing it with the surge of ocean swells, which would lift first the canoe, then the seal. Ben Johnson, a Makah elder from Neah Bay who has always drawn his living from the sea, told me:

A good spearman could throw that spear fifty feet or more. But not everybody was any good. Gotta go straight, and a small wobble on the end you're holding, why that throws everything way off target.

If the wind is blowing you can get right up close. The seals are sleeping and they're listening to the wind. They hear the slap of the water so don't notice the canoe coming. Them canoes, they used to burn [char] them before they went seal hunting; burn off the slivers so the canoe won't make any bubbles. We had special paddles too: sharp deal on the end so when you lift it all the water runs off that tip and isn't making any noise.

The skipper has gotta be really good. It's choppy out there. The swells raise the canoe up and the skipper's got to lift himself—shift his weight—so the bow stays in the water and doesn't slap as it comes off the crest of the wave. When the seal is on the top of the swell, you paddle. He won't see you [in the trough of the waves]. You wait, and when he goes up again you can paddle again. You can't get right up to them when it's calm weather unless you're a real sharp man.

The spear slides along the water with the short prong underwater. It's gotta be just right. I've been out there when it's real choppy; you're bouncing all over in that canoe, so it's really hard to throw accurately. They'd try to hit under the [seal's] arm, I guess you'd say. Not hit that flipper, the shoulder. That's all bone there and the harpoon won't go in. One thing they taught me right away is: "Never put your hands on the gunwale." A seal that's been hit, why he can bite your hand right off.

Them fur seals are delicious. Even the liver. Way better than hair seal; hair seals eat too much bottom fish. Fur seals eat salmon and herring. Well, they're both good if you like seal meat. Especially that blubber. Man!

Sealing was one of the few instances of the white wage economy directly incorporating a traditional skill. But in 1911 an international treaty ended the

*Alice Paul lived in Victoria for years and now has returned home to Hesquiat.* RUTH AND LOUIS KIRK

hunt as a conservation measure.

By the end of the nineteenth century village economies had largely shifted from drawing independently on the resources of land and sea to sending men aboard boats to exploit fish and fur seals as employees of white men. Clanking, hissing machinery at logging operations and canneries also drew people away from their traditional locations and activities. Natives cut trees that were hauled off, and they preserved fish in the white way, filling cans with flesh that Animal People had granted their ancestors. Alice Paul, a Hesquiaht elder, told me about working shift at a Clayoquot cannery, sending cans rattling down conveyor belts and through a steam preservation process:

Herring time, it's day and night work—twenty-five cents an hour. Some of them thirty cents. The Nootka

223

*Each summer people left their home villages to work at canneries, employment that gave individuals, not just chiefs, access to wealth. As canneries closed in the mid-twentieth century, owing to the depletion of fish runs, many native people who had become dependent on cash had no way of earning wages. Many of them moved to cities, resulting in a great social and psychological dislocation.* BRITISH COLUMBIA PROVINCIAL MUSEUM, ETHNOLOGY DIVISION, PN 11763

Company had two shifts, maybe a hundred workers. They used to send me around to pick up the ladies when the season started, and I represented them to the manager. I never was afraid of him. When he was talking he used to be chewing tobacco and he'd shoot that juice right at me. But I didn't let him scare me.

My mother and my sister from her previous marriage worked at a cannery too. . . . Worked real hard. So she never had much time to teach me things. But she could say the ABCs and the counting. Say them frontwards, then backwards. Real fast.

## Social Change

By the 1880s many of the parents and grandparents of today's Indian elders were financially comfortable. "My mother said we always had gold coins in our pockets," an elderly Makah woman told me. The wealth that had come a century earlier with the maritime fur trade seemed to have returned. Yet, actually, daily continuity with the past was broken. Native men and women might still be hunting fur seals or rendering dogfish oil, catching salmon or cutting cedar and spruce; perhaps they even laboured on the same waters and hillsides known to their parents and grandparents. But, overall, methods had changed, and the old order based on rank had nearly collapsed. Even commoners received wages and had access to wealth goods.

Appalling epidemics aggravated this economic and social dislocation. Smallpox, measles, syphilis, tuberculosis and other infectious diseases, virtually unknown on the Northwest Coast until contact with Whites, became a scourge, and Natives had almost no immunity to check their ravage. The overwhelming anguish of epidemics began in the 1860s and went on for decades; the devastation was psychological as well as physical. Nobody knows its full dimensions, although commonly quoted reports say that by the late nineteenth century successive epidemics had killed perhaps half of the Nuu-chah-nulth, two-thirds of the Southern Kwakiutl and three-quarters of the Nuxalk.

No dependable census of coast Indians exists from before about the 1870s but what figures there are claim a combined total population of 20 000 for the Nuu-chah-nulth, Southern Kwakiutl and Nuxalk. However, archaeologists now conclude there must have been 20 000 people on the west side of Vancouver Island alone. If so, 90 per cent perished during epidemics and nineteenth-century conflicts, for reasonably plausible census figures from the late nineteenth century give a Nuu-chah-nulth population of only 2000. Tragically, from Mexico northward, this 90 per cent death rate holds grimly true following Native contact with white people. So overwhelming was this loss that it shattered the ancient pattern of many small, independent groups: too many people lay dead. Remnant handfuls of survivors were forced to band together.

Nothing can express the terror that seized the coast. The dead lay where their last breath left them. Or—worse—as Nuu-chah-nulth elder Alice Paul told me:

Somebody wrapped that body in a blanket or old mat and put it into the canoe. Body after body. Spread the contamination. . . .

From long time ago, there was nothing: just old age [to cause death]. Now along come the smallpox, measles. When they used to go to Washington, pick hops, that's the time my mother caught the measles. The white people said, "Don't go while you got the measles." They talked Chinook Jargon. They used to come around and say, "You got to stay. You're not going if you want the children to be all right."

But some didn't listen. All the way home, they'd land and bury children.

Southern Kwakiutl Chief Martin Smith had similar memories, which he told to anthropologist Wilson Duff:

When I was small, I can remember as we came home from Seattle year after year that as we advanced on our way homeward, it was as if little "towns" of newly made graves had suddenly sprang up everywhere, the people of all coastal nations died out so quickly and in such vast numbers. It went on all through my childhood.

# Smallpox

In 1853 a trader named Samuel Hancock was living in Neah Bay. That spring a brig arrived from San Francisco with a crewman on board who had smallpox. Also on board were two Makah men returning home. After going ashore, these two fell ill. Hancock wrote:

One soon died and the other recovered, but the disease [smallpox] spread among the natives, proving very disastrous, for in a majority of instances it was fatal.

After resorting to every means in their power to arrest its progress and fatality in vain, for their friends were dying in vast numbers daily, those who had escaped became almost frantic with grief and fear, and conceived the idea of crossing the Strait and going to the Nitanat [sic] tribe living on Vancouver's Island [sic]. They crossed over to this place, carrying the infection with them, and soon nearly all those who fled from Neaah Bay [sic], besides a great many of the native tribe, became victims to the epidemic.

In was truly shocking to witness the ravages of this disease here in Neaah Bay. The natives after a time became so much alarmed that when any of their friends were attacked, all of the other occupants who lived in the house would at once leave it and the sick person with a piece of dried salmon and some water, laying all their personal effects by the sick persons, not intending to ever approach them again; sometimes the retreating ones would lie down anywhere on the beach till they died. I have, in walking along, encountered them lying in this situation when they would beg in the most supplicating manner for medicine or something to relieve them, promising to serve me as slaves all their lives should they recover, if I would contribute in some way to their recovery. . . .

In a few weeks from the introduction of the disease, hundreds of the natives became victims to it. The beach for a distance of eight miles was literally strewn with the dead bodies of these people. . . . In their distress [they] concluded I might afford them some relief, and as soon as they would feel the symptoms of the disease, they would come about my house and lie down in the yard to die.

They continued this until the dead were so numerous I could scarcely walk about round my house, and was obliged to have holes dug where I deposited fifteen or twenty bodies in each. Still they continued to come about me to die, in such numbers that I finally hauled them down the beach at a time of low tide, so they would drift away. . . .

The disease . . . raged here in its most violent form for about six weeks.

*A frequent burial pattern was to place coffins in spruce trees, as here at Blunden Harbour.* ROY L. CARLSON

"The wonder is that Indians kept their sanity," is how Bill Reid, renowned Haida carver and artist, expresses the almost incomprehensible anguish of the era.

To some extent it was a society of broken souls and minds that missionaries and government officials set about reshaping and administering. Families had lost more people to disease than remained alive and lacked the strength to properly hand down rank and ceremonial privileges to their young people. Survivors faced chaos within their own systems of rank and, economically, were forced to fit into new patterns and even to compete with the white newcomers for traditional resources and rights. Natives were no longer as necessary to Europeans as they had been during the fur-trade decades. Church and government officials alike did recognize, however, that Indian people belonged to humanity and worked to save them from what missionaries mistakenly called their "heathen darkness."

Changes in native ways of life intensified. Indians began to live in "white-man houses" and, with the old communal dwellings empty, large families no longer shared daily life as closely as in the past. Traditional families were even outlawed. A Makah friend once told me:

My mother had to translate for the Indian agent. . . . He called her out of school and told her to explain to her father that he could only have one wife. He had to choose. Well, he didn't pick my grandmother, so she had to move. But we all used to get together at night sometimes anyway. Tell stories. Sing.

Old concepts of land tenure, derived from 10 000 years of coast life, were not considered valid. "Pre-emptions" and "reserves" created new realities, confusion, heartbreak, frustration, indignation, awareness of injustice—and submission.

*Finely carved welcome figures, photographed in 1902 at the village of Kiixin, near Bamfield. Later, the figures were shown at the Diamond S Department Store in Vancouver during the city's Golden Jubilee in 1936. They are now on display at the British Columbia Provincial Museum.* BRITISH COLUMBIA PROVINCIAL MUSEUM, ETHNOLOGY DIVISION, PN 494 AND PN 10509

*A feast dish belonging to South-
ern Kwakiutl chief George Scow
was photographed at Gwayasdums in 1955.* BRITISH COLŒ
UMBIA PROVINCIAL MUSEUM,
ETHNOLOGY DIVISON, PN 2163

*At Bella Coola, the carving of
an Eagle holds a coffin identified as that of the Indian wife
of John Clayton, a Hudson's
Bay Company trader. The
photograph was taken in 1895.*
BRITISH COLUMBIA PROVIN-
CIAL MUSEUM, ETHNOLOGY
DIVISION, PN 4588

Entries taken at random from George Blenkinsop's report to government officials concerning conditions at Barkley Sound in 1874 tell the tale:

I endeavoured to impress on them the necessity of closing at once with the [land] offer of the Department, as in the course of a few years the country might become more settled by the Whites and that they could then be obliged to occupy lands much less convenient for their fishing and hunting. They gave in after a hard struggle. . . .

Strange to say these Indians prefer grubbing around their old village sites to utilizing this fine soil for potatoes. . . .

They certainly seem to aim at accomplishing great things in the way of improvement, such as painting their houses, having glass windows, and ornamenting them in various other ways. One or two ambitious damsels went so far as [to request] sewing machines. . . .

It was certainly a pleasing feature in the character of these Indians that, prior to my addressing them on the subject of my mission [to check on land requirements] men, women, and children both old and young united in singing a Chinook Hymn taught them by the Priests, and although much is probably due to its novelty yet the desire seems general to accept instruction from both the Priest and Schoolmaster.

Thirteen years after Blenkinsop wrote his report, missionary Kate Hendry at Bella Coola entered in her diary for 25 February that her hus-

*Early twentieth-century photographs document changing native architecture. Vertical planks still wall the house of Chief Klaklilikla on Harbledown Island. Above the entry, a carved canoe prow projects from painted boards along with two carved columns and a Hokhokw (supernatural Cannibal Bird).* BRITISH COLUMBIA PROVINCIAL MUSEUM, ETHNOLOGY DIVISION, PN 245

band was visiting "some of our People who are working down by the salt water about 50 miles from here." Left in charge at the mission, she reported going from house to house, holding services and feeling gratified by the Natives' attendance and attention:

Oh, it was a good Sabbath. . . . There is a gracious influence at work on the hearts and consciences of many [Nuxalk], more especially the young men which are a very fine specimen of the human race. I think we would have a large number of them on our side were it not for the wicked old chiefs. We have been praying for their removal and already one has been taken away very suddenly. He was here, well, as usual one P.M. & the next A.M. he started to see [to] his canoe but ever he

reached it he fell down and expired. . . .

If the people here knew we had been praying thus I doubt not that they would want us to leave this place but we feel the Lord has done this for some wise purpose. Better one or two should be lost than that many should perish Eternally.

Inevitably, the old culture of the coast collided with the new one. A missionary named the Reverend Mr. Swartout, under the pseudonym C. Haicks, wrote about the transition in a manuscript titled *On the West Coast of Vancouver Island*. A Sheshaht chief told the missionary that his medicine and education for the children were welcome and that he even hoped the man would stay. It was exceedingly difficult, however, the chief

*At Quatsino Narrows, horizontal milled lumber replaces—or covers—traditional vertical planks, and a hinged door and glass-paned windows have been added. Painted and carved crests remain, but the symbol over the door is a ship's figurehead.* BRITISH COLUMBIA PROVINCIAL MUSEUM, ETHNOLOGY DIVISION, PN 114

231

*Leonard, age eighteen, and Catherine, age sixteen, were married at Hesquiat in 1913. Missionary concepts of family differed radically from traditional views, and the new system —each man and wife living in their own home—forever changed native society.* MOUNT ANGEL ABBEY ARCHIVES,

said, to accept Christianity, as the religion destroyed families and values:

"A Christian is a man who never eats with his friends but always sits down alone with his wife to eat. He never invites other Indians to eat with him. He never gives a potlatch. That is a Christian. Missionary, I do not want to try to make Christians of my people."

Church effort concentrated especially on the young, and wage opportunities and schooling also drove a widening wedge between generations. School education tended to be authoritarian and based overwhelmingly on ability to use English, handle arithmetic and memorize standardized "facts." The process held a certain exotic appeal for some. For instance, in Alert Bay, Southern Kwakiutl elder Flora Sewid told me:

I sneaked away to go to school. I used to see my friends from the residence school marching down the road, and I wanted to be like them, with their black hats and black skirts. . . . My parents didn't want me to go, so I sneaked off and went. We were fenced in at the school and they really watched us, so we couldn't visit our people. We just got out one time a week, on Thursday. They'd let us go right after dinner and we had to be back by seven o'clock. But, still, it was good. We learned how to work in a house. Bake bread. Milk cows.

My parents didn't want me to go because they were afraid I'd learn bad things and forget Indian things.

Inevitably, parents themselves were re-evaluating traditions. Nuu-chah-nulth elder Winnifred David mentioned an instance of this while telling me about her puberty potlatch:

My dad wouldn't have anything to do with it. He had rejected potlatching and the winter dances because his father died as a result of participating in a Tlu•kwa•na ceremony. They had to do something difficult, a topati. Different families did different things, and he had to float down the river. Not supposed to paddle, just lie on his back in the water and float from way up near the bridge to the pulp mill. He got pneumonia and died.

So my great-grandmother gave my party. She used to weave baskets all the time; buy pots, pans, shirts [to give] the men, socks and sweaters for the ladies. She even got jewellery. She had a big pile. As soon as I was born, that's when she started putting away things. . . . Buy material; make dresses, aprons. . . .

I was thirteen and thinking maybe my dad would do it [give a puberty potlatch]. I didn't know my great-grandmother was putting things away for me. They used to keep it a secret. . . . I used to think, "Gee, she has a lot of stuff. She has trunks and trunks and suit-cases all filled. I wonder why she's keeping so much." But kids didn't ask questions in those days. My daughter didn't ask either. She knew we had boxes of cups put away but she didn't ask about it.

Well, when my great-grandmother gave my party at Village Island [Effingham Island] we didn't know nothing about it. We weren't even down there; we were up here having our summer holiday. I guess she knew my father wouldn't let us come. Maybe my mother knew about it but she never mentioned it till afterwards, and then my dad was sore. "Why did she have to do that?" He was thinking it was nobody's business that I'd become a woman. As soon as that was announced there'd be people coming to ask for the girl's hand.

But when my husband came he came by himself [without a traditional delegation of negotiators]. My father told him, "I don't want any Indian-style marriage. My daughter is not for sale." Because as soon as a girl becomes a woman they used to have to get married to an old man whose family asked for her. My father didn't want that.

After a century of contact with white people, virtually all aspects of native culture had become a compound of old ways and new. The potlatch, central to traditional life, underwent particularly great upheaval and was buffeted in several directions at once. Beginning in 1884, successive versions of the federal Indian Act were deliberately intended to suppress the practice. At the same time, however, increased access to wealth goods was facilitating the potlatch on an ever-grander scale. Economic enrichment from wages, along with more—and in some ways better—tools, were helping to foster the proliferation of totem poles and other artwork now widely regarded as symbolic of the whole 10 000 years of Northwest Coast Indian culture.

Disease had emptied ceremonial positions and left honoured names unclaimed. People scrambled to fill vacancies, and some previously without high rank enhanced their stature. True chiefs added even more prestige to their names and gained additional ceremonial positions, for only they fully knew the rules. Customs inflated. Simultaneously, however, other forces ran counter to the growing elaboration. Some villagers rejected potlatching, as government officials and missionaries made it a particular target.

On a tape, the late Bill Scow, a Southern Kwakiutl chief, spoke about potlatching in spite of government disapproval. The answer was to head for remote villages, beyond easy surveillance:

Kingcome. [It was] a place where . . . they got their winter supplies, like salmon, berries in the summer, bear hunting, and one thing and another. And later on they started to practice the old customs up there too, you know. In the twenties they really moved up there, the four tribes, and stayed and made it their permanent village. It was due to the suppression of the old customs, you know, when the government really put their foot down and prohibited them from practising the potlatch. . . .

At the height of their customs, they'd wait till the river was frozen and then they used to post people down on the flats there to watch if there was any strangers coming up the valley or the inlets. And then they [government agents] approached the heads of the tribes and said, "You don't suppose to live here. Your reserve is in Gilford, or your reserve is in Wakeman, or yours is in Hopetown." So they kind of divided the people that was in the habit of living together. . . . It was one means of depriving them of practising the old customs. Mind you, this is my interpretation. Because you can't practice [potlatching] very well within your own family. You have to have an audience. So with four bands living together you naturally have three being your audience any time you conduct this ceremonial, or potlatch.

As a child I didn't know that it had been forbidden. I thought that it was the general practice of all the human beings to be active with these feelings, that you must forever perpetuate the name and traditions of your family.

233

# Halting the Potlatch

Daisy Sewid Smith, daughter of Southern Kwakiutl elders James and Flora Sewid, taped the memories of elders who had experienced the loss of land and potlatching. Before writing her book, *Prosecution or Persecution,* she felt she had to get hatred out of her heart, so she read what Indian Agent William Halliday had written, "trying to find what was good" in it. She didn't want to hurt his family, still living in the Campbell River area, and supposed he had been obeying orders (although actually his superiors had told him to desist long before 1922 when charges of potlatching were brought against members of her family).

Excerpts from the official correspondence of Alert Bay Indian Agent William M. Halliday published in Mrs. Smith's book include the following:

*Southern Kwakiutl Agnes Alfred remembers the jailing of potlatch participants in 1922.* RUTH AND LOUIS KIRK

1 September 1914 [Halliday to various chiefs]: The law against the potlatch has been passed because it has been seen that where the potlatch exists there has been no progress and the Government wants to see the Indians advance so that they are on the same footing as the white men, and this can not be as long as the potlatch continues.

21 September 1914 [one of the replies]: Not one of these Indians were satisfy with the statement you sent us because we all known that we wont good for anything if we quit the potlatch. . . . Well, as we are an Indian, our name will never change. That why we wont quit our good business, the potlatch.

29 May 1918 [Halliday to the Department of Indian Affairs, Ottawa]: I realize the evil of the potlatch and at the present time the Indians themselves are in a proper mood to accept something different as they will be gathering here in a week's time to embark for the canneries at Rivers Inlet. I want to be in a position to advise them on this matter as well as others. If the Idlers' Act is framed to suit the occasion, it will do good work.

24 January 1922 [Halliday to the Department of Indian Affairs, Ottawa]: As indicated in a previous letter, what is reported to be the biggest potlatch that has ever occured in the agency took place at Village Island on or about Christmas Day. Sergt. Angermann has been busy collecting evidence but as both some of the defendants and some of the witnesses are widely scattered, the case will probably not come up for hearing until about the middle of February. . . . A number of Indians have told me that . . . they are both old and young in a state of fright as they do not know who will be prosecuted in this case and who will not.

10 April 1922 [Halliday to the Deputy Superintendent General of Indian Affairs]: Strictly speaking all concerned in this gathering should have been given six months imprisonment but it would have left me with a very small agency to look after and a big burden of expense for the care of families and

when the result was accomplished by milder means [jailing only some of those who had potlatched] I think it should meet with your full endorsement.

In addition to compiling written documents, Daisy Sewid Smith taped Southern Kwakiutl

*Following the 1922 potlatch of Chief Dan Cranmer, the Reverend V. S. Lord photographed regalia taken to the parish hall in Alert Bay. The masks—proud symbols of heritage, belief and ceremonial wealth—were then sent to the Royal Ontario Museum, the National Museum in Ottawa and the Museum of the American Indian in New York. Recently, the National Museum returned its part of the collection, and the Southern Kwakiutl are now negotiating a similar return from the other museums.* BRITISH COLUMBIA PROVINCIAL MUSEUM, ETHNOLOGY DIVISION, PN 12189

elders' accounts of the events Agent Halliday reported. Agnes Alfred, grandmother of Mrs. Smith, recalled:

We sure suffered when we were all arrested. . . . They would make us sit down on chairs and they would call out our names. We would answer "Tooh [Hello]." This is all we did and they would file us back out. At one time they brought us to the jail at the other end of the Island, and we repeated this again. It took forever. . . .

[Later on] they brought us back to the day school. They stood us all up, Noo-la-gah [Mrs. Alfred's sister, Florence Knox] and I. They made one go left and the other right. They put those who were not going to prison to one side. They put those who were going to prison to the other side. . . .

They really suffered when they first arrived at prison. They were told to take all their clothes off. They would examine their whole body. They say poor Noo-la-gah really cried. We do not do that. We never ever do that, examining each others' bodies.

Chief Herbert Martin, sentenced to Oakalla prison in 1922, also taped his memories:

We started to work again. We were told to go and cut a cedar tree. There was me, Spruce Martin, Jerry Brown. They would send me to go and get the tools. Handyman!
I went and got the wedge and sledge hammer. Also the axe. To my surprise I saw the chieftains of the Kwakiutl—High-yahlth-kin Whonnock—feeding the pigs. Also Billy McDuff was feeding the pigs. James Knox, the youngest, was with them. Three of them were feeding the pigs! We started to cry. Imagine. The great chieftains of the Kwakiutl degraded to feeding the pigs.

235

A Makah friend in his late sixties told me:

I know when I was young here we had to find places to hide to have our old Indian dances and bone games. If we were caught we were arrested. The government didn't really go along with the type of culture that the Indians had in those days. I think it was just because they didn't understand it then, as much as they do now. I think that was why they more or less made us—or tried to make us—change our way of life. Forced us to forget a lot of the old culture, or to try to forget it.

Many official memos and reports reflect adamant objection to the potlatch. William Halliday, Indian Agent in Alert Bay, wrote to his superiors in Ottawa in 1918:

During these gatherings they lose months of time, waste their substance, contract all kinds of diseases and generally unfit themselves for being British subjects in the proper sense of the word.

The Reverend R. C. Scott of the Crosby Marine Mission reported in a letter to Agent Halliday a few years later:

There have been none of the old time festivities here or at Campbell River. The young folks have done all the dancing, and they are doing it in the accredited White fashion, Fox Trotting, Waltzing, etc. etc.

In the spring of 1929 the superintendent of the Columbia Coast Mission at Kingcome held a meeting to discuss the potlatch. There, Southern Kwakiutl chief Herbert Martin spoke:

I lately visited Vancouver and went to the Pantages Theatre and saw a white woman dance. She was an actress and naked. It seemed real to me, but it might have been done by a trick, the same as the eating of flesh in our [Hamatsa] dance. . . .
There was a time when there was no white man in Canada. Canada was given to us by Almighty God. . . . The rivers and seas, teeming with fish, were ours. Then Columbus reached Canada and the white men came to find the gold in our mountains and the oil in our fields, and the spruce in our forests to make their flying machines, and many millionaires were made by the wealth of Canada which was given to the Indians by God.

Now all this has been taken away from us, and only little plots of land called reservations have been left to us, and we are only asking that . . . we may be able to live happily in our villages and entertain one another, and that we may be able to keep poverty also outside our villages.

In 1951, after many years of native protest, the Indian Act was rewritten, omitting the edicts against potlatching. People were free to resume traditional ways, but noted there was no admission that the ban had probably been wrong.

## Land Problems

The situation at Bella Coola is typical of how problems concerning land began. Throughout the 1850s and 1860s smallpox emptied entire villages dotting the lush bottomlands of the valley; and in the 1880s measles, whooping cough and influenza repeated the onslaught. About this time, B. Fillip Jacobsen, a Norwegian, arrived on the coast with his brother Adrian Jacobsen, who was collecting Indian material for museums in Germany. Fillip wrote articles for Norwegian-language newspapers, praising the valley and making it sound like a Scandinavian landscape lacking only blond, blue-eyed farmers and timber cutters. Partly in response to these accounts, Norwegian colonists arrived at Bella Coola in the 1890s.

They had farmed briefly in Minnesota but been forced out by the widespread financial panic of the time. The Canadian Pacific Railway gave them reduced fares and the Minister of Immigration promised them free land. He further indicated that a wagon road would be built as soon as thirty families were established on farms and that all government land in the valley would be held for future Norwegian immigrants and their descendants.

Thus did the Nuxalk formally lose most of their domain. Yet recently at Bella Coola, Mrs. Felicity Walkus—now in her late seventies—shared with me various accounts of "before white people were around to spoil things." She mentioned:

This whole valley was ours, right up to the precipice [64 km or 40 miles from tidewater, where an abrupt pass leads up to the Chilcotin Plateau]. Now they only let us fish four miles [6.5 km] of the river, though it was all ours!

Thinking of those days before the Norwegians had come, Mrs. Walkus's grandson Edward Moody, elected chief councillor of the Nuxalk, said:

It's kind of a bum deal . . . I guess the British government was afraid of colonization by other countries, so they started encouraging their travellers, I guess you'd call them, to explore land, and survey it, and occupy it. They'd survey the Hudson's Bay Company land and after that they'd establish the reserve land. But that's backwards.

John Clayton was the trader and he was living here with a Native woman; our people had said to him, "Sir, you have our permission to stay here." There was a village there [by the Company store]. There were long-houses. And then later we found out, "That's not your land anymore." We've done a lot of research and when we bring our land claims, this will all come out.

I looked at the McKenna-McBride [Commission] minutes. They didn't even let the Indian people know what was happening. . . . The population of the valley today is about eighteen hundred and we make up eight hundred of the eighteen hundred. We occupy just over three thousand acres and the others have six hundred thousand acres from the head of the valley to here. Yet [when Alexander Mackenzie arrived] we had thirty-four villages from the mouth of the river to the precipice. We know where they all were; we've got them all worked out on the map.

For Southern Kwakiutl and Nuu-chah-nulth Indians, the pattern regarding land loss parallels the Nuxalk experience. Early in the twentieth century,

In 1895 a Norwegian settler in the Bella Coola Valley photographed the native village at the river mouth. In the foreground stands the house of Chief Klalameen; next to it, that of a chief in the Mack Family. Exceptionally wide boards, a prized possession to pass from generation to generation, decorate the gable plates of Klalameen's house. BRITISH COLUMBIA PROVINCIAL MUSEUM, ETHNOLOGY DIVISION, PN 4575

*After British Columbia joined Canada in 1871, government agents allocating reserve lands travelled the coast to talk with native people. In this 1879 photograph of Ma-ate on northern Vancouver Island, a man in a frock coat—probably Dr. Israel Powell, British Columbia commissioner for Indian Affairs—addresses a seated group.* BRITISH COLUMBIA PROVINCIAL MUSEUM, ETHNOLOGY DIVISION, PN 1980

timber leases began to cover vast areas selected by logging companies, and a few farms belonging to white men dotted the land. Describing this loss of access to resources, Nuu-chah-nulth elder Peter Webster says in his autobiography *As Far as I Know:*

Fisheries officers demanded licenses for fishing and arrested us for shooting seals. . . . The lumber people . . . seemed to own the entire forest. This made it illegal for us to get trees for canoes and cedar bark for weaving, except from our tiny reserves. When the loggers moved in, the animals we hunted and trapped disappeared. The destruction of the forests is easy to see. Our use of the woods was hardly noticeable.

All these things made it easy to get into trouble with the law. I think a lot of us became "criminals" without really knowing the reason. Once I was arrested for possession of the fur of fur seals. Another time, when I was about thirty years of age, a group of my friends and I were sent to Oakalla Prison on the mainland for

*The McKenna-McBride Royal Commission, appointed to finalize reserve allocation, meets in Victoria sometime between 1912 and 1916.* BRITISH COLUMBIA PROVINCIAL MUSEUM, ETHNOLOGY DIVISION, PN 12326

one month for refusing to pay the provincial seine tax. . . .

I can look back to a time when we lived pretty much . . . the way it was before the white people took away our land and made so many rules and regulations that I sometimes wonder if it will end when we have to buy a license each time we want to sleep with our wives.

Although native people had not surrendered their land rights, government officials opened British Columbia to settlers and reserved mere patches of land for Natives. Individual white people could claim 320 acres (130 ha) and buy an additional 320 acres, but native people received reserve lands according to "needs." In 1873 these were defined by federal recommendation as 80 acres (32 ha) per family of five. To this the provincial government responded that 80 acres was too much; 20 acres (8 ha) should be enough for Indians.

Confusion compounded for decades, finally leading to the appointment of a joint federal and provincial commission, the McKenna-McBride Royal Commission of 1912–16. Its task was to draw reserve boundaries once and for all. Its procedure was for Indian leaders to testify and white commissioners to listen.

Read transcripts of these hearings and you find pathos and frustration, as representatives of one culture met those of another. At a Southern Kwakiutl hearing, one of the commissioners tried to explain that a certain claim could not be accepted since the land already was "all covered by timber limits." Southern Kwakiutl chief Dawson of Mamalillikula responded by asking who had sold that particular land out of Indian ownership. None of the commissioners knew. They could only say that their map showed it as "purchased and therefore we cannot give it to anyone else," although perhaps the owner would permit use of the "five or 10 acres on which your houses are built."

Transcripts of the hearing record Chief Dawson's reply:

"We can't allow the place to go that way. We never sold it. . . . What right has [the government] to sell it before I was through with it, because I was the owner of it."

Similarly, at Blunden Harbour, Chief Tsukaite reminded commissioners:

239

"It is not just now that I came into possession of the country. It has been mine from the beginning of time, . . . when there was no whiteman in the country. . . . What has been done . . . [might] be the other way. I [might] have measured pieces off for the whitemen instead of the whitemen measuring off pieces for me."

Everywhere, commissioners heard such statements together with pleas that reserve lands be increased rather than reduced. A Mowachaht chief said:

"The lands that we have are not very much, and all that we have got we want to keep. We have been on these reserves for a very long time. . . . We are not very well off and we will be very pleased if you gentlemen will see to it that the reserves that we have . . . are kept for us."

At Clayoquot, Chief Jimmy Jim told the commission:

"They had a big place then, the Indians had. Then comes a priest, that was the first white man that came here . . . and Mr. Gilliod came. He was the first agent. He divided up the land and gave us a reserve. . . . [He] used to say to the Indians that there would not be any white people here. They will not come here: it is too wild. . . . This is all your land. You can do what you like with it, because there will be no white people come around here.

Now the Indians are beginning to know. They have education from the Catholic and other missionaries. They know they only have a small place here. . . . Some white men have 200 acres or more, and some have 80 acres. And why have we such a small place here? We were born here, and white settlers have a bigger place. . . . We cannot sell timber or we can't cut down the timber on our own reserves. It is just like holding us as blind men."

The chief of the Sheshaht people spoke:

"What fish we caught, they were distributed amongst the tribe. . . . The whites came in here and . . . thought they would run the place better and thought they would have more fish by having the Indians not use traps. The purse seine came and began fishing at the mouth of the river, and sometimes they caught 10,000 and 15,000 salmon and they caught the salmon before they got to the spawning grounds. . . . If they keep on fishing with the purse seine they won't have any salmon to take out of the river."

*The Broken Islands of Barkley Sound characterize the protected waters and winding shorelines of the Northwest Coast—a remarkable topography not repeated south of it until Tierra del Fuego.* BRITISH COLUMBIA PROVINCIAL MUSEUM, ARCHAEOLOGY DIVISION, 84B-320

Chief Adam Shewish, a descendant of the Sheshat chief who testified before the Royal Commission, told me:

Some Ottawa men were trying to get us to give up land in the Broken Island group recently. That's part of the national park now, you know. We had a new band manager, and he thought it might be okay to swap because we'd get more acreage that way. They were offering ten for one. But I want to go to our beach and dig enough clams to give to my people. We've always done that.

So I waited for a really beautiful day, and then I took the band manager down there on my boat. We walked the beach and talked. We cooked corn in a big pot and had seafood. I said, "Just think. Some people go all the way to Hawaii and stay in a condominium. And we've got this." The band manager changed his mind.

Land rights was the issue that the McKenna-

# The Modern Salmon Dilemma

Chief Edward Moody of Bella Coola summarized for me his future expectations:

I guess I'd say respect for Indian ways. I was arguing with Fisheries last month. They wanted to cut our fishing down to two days, from four days. I said, "No. I can't do that. Not when it's the economy of our people. If you can cut your [white] economy in half for the benefit of my people, then maybe we can consider this.

We used to use the weir system [of fishing] where we could keep track of the salmon runs and if there were not enough going upstream we wouldn't take so many. We had to let enough escape to get upriver to the villages farther up. We looked after the river. The old people walked up and down the creeks [checking conditions throughout the entire system].

Who is doing that today? I don't see anybody looking after the river. All they [the officials] do is look after their figures and their closures. . . . To humour the group at one of our meetings, I said, "I know what we'll do: We'll give up spring salmon and [instead] smoke baloney and weiners!"

Fishing is the heart of our people. It's lifestyle. It's the economy. Our boys, they see their fathers have to get up and go and get the salmon; bring them in. Then they have to get the wood for the smoke-houses. Repair the smokehouses. And the ladies have to prepare the fish, dress them, get them ready for smoking and canning. That's *work*. It's better than $200 a month welfare in your pocket. . . .

Longterm, what's needed is to get our own people back in the management of the resources.

*Cecilia Siwallace uses a measuring box to cut salmon into lengths suitable for canning.* RUTH AND LOUIS KIRK

*A figure newly carved by Clayoquot artist Joe David stands in front of the British Columbia Legislative Buildings, where in 1985 Natives, joined by non-Natives, urged that Meares Island not be logged. Pointing out that land and heritage are inseparable, Nuu-chah-nulth Tribal Council Co-chairman Simon Lucas said:*
*"What really is on that island? All the things we need to sur-*

*vive. . . . [There is] a heritage group in this country where they say, 'Here's a historic property; we want to spend a million dollars on it.' That's OK, but when we say that, we have to start negotiating, trying to convince the non-Indians that it was ours from the start, that there were no transfer papers."* ROBERT SODERLUND (NUU-CHAH-NULTH TRIBAL COUNCIL)

McBride Commission tried to deal with once and for all, yet chiefs today still feel a need to defend their land. Their people went through a staggering population loss owing to disease and then went through a drastic dislocation as survivors amal-gamated villages and adapted to a wage economy. Native people saw most of their land alienated a century ago, and they find their reserves coveted today.

# CHAPTER NINE
## Today and Tomorrow

Today's Indian elders are the children and grandchildren of the people who were put through the cultural wringer of transition. Several of these elders recorded their memories about the time of change along with tales told them by parents and grandparents about earlier times for the Linguistics Division of the British Columbia Provincial Museum.

Prejudice dies hard. So does memory. A city high school teacher in his mid-twenties recalled his childhood for me:

It was rather sad. I was taught not to acknowledge that I'm Indian. Then in high school I was good at athletics, and they used to say "Let's get the Indians on our team." So then I accepted that I'm Indian, and admitted it even against my mother's advice.

Ruth Tom, the granddaughter of Virginia Tom who posed for Edward Curtis wearing cedar-bark clothing, said:

Growing up I felt sorry I was Indian. You keep hearing you're not much good. So I always was a loner. I was fourteen by the time Christie School got a headmistress who'd let me go home to my mother, summers. By then it was too late. I never got close with my mother. I wanted a better life.

When my daughter came, I didn't want her to know the pain I've had so I worked two jobs and sent her to private, Catholic school. I shielded her from being Indian. But when she turned fourteen she joined the archaeology project at Hesquiat. And the first time she stepped out on the beach there she said, "I'm home!"

That daughter, Marina Tom, a graduate of the University of British Columbia Law School, said:

It's not me, it's my whole family that's nurtured me. I feel like when I graduate, they should be the ones up there getting the degree.

At court I speak on behalf of a client. And the judge will say to me, "Does your client understand English?" He thinks I have this universal tongue and should be translating. He doesn't even realize there are different languages native to this province.

The government asks Indians: "What do you want?" But they don't understand we're different cultures and have different answers to the question.

In Bella Coola, Nuxalk elected chief Edward Moody, who is also a hereditary chief, commented:

My parents were told not to speak their language or to practice the dances, the songs. Now that has got to be stripped away. Our people are growing up to realize we mean more to this earth than just a welfare case. We have a history and a language, and nobody else has this particular history and language but us. We're not like the watered-down citizenship of white Canadians. We don't say, "I got a hundred spring salmon," and the old lady sitting there is saying, "I can't fish." We have to work together. We have to fish for the ones who can't.

Relations are getting better. Racial prejudice begins with saying: "I'm better than this other person." We're not going to use uncertain standards comparing us with somebody else. . . . I realize now that a seagull is a seagull. It has its own certain colour, its own certain food, its own certain ways. And it's the same for us. We're going to just be ourselves. That's all.

Hilary Irving, a Makah elder, said:

In our schools instead of studying what the white man is, we should be studying what the Indian is. What good is it for me to know what Columbus did? Why shouldn't I be studying about Maquinna and the chiefs around here? That would lift my pride to the point where I'm not a drunken old Indian: I'm an Indian. If the kids are taught this . . . they will realize they are somebody.

I didn't get an education so I've done everything the hard way, and I've got away with it. But I don't think anybody can get away with it in this present age.

Ron Johnson, a Makah teacher and basketball coach, said:

Our parents were taught to forget everything and now we're trying to get it back. To find out who we are.

Lloyd Colfax, a Makah directing native studies at

*Ditidaht elder Effie Peter collects basketry material from traditional sites near Clo-oose, a major village emptied as people moved away for jobs and schools.* RUTH AND LOUIS KIRK

Evergreen State College in Washington, added:

Among the many things that make Indian people different from other members of society is our legal status, shared only by Indians. Belonging to any organization binds people closer to each other, both on a social basis and—many times—through acceptance of the same philosophy . . . the same understanding of fears and aspirations. In the past, most of our employment was the same. Tribal members ate the same things and shared the same food-gathering techniques.

Indian people were among the most spiritual ethnic group in the world and that is reviving. We also share the same weight of discrimination. I'm of the opinion that all of these circumstances together commit Indian people to be a more cohesive group than any other in society today.

## Education Today

Lloyd Colfax, a Makah friend who is a teacher in Washington, told me:

To make the Indian comply with European principles of social behaviour it became necessary to separate him from his own values, which had successful propagation over thousands of years. The main threat was to individualize the thinking of each Indian person, to disengage him from his natural tendencies of pluralism.

The school system was born of the Industrial Revolution. The philosophy appears to be to turn out a product that will fit into the industrial machine of our times. The implication is a strengthening of the idea of pursuing [mainstream] careers.

But there are very few careers on Indian reservations. Attempts to continue education on this theory increase the possibility of conflict. If an Indian child is going to abandon his values as handed him from generation to generation . . . he must then be prepared to accept the consequences of his decision. This is extremely hard to do, especially because of the legal aspect by which he is bound. He is still an Indian, with a definable relationship to his tribe.

The very promise of democracy is contrary to tribalism in that it advocates a respect and concern for individualism as a birthright. Tribalistic approaches are more of a self-sacrifice, a self-fulfillment with close relationships to family and community. If the promise of an optimum education means that teaching and learning should be individualized . . . then schools must take another look at their position. By being Indian, we have different values than non-Indian society, a different philosophy of life, different aspirations in life and the real possibility of different goals.

Ben David, a Nuu-chah-nulth who works with an alcoholism program in Alberni, commented that mainstream society

worries over dressing right. Colours matching. Hair in place. Ritual grooming. That's what makes people comfortable. Natives are more relaxed. We feel our belonging. We say, "This is where I am, so I feel comfortable." We can keep our values as Natives and work parallel with Whites. Take the best of both worlds.

I've learned discipline from Whites. The way to deal with bureaucracy, to go through formalities. Sit down and go over things, not raise voices. Paperwork. Get it done. Our greatest native strength is the family.

Bernice Touchie, a Ditidaht in charge of the native culture program of Alberni schools, said:

Historic events have made socioeconomic differences. Whites strive more for financial success; they're more oriented toward tomorrow over today. Native people now are thinking deeply. We are going headlong into accepting what white society had to offer. Now we're thinking that's not necessarily right and we're reinterpreting our philosophy for the future.

The physical setting is different for native people than among Whites. We still have the extended family system so we're not in a panic. We still have assurance that relatives will help.

Jane Sterritt, a Nuu-chah-nulth who lives in Campbell River, told me:

Whites look at forests or copper ore and see money. A native person looks and sees trees and rocks and thinks of beauty, of how they're part of nature. It's hard to change from loving nature to having to deceive your brother.

But when the loving gets to be for money, you have to change. It's a long step.

Nella Nelson, a Southern Kwakiutl born in Alert Bay and now teaching in Victoria, summed up her expectations of the present and future:

I really resent special programs in school. If classes are only for Natives, how are we going to educate non-

Natives? We need to take the best from both cultures.

History has transplanted us. But we haven't forgotten where we came from. Sometimes lawyers say emotional argument doesn't mean anything. But I say, "Don't give me that. People have always been talking with each other."

Nuxalk elected chief Edward Moody told me:

The first generation [the elders], they have their culture. It's solid for them. The next generation, they're the ones who got it stripped away through the residential schools. The third generation—my generation—we're lost. The fourth generation—our kids—there's real pride with the elders now as they see the fourth generation coming on.

I can never commend the elders enough. The things they have gone through and seen. The way they restrain themselves. I'd like to have a total immersion in the culture. But I can't. I have to do the legwork for the elders.

Top. *Nella Nelson, a Southern Kwakiutl, teaches native studies in Victoria—a subject she feels* all *students should be equally eligible to take.* RUTH AND LOUIS KIRK

Bottom. *A Nuxalk dancer performs at a competition held at Esquimalt, with participants from the entire coast.* BRITISH COLUMBIA PROVINCIAL MUSEUM, ETHNOLOGY DIVISION, PN 5443-25

*Chief Adam Shewish speaks at a potlatch. Native people today belong to the present, yet also are aware of the long continuity of their presence on the coast. Increasingly, they are taking charge of their reserves and destinies rather than blindly accepting direction by the Department of Indian Affairs. A new transition is underway.*
ROBERT SODERLUND
(NUU-CHAH-NULTH TRIBAL COUNCIL)

*Elders safeguard the wisdom of past millennia and hand it on.*
RUTH AND LOUIS KIRK

Robert Joseph, a Southern Kwakiutl who is a district manager for the Department of Indian Affairs, said: "It didn't all stop with Boas, you know." Then he went on:

I thought my fortune was "out there" someplace, not here where my people have been for the last thousands of years. So I went in a big circle. I learned some good things but then it dawned on me: my search really has to be within. I'd just been searching externally.

So I came back home and I began looking for ways of existing with whatever there is here, and making it develop. Many of the elders are very old. There are so few, they'll soon be gone. So young people are finding it necessary to give potlatches now, while the elders are here to teach and also because we want them to know that somebody is going to carry on that legacy.

We're saying: "I'm responsible and will pass this on."

249

# Selected Bibliography

## Archaeology

Bunyan, D. E. *Pursuing the Past: a General Account of British Columbia Archaeology.* Museum Notes, no. 4. Vancouver: University of British Columbia Museum of Anthropology, 1978.

Carlson, Roy L., ed. "Archaeology in British Columbia— New Discoveries." *B.C. Studies* (Special Issue no. 6–7, 1970).

Dewhirst, John. "Nootka Sound: A 4,000 Year Perspective." In *Nu·tka·: The History and Survival of Nootkan Culture,* edited by Barbara S. Efrat and W. J. Langlois, *Sound Heritage* VII: 2.

Fladmark, Knut, ed. "Fragments of the Past: B.C. Archaeology in the 1970s." *B.C. Studies* (Special Issue no. 48, 1980–81).

———. *Prehistory of British Columbia.* Ottawa: National Museum of Man, National Museums of Canada, 1986.

Hobler, Philip M. *Papers on Central Coast Archaeology.* Publication no. 10. Burnaby, B.C.: Simon Fraser University, 1982.

Kirk, Ruth, with Richard D. Daughtery. *Exploring Washington Archaeology.* Seattle: University of Washington Press, 1978.

Kirk, Ruth, with Richard D. Daugherty. *Hunters of the Whale, an Adventure in Northwest Coast Archaeology.* New York: Morrow, 1974.

Stewart, Hilary. *Indian Artifacts of the Northwest Coast.* Seattle: University of Washington Press, 1976.

## Biographies and Books by Native People

Clutesi, George. *Potlatch.* Sidney, B.C.: Gray's Publishing, 1969.

———. *Son of Raven, Son of Deer: Fables of the Tse-shaht People.* Sidney, B.C.: Gray's Publishing, 1967.

Ford, Clellan S., with Chief Charles Nowell. *Smoke from Their Fires: The Life of a Kwakiutl Chief.* New Haven: Yale University Press, 1941.

Jones, Chief Charles, with Stephen Bosustow. *Queesto, Pacheenaht Chief by Birthright.* Penticton: Theytus Books, 1981.

Sewid-Smith, Daisy (My-yah-nelth). *Prosecution or Persecution.* Cape Mudge: The Nu-Yum-Balees Society, 1979.

Spradley, James P., with Chief James Sewid. *Guests Never Leave Hungry: The Autobiography of James Sewid, a Kwakiutl Indian.* New Haven: Yale University Press, 1969.

Swan, Luke, and David W. Ellis. *Teachings of the Tides.* Penticton, B.C.: Theytus Books, 1981.

Wallas, J. J., as told to Pamela Whitaker. *Kwakiutl Legends.* Victoria: Hancock House, 1981.

Webster, Peter S. *As Far as I Know: Reminiscences of an Ahousaht Elder.* Campbell River Museum and Archives, 1983.

## Ethnography

### Nuu-chah-nulth

Arima, Eugene Y. *The West Coast (Nootka) People.* Special Publication no. 6. Victoria: British Columbia Provincial Museum, 1983.

Drucker, Philip. *The Northern and Central Nootkan Tribes.* Bureau of American Ethnology, *Bulletin,* no. 144. Washington: Government Printing Office, 1951.

Haeggert, Dorothy. *Children of the First People.* Vancouver: Arsenal Pulp, Tillacum Library, 1983.

Jewitt, John R. *The Adventures and Sufferings of John R. Jewitt, Captive among the Nootka, 1803–1805.* Edited by Derek G. Smith. Toronto: McClelland and Stewart, 1974.

Mozino, José Mariano. *Noticias de Nutka: An Account of Nootka Sound in 1792.* Translated by Iris H. Wilson. Seattle: University of Washington Press, 1970.

Sapir, Edward, and Morris Swadesh. *Nootka Texts.* Linguistic Society of America. Philadelphia: University of Pennsylvania, 1939.

Sendy, John. *The Nootkan Indian.* Port Alberni, B.C.: Alberni Valley Museum, 1977.

### Nuxalk

Davis, Philip W., and Ross Saunders. *Bella Coola Texts.* Heritage Record no. 10. Victoria: British Columbia Provincial Museum, 1980.

McIlwraith, T. F. *The Bella Coola Indians.* 2 vols. Toronto: University of Toronto Press, 1948.

### Southern Kwakiutl

Boas, Franz. *Kwakiutl Ethnography.* Edited by Helen Codere. Chicago: University of Chicago Press, 1966.

———. *The Kwakiutl of Vancouver Island.* Memoir of the American Museum of History, The Jesup North Pacific Expedition, vol. V, part II, 1909. Reprint. New York: AMS Press, 1973.

———. *Religion of the Kwakiutl Indians.* Part 2. Columbia University Contributions to Anthropology, vol. 10, 1930. Reprint. New York: AMS Press, 1969.

———. *The Social Organization and the Secret Societies of the Kwakiutl Indians.* 1895. Reprint. New York: Johnson Reprint, 1970.

Hawthorn, Audrey. *Kwakiutl Art.* Vancouver: Douglas & McIntyre; Seattle: University of Washington Press, 1979.

Holm, Bill. *Smoky-Top: The Art and Times of Willie Seaweed.* Seattle: University of Washington Press, 1984.

# General

Drucker, Philip. *Indians of the Northwest Coast.* Garden City, N.Y.: Natural History Press, 1963.

Hill, Beth and Ray. *Indian Petroglyphs of the Pacific Northwest.* Seattle: University of Washington Press, 1975.

Macnair, Peter L., Alan L. Hoover and Kevin Neary. *The Legacy: Tradition and Innovation in Northwest Coast Indian Art.* Victoria, B.C.: British Columbia Provincial Museum, 1980. Reprint. Vancouver: Douglas & McIntyre; Seattle: University of Washinton Press, 1984.

Steltzer, Ulli. *Indian Artists at Work.* Vancouver: Douglas & McIntyre; Seattle: University of Washington Press, 1976

Stewart, Hilary. *Indian Fishing: Early Methods on the Northwest Coast.* Vancouver: Douglas & McIntyre; Seattle: University of Washington Press, 1977.

———. *Cedar: Tree of Life to the Northwest Coast Indians.* Vancouver: Douglas & McIntyre; Seattle: University of Washington Press, 1984.

Turner, Nancy J. "Plant taxonomic systems and ethnobotany of three contemporary Indian groups of the Pacific Northwest (Haida, Bella Coola and Lillooet)." *Syesis* 7: supplement 1. Victoria: British Columbia Provincial Museum, n.d.

Turner, Nancy J., and Barbara S. Efrat. *Ethnobotany of the Hesquiat Indians of Vancouver Island.* Cultural Recovery Paper no. 2. Victoria: British Columbia Provincial Museum, 1982.

Turner, Nancy J., John Thomas, Barry F. Carlson and Robert T. Ogilvie. *Ethnobotany of the Nitinaht Indians of Vancouver Island.* Occasional Papers Series no. 24. Victoria: British Columbia Provincial Museum, 1983.

# History

Cole, Douglas. *Captured Heritage: The Scramble for Northwest Coast Artifacts.* Vancouver: Douglas & McIntyre; Seattle: University of Washington Press, 1985.

Duff, Wilson. *The Indian History of British Columbia.* Vol. 1, *The Impact of the White Man.* Memoir, no. 5. Victoria: Provincial Museum of British Columbia, 1964.

Fisher, Robin. *Contact and Conflict: Indian-European Relations in British Columbia, 1774–1890.* Vancouver: University of British Columbia Press, 1977.

Gunther, Erna. *Indian Life on the Northwest Coast of North America As Seen by the Early Explorers and Fur Traders during the Last Decade of the Eighteenth Century.* Chicago: University of Chicago Press, 1972.

La Violette, F. E. *The Struggle for Survival: Indian Cultures and the Protestant Ethic in British Columbia.* 2nd ed. Toronto: University of Toronto Press, 1973.

# *Index*

References to photographs and illustrations are in *italic type.* References to sidebars are in **bold type.**

## A

Abalone shell, *140, 207*
Adzes, 112, **113,** *211*
Ahousat, *190*
Albatross, **170**
Alberni Canal, 218
Alder, 115
Alert Bay, 25
Alfred, Agnes, 122, **152, 235,** *235*
Alfred, Moses, 32
Alquntam, 21–22, 39, **41,** 161. *See also*
    Legends; Spirits
Amos, Alex, *39, 170*
Amos, Mary, *39*
Amulet, 146
Ancestors, 17–18, 39–40
Andrews, Ben, *16, 39*
Animal People. *See* Spirits
Animals, land. *See* Bear; Deer; Elk;
    Mountain goats
Animals, marine. *See* Sea lions; Seals;
    Sea Otters; Whales
Archaeological sites. *See* Bear Cove;
    Hesquiat Harbour; Hoko River;
    Kwatna Bay; Namu; Ozette; Sequim;
    Yuquot
Archaeology, *112, 114,* 143, 158–75,
    184, *191, 192*
Arima, Eugene, *47,* 117, **125**
Armour, *147*
Arrows, 115, 127
Art, 49–50, *90, 91, 93, 99,* 165,
    **166–67,** *166, 167, 198–99,* 233
Athapaskan Indians, 177–78
Athapaskan Language Family, 177–78
Awl, *175*

## B

Bald eagle, *93*
Barkley Sound, 145–46, *146,* 220–21,
    230, *240–41*
Basketry, *24, 102, 103,* 109–10, *111,*
    *129,* 165
Bear, *83,* 127
Beargrass, *142,* 143
Bear Cove archaeological site, 161
*Beaver,* **53,** 214, *214*
Becomes-Ten, Chief, 108

Beliefs. *See individual groups;* Legends;
    Spirits
Bella Bella Indians. *See* Heiltsuk
    Indians
Bella Coola, 17, 144, *197,* 205, 215, **216**
Bella Coola Indians. *See* Nuxalk
    Indians
Bella Coola language. *See* Nuxalk
    Indians; Salishan Language Family
Bella Coola River, 17, *82*
Bering Strait, 158
Berries, 128, *129,* 132, **132**
Birds, *93. See also* Waterfowl
Blenkinsop, George, 220–21, 230
Blunden Harbour, *14*
Boas, Franz, 30, 43, 65, 81, 86, *126,*
    128, *130,* 141, 151, **219**
Boehm, Gay, **170–71**
Boit, John, 212
Bone, 112, *112,* **113,** *175*
Bone game, *39,* 188–89
*Boston,* 213
Bosustow, Stephen, 45
Bowls, *91*
Bows, 127
*Boxer,* HMS, *19*
Boxes, 110–111, *110, 111*
Bracken fern, *131,* 203
*British Colonist,* **218**
Broken Islands, *240–241*
Brooks Peninsula, 178
Burial practices, *227, 229*
Butler, Mary, *109*
Button blankets, *28, 58, 200*

## C

Calendar, **125**
Callicum, *207,* 212
Camas bulbs, 141–42, *141*
Canneries, **121,** 223–25, *224*
Cannibal Dance. *See Hamatsa*
Canoes, *12, 59, 104,* 115–18, *115, 116,*
    *151,* 165, 230
    names, 56
    sealing, 221, *221,* 223
    and sea otter hunt, **206**
    travel by, *12,* 117–18, 143–44
    *See also* Seamanship

Cardero, José, *204*
Car-li-te, Chief, *58*
Carrier Indians, 144, 215
Cattail, *102,* 143
Cedar, 163
    bark, **15,** *65, 103,* 110, *110, 114*
    wood, **113,** *114,* 115, 116, 163, 165
Ceremonial contests, *154,* 155
Ceremonial rights, 37, **38,** 40
Chiefs
    and ceremonies, 49
    head, 39, 43–44, 48, 120
    and marriage, 146, 149, 152–56
    names of, 52–56, **55,** 56
    responsibilities, 26–27, 120, 132–33
    rights, 33, 39, 43–44, *43,* 48, 49, *97,*
        108, 212
    and trade, 204, 205, 210, 211, 215
    *See also* Kinship; Potlatches; Rank;
        Whaling
Chilcotin Indians, 144, 215
Chilkat blankets, *48, 97*
Chinook Jargon, 59, **180,** 218–20
Chisels, 112, **113**
Christianson, Capt. James, 221
Cinquefoil, 24, 43
Clayton, John, 237
Clayton, Mrs. John, *229*
Clo-oose, 24
Clothing, 65, *110*
Clover root, 132
Clowns, 44
Clubs, *148*
Coast Salish Indians, 33, 141, 143–44,
    213
Colfax, Lida Butler, *109*
Colfax, Lloyd, 245, **246**
Colfax, Roger, 109
Comekela, 210
Commoners, 37, 39, 44, 60, 70, 154.
    *See also* Rank
Conflict, 144–49
    and guns, 145
    intertribal, 213
    with Royal Navy, *212,* 213
    with Whites, 211–13
    *See also* Warriors

Cook, Capt. James, 18, *19*, 36, *148*, 201, *202*, 203–4, 210
Cooking, 24, *100*, *110*, 111, 128–30
Coppers, *62*, *63*
Cradles, 109–10, *109*
Cranmer, Agnes, 32
Cranmer, Chief Dan, *234*
Crests, *40*, 49
Crooked-Beak-of-Heaven, 76, *76*
Curtis, Edward, **15**, *15*, *54*, 108

**D**
*Daedalus*, HMS, 213
Dances
  *Hamatsa*, 76, *76*, 77, 79–80, 81
  *kisiut*, 78
  *sisaok*, 78
  thunderbird, 79
  *tla'sala*, *48*, 76–78
  *tlu·kwa·na*, *72*, 73–74, *73*, *94*
  *t'seka*, 74–76, *74*
  war, *80*
  *See also* Winter ceremonials
*Daphnae*, HMS, 213
David, Ben, 246
David, Joe, *243*
David, Winnifred, 36, **38**, 73–74, 84–86, 201, 232–33
Davis, Agnes, 22
Davis, Philip W., 22, **132**
Dawson, Chief, 239
Deer, 127, *175*
Dentalia shells, 139, 143, *143*
*Der Berliner Tageblatt*, **219**
De Suria, Tomas, *45*
Devil's club, 115
Dick, Jim, *42*
*Discovery*, HMS, **216**
Dogfish oil, 218–20, 221
Dogs, *110*, 127, 133, 139, 141
Douglas, James, 33, 213
Drucker, Philip, 44, 56, **125**, 133
Drums: box, 111; log, *28;* tambourine, *39*
Duff, Wilson, **20**, **29**, *73*, 158, 225
Dzoonokwa, *90*, 151

**E**
Economic change, 219–25, 233
Edgar, Agnes, **132**
Edgar, Joshua, *89*
Education
  modern, **15**, 176, 245, **246**
  schools, mission and residential, 16, **22**, 86, 175–76, 232, 244
  traditional, **22**

Efrat, Barbara, *181*
Elderberry, 115
Elk, 127, 139, *178*
English language, 12, 16, 27
Environment, 16–17, *90*, 92, 95, *159*, *160*, 178, *178–79*, *182*, *183*, 240–*241*
Epidemics, 225–28, 233, 236
Espinosa y Tello, José, 205
Euclataw, 213
Eulachon, 120, *122*, *123*, *124*

**F**
Feast dishes, *70*, 229
Feasts, 69–70, 167
Figurines, *167*
First People, 17, 21–22, 39, **41**, 161
Fish, **170–171**, **172**. *See also* Dogfish oil; Eulachon; Fishing; Halibut; Herring; Salmon; Shellfish
Fishing, 118, 120–126, *120*, **121**, *194–95*
  gear, 115, 169, *171*, *193*, 210
  rights, 25
  trap, *192*
Food. *See* Animals, land; Animals, marine; Birds; Fish; Fishing; Plants; Resources; Shellfish
Ford, Clellan, S., 21
Fort Langley, 215
  McLoughlin, 215
  Rupert, 33, 141, 215
  Simpson, 215
  Vancouver, 214
  Victoria, *215*
Friendly Cove. *See* Yuquot
Frontlet, *37*
Furs. *See* Seals; Sea otters; Trade

**G**
Gleeson, Paul, **113**
Gray, Robert, 212
Grease feasts, 66
Guns, 145, 210, 212, 213
Gunther, Erna, 138
Gwayasdums, *106*, 229

**H**
Haicks, C. *See* Swartout, Reverend
Haisla Indians, 17
Haisla language, *9*, 17
Halibut, 21, 120, *126*, *127*
Halliday, William, **234–35**, 236
*Hamatsa*, 16, *76*, 77, 79–80, 81
Hancock, Samuel, **226**
Hans, Willie, **121**

Hanuse, Roy, 112
Harbledown Island, *230*
Harpoon, 135–36, *135*
Hat, *43*, *45*
Head-binding, *164*, **166**
Headdresses, *37*, *48*, *49*, *54*, *57*, *72*, *73*, *76*
He'gams, 213
Heiltsuk Indians, 17, 149, 213, 215
Heiltsuk language, *9*, 17
Hemlock, 115
Hemlock bark, 131–32
Henderson, Jim, *176*
Hendry, Kate, 230–31
Herring, 119–20, *120*, 223–25
Herring roe, *101*, 118–19, *119*, 120
Hesquiat dialect, **20**
Hesquiat Harbour, 33, 201, *232*
  archaeological site, 169, **170–71**, *170*, *171*
Hill, Matha, *52–53*. *See also* McNeill, Capt. William Henry
Hoko River archaeological site, **166**, **172**, *172*
Hokhokw, 76, 77, *230*
Holm, Bill, *42*
Hottowe, Jeff, *94*
Hottowe, John, *109*
House groups, 36, 39, 48–49
Houses, 13, 39, 67, 105–9, *230*, *231*.
Hudson, Ted, *104*
Hudson's Bay Company, 33, **53**, *208–9*, 213, 214–17. *See also individual forts;* Trade
Hunt Family, *48*
Hunt, Calvin, 79
  , George, 63, *130*, *134*
  , George Jr., *42*
  , Henry, 27
  , Richard, *198*
  , Thomas, *42*
  , Tony, 27, *186–87*
Hunting. *See* Animals, land; Animals, marine; Ritual; Waterfowl

**I**
Ice age, 158–60, *159*, 161
Ides, Harold, 136–37
Indian Act, 233, 236
Irving, Hilary, 118, 245

**J**
Jack, Jackson, *221*
Jackson, Ella, *13*
Jacobsen, B. Fillip, **219**, 236
Jacobsen, Capt. J. Adrian, **219**

Jewitt, John, 45, 63–64, 108, 120, 124–26, 139, 143
Jim, Chief Jimmy, 240
Jim, Old, *115*
John, Leslie, 201
Johnson Family, *106*
Johnson, Andrew, 138
Johnson, Ben, 223
Jones, Chief Charles, 24, 45, 117
Jones, Ida (Mrs. Charles), 24–25, *24*, **68**, 86–87, 105
Joseph, Chief, *49*
Joseph, Robert, 175–76, 249

**K**
Kelp, 120, *131*
King, James, *42*
King, Sam, **55**
Kingcome, 233
Kinship, 36–40, 48–49, 149. *See also* Ancestors; Marriage
Kisiut, 78
Klaklilikla, Chief, *230*
Klalameen, Chief, *237*
Knives, 112, **113**, *172*, *172*
Koon, Daniel, *101*
Koskimo Indians, 65, 108
Krause, Aurel, **219**
Kwakiutl Indians, 17. *See also* Southern Kwakiutl Indians
Kwa-kwa-ka'wakw, 17
Kwakwala language. *See* Southern Kwakiutl Indians
Kwatna Bay archaeological site, **166**, *167*
Kwiistuh, Chief, **144–45**
Kyuquot, **38**

**L**
LaChester, Chief, *185*
*Lahal. See* Bone game
Lamb, Donna, *176*
Land
  agreements, 33
  problems, 236–43
  rights, 32, 33
  *See also* McKenna-McBride commission
Land Above, 21, **41**
Leeson, Benjamin, *222*
Legends, 21, 23
  Chief who lived in North, 161
  Giant Halibut and first man, 21, 161
  Raven and Bella Coola River, 17
  Raven brings soapberries, **132**
  Raven gets things ready, *159*

Raven, Wren and Animal Chiefs, 43
  Three brothers, 23–24
  Why Salmon bones are returned, **82–83**
  *See also* Alquntam; Beliefs; Spirits
Lightning Snake, *50*, *57*
Logging, 223, *243*
Loon, *54*
Loy, Thomas, **172**
Lucas, Matthew, *57*
Lucas, Simon, *243*

**M**
Ma-ate, *238*
McCarty, Harry, *118*
McIlwraith, Thomas, 21, **41**, 45, **55**
McKenna-McBride commission, 237, 239–40, *239*
Mackenzie, Alexander, 141, 205, **216–17**, *217*
McNeill, Capt. William Henry, *53*. *See also* Hill, Matha
Mack Family, *237*
Mack, Chief Orden, **216–17**
Maguaa, *204*
Makah Indians
  art, **166**
  beliefs, 23–24
  canoes, 117, 118
  dances, 28, *73*, *94*
  education, 245, **246**
  epidemics, **226**
  fishing, *126*, *127*, *172*, *194*
  houses, *109*
  language, *8*, 17, 23–24, 183
  names, 221
  rank, *26*
  sealing, *220*, 221, 223
  social change, 228, 236
  trade, 139, *142*, 143, **144–45**
  whaling, 133, *135*, 136–37, *136*, 138
  *See also* Hoko River; Neah Bay; Nuu-chah-nulth Indians; Ozette
Maquinna, Chief, 45, 64, 79, 80, 108, 140, *203*, 204, *207*, 211, 212–13
  , Chief Ambrose, 45
  , Chief Mike, 45
  , Jessie (Mrs. Napoleon), 65
  , Chief Napoleon, 64, 65–66, *65*
Markishtum, Hubert, *194*
Marriage, 67, 68, 149–56, *150–151*, **152**
  bride price, 149, 151, 155
  dowry, 149–51, *152*, 156
  and ceremonial rights, 152–55, 156

and resource ownership, 149
  *See also* Kinship; Rank
Martin, Chief Herbert, **235**, 236
Martin, Chief Mungo, 27–28, *27*, **29**, *73*, *90*, 111–12, 213
Masks, 50, 81, *186*, *187*, *234*
Mat creaser, *166*
Matilpi, Diane, *176*
Mats, 110
Mauls, **113**, 165
Meares, John, 209–10
Metal, 112, **113**, 203, 209, 210, *211*
*Mexicana*, 204
Microblades, 162, *162*, 163
Middens, 163, 169, 171–73, 175, 184, 221
Midshipman, *170–71*
*Minmint*, **41**, 43
Missionaries, 25, 30, 86, 228, 230–232, *232*, 236
Mission schools. *See* Education
Moody, Chief Edward, 237, **242**, 245, 247
Moon, Johnny, **52–53**, *53*
Moser, Charles, 221–22
Mountain goats, *96*, *97*, 110, 127, 133, 141
Moziño, José Mariano, 141
Murphy, August, 108, **206**
Mussel shell, 112, **113**, 135

**N**
Names, **55**, 56
  "baby," **55**
  ceremonial, 29, 52
  group, 17–18
  place, 17–21, 201
  *See also* Chiefs
*Namima*, 40, 43, 48
Namu archaeological site, 161–62, 163
Native languages, *8*, *9*, 17, **20**, 24, 175–84, **180**. *See also individual groups;* Chinook Jargon
Nawitti, 213
Neah Bay, 23–24, **226**
Neck rings, 77
Needle, *175*
Nelson, Leslie, *53*
Nelson, Nella, 246–47, *247*
Nettle, 120, 128
Nitinat language. *See* Nuu-chah-nulth Indians
Nootka Indians. *See* Nuu-chah-nulth Indians
Nootka language. *See* Nuu-chah-nulth Indians